APPEASEMENT

IN

International Politics

STEPHEN R. ROCK

THE UNIVERSITY PRESS OF KENTUCKY

Publication of this volume was made possible in part by a grant
from the National Endowment for the Humanities.

Editorial and Sales Offices: The University Press of Kentucky
663 South Limestone Street, Lexington, Kentucky 40508–4008

04 03 02 01 00   5 4 3 2 1

Library of Congress Cataloging-in-Publication Data

Rock, Stephen R.
  Appeasement in international politics / Stephen R. Rock.
    p.   cm.
  Includes bibliographical references and index.
  ISBN 0-8131-2160-4 (cloth : alk. paper)
  1. Diplomacy. 2. Detente. 3. International relations. 4. Deterrence (Strategy) I. Title.
JZ5599 .R66 2000
327.1'1—dc21   99-087216

Manufactured in the United States of America

For Jenny

CONTENTS

TABLES

PREFACE

About a decade ago, I decided I wanted to do a study of appeasement—not an analysis of the failed efforts to conciliate Germany and Italy during the interwar period, but a much broader work examining appeasement as a type of diplomatic strategy. The project suggested itself to me as I was writing an earlier book. While researching one of the chapters for that volume, I realized that a series of concessions on the part of the British government had played an important role in the reconciliation between Great Britain and the United States around the beginning of the twentieth century. Here, in contrast to the notoriously futile efforts to conciliate the European dictators in the 1930s, was a case in which the policy of appeasement not only brought two countries back from the brink of war but helped to produce a dramatic, positive transformation of their relationship. I was fascinated by this comparison. Why were the outcomes so different? Why did appeasement succeed in some cases, but not in others? This study represents my attempt to answer these and other related questions.

My interest in appeasement is actually more longstanding than the previous paragraph would suggest. I owe much of it to my father, William R. Rock, a historian of British foreign policy in the 1930s. Although not a frequent subject of dinner-table conversation in our home, Dad's enthusiasm for appeasement (the topic, not the policy) and for diplomacy more generally clearly rubbed off on me. When I was in my teens, he asked me to help him read proofs of one of his manuscripts. When I was a graduate student in government at Cornell University, my father suggested that I consider doing a comparative study of appeasement. At the time, I was more interested in other things. However, as I have said, I eventually became intrigued by the possibility of engaging in just such a study.

I am grateful to a number of persons and institutions who made this project possible. Peter Volpe, Dean Rogers, and other staff members of the Interlibrary Loan Office at the Vassar Libraries procured for me numerous materials not in Vassar's collection. A series of student assistants— Cheryl Wood, Ethan Cohen, Caitlinn Khemka, Manoj Zacharia, David Gong, Ingrid Stegeman, Julie Clover, Carl Cade, and Jerome Sherman— did everything from bibliographic research to footnote checking. Paul Huth provided helpful data from his work on extended deterrence. William Rock and Alexander George read the manuscript, offered suggestions for improvement, and saved me from potentially embarrassing errors. Alex George deserves special thanks for his continual expressions of interest and encouragement, and for providing me with funds from a Carnegie Corporation grant, which enabled me to buy a reduction in my teaching load and thus devote more time to my research. Vassar College's generous leave policy permitted me to take paid sabbaticals totaling three semesters during the time I was working on this project.

Finally, I would like to thank my family. My two children, Andrew (eight) and Julia (five), were a welcome diversion from my writing, providing me with affection and the pleasures of watching them learn and grow. No matter how frustrating my day at the office computer, going home to them gave me a boost. My wife, Jenny Arden, contributed to this project in ways far too numerous to mention. This is not the place to express my feelings for her, and in any event I doubt I could find the words. Let me say simply, then, that it is a great joy to share the publication of this book—and, more important, my life—with Jenny.

1

THE STUDY OF APPEASEMENT

Since the Munich Conference in 1938, "appeasement" as a policy has been in disrepute and has been regarded as inappropriate under every conceivable set of circumstances. This is unfortunate, because there are historical examples in which appeasement has succeeded. Contending states have not only avoided conflict but also achieved a relationship satisfactory to both.

Robert Gilpin, *War and Change in World Politics*

For the present era, it is critically important to understand how appeasement can succeed or fail, without being swayed by false lessons from the 1930s.

Fred Iklé, *Every War Must End*

On 30 September 1938, Neville Chamberlain returned to London from his conference with Adolf Hitler in Munich. Appearing at the window of his official residence at 10 Downing Street, the British prime minister waved a slip of paper bearing Hitler's signature and triumphantly declared to the cheering crowd the achievement of "peace for our time." Chamberlain believed that by permitting Germany to annex the Sudetenland region of Czechoslovakia he could satisfy her territorial ambitions and avert a European conflict. History records that he was wrong. In short order, German forces not only seized the remainder of Czechoslovakia, but invaded Poland as well. Less than a year after his meeting with the German chancellor, the war Chamberlain had tried so hard to avoid began.

Chamberlain's failure etched itself indelibly on the minds of post-war scholars and policymakers. Heeding Santayana's famous dictum that "those who cannot remember the past are condemned to repeat it,"[1] many in the West embraced the so-called "Munich analogy," the chief lesson of which was that making concessions to a hostile state could not succeed in pacifying it and thus preventing war. Instead, a policy of "appeasement" only made conflict more likely by emboldening the aggressor and encouraging him to put forth ever increasing demands. In the words of the French proverb, "L'appetit vient en mangeant"—appetite grows with eating.[2]

The futility of appeasement and the dangers of appearing weak were elaborated by American scholars in what became known as the "deterrence model" of international politics, a perspective which reigned almost unchallenged for several decades, and which remains widely accepted even today.[3] This model, implicitly or explicitly, was also adopted by U.S. officials and provided much of the intellectual foundation for the strategy of "containment" pursued by the United States with respect to communism throughout the Cold War.[4] In particular, it strongly influenced Washington's strategy in relations with the Soviet Union, in the minds of many policymakers the postwar reincarnation of Hitlerian Germany.[5] As historians have noted, the decisions of various administrations not to share the secret of the atomic bomb with the Soviets, to intervene in Korea, to take a hard line in Cuba, and to fight in Vietnam were in large part determined by the perceived need to maintain a resolute opposition to the expansionist aims of the Soviet Union.[6] The guiding principle of America's Cold War policy was stated clearly by Clark Clifford, special counsel to President Harry Truman, in a 1946 report: "The language of military power is the only language which disciples of power politics understand. The United States must use that language in order that Soviet leaders will realize that our government is determined to uphold the interests of its citizens and the rights of small nations. Compromise and concessions are considered, by the Soviets, to be evidences of weakness and they are encouraged by our 'retreats' to make new and greater demands."[7]

American policymakers have, of course, applied the "lessons of Munich" in relations with other states as well. The decision by the Bush administration to intervene in the Persian Gulf after the invasion of Kuwait by Iraq in August of 1990 was, for example, clearly informed by memories of the 1930s. Within a week of the attack, President Bush, explaining to the American public his decision to send U.S. military forces into the region, compared Iraqi leader Saddam Hussein to Hitler and stated flatly that "if history teaches us anything, it is that we must resist aggression, or it will destroy our freedoms. Appeasement does not work."[8] Two months later, Bush repeated this message, telling a gathering of military personnel that Iraq would not be allowed to retain Kuwait. Said the president, "In World War II, the world paid dearly for appeasing an aggressor who could have been stopped. Appeasement leads only to further aggression and, ultimately, to war. And we are not going to make the mistake of appeasement again."[9]

Despite this anti-appeasement mindset, the government of the United States has from time to time pursued policies of conciliation. Examples include, somewhat ironically, the Bush administration's attempts during the late 1980s to secure the friendship of Saddam Hussein, as well the strategy of "engagement" it applied to China in the aftermath of the 1990 massacre in Tienanmen Square.[10] Nevertheless, American officials have scrupulously avoided attaching the label "appeasement" to any of these policies. Their caution in this regard seems justified, for in the United States appeasement has acquired such an odious reputation that any policy that remotely smacks of it is suspect. As Jack Plano and Roy Olton observe, "The charge of appeasement is often invoked as a term of opprobrium applied to any concession granted to a diplomatic opponent."[11] Thus, during the 1970s, conservative critics of détente sought, with some success, to discredit the policy by equating it with appeasement in the public mind.[12] Throughout the Cold War, arms control negotiations and agreements were tarred by their opponents with the appeasement brush. Even the 1987 Intermediate-range Nuclear Forces (INF) Treaty, a relatively modest pact, and one concluded by the most aggressively anti–communist administration since the Truman era, was labeled "appeasement" by prominent members of the president's own party. Congressman Jack Kemp termed it a "nuclear Munich," while evangelist and fellow presidential candidate Pat Robertson charged that Ronald Reagan, in his advocacy of the treaty, "sounded like Neville Chamberlain."[13] Howard Phillips and Richard Viguerie, leading conservatives, formed an "Anti-Appeasement Alliance" in an unsuccessful attempt to block the treaty's ratification.[14]

THE CRITIQUE OF APPEASEMENT

Clearly, as Gilpin writes, appeasement is "in disrepute."[15] Indeed, there exists in the United States a widespread belief in a kind of iron law: "If appeasement, then World War III."[16] Why should this be true? What exactly is wrong with appeasement? The conventional wisdom, grounded in the experience of Munich, holds that the policy is flawed in two fundamental respects. First, dissatisfied states and their leaders cannot be appeased. The offering of inducements cannot redress grievances and turn a disgruntled adversary into a friend or even a benevolent neutral. As one author states, "When faced with an aggressor, threats and force are necessary. Concessions may serve important tactical needs, but they will not meet the underlying sources of dissatisfaction."[17] Second, appeasement is dangerous because it undermines subsequent attempts at deterrence. Rather than simply failing to prevent aggression, it actually serves to promote it.

It does so in either (or both) of two ways. First, by ceding strategically valuable territory or abandoning certain of its defenses, the appeaser allows the military balance to shift in favor of the potential aggressor, eroding the former's deterrent capacity. This might be called the "material effect" of appeasement. Thus, for example, the abandonment of formidable Czech defenses in 1938 at Munich and the loss of the Czech Army in March of 1939 shifted the military balance toward Germany and rendered her attack on Poland more likely to succeed.[18]

Second, and much more critical, is what one can term the "psychological effect" of appeasement. Specifically, it is argued that appeasement gravely weakens the credibility of deterrent threats. Once it has received inducements, the adversary refuses to accept the possibility that the government of the conciliatory state will later stand firm. It thus advances new and more far-reaching demands. When the government of the appeasing state responds to these demands by issuing a deterrent threat, it is not believed. Ultimately, deterrence fails, and the appeasing state must go to war if it wishes to defend its interests.[19] The real tragedy of Munich, from this perspective, was not that Anglo-French concessions failed to satisfy Hitler in September of 1938—although that was bad enough—but that they encouraged him to attack Poland a year later, in blatant disregard of warnings from London and Paris that they would intervene.[20]

THE NEED FOR RECONSIDERATION

Although this critique of appeasement is deeply ingrained in the American consciousness, there is surprisingly little evidence to support it. No systematic analyses of cases of attempted appeasement exist, and there is no reason to believe, *a priori,* that concessions never work, that it is impossible to satisfy a dissatisfied state or leader.[21] Indeed, simple logic suggests otherwise. Not every statesman is a Hitler or even a Stalin. Not every state that makes demands has unlimited ambitions. As Robert Jervis notes, "Our memories of Hitler have tended to obscure the fact that most statesmen are unwilling to pay an exorbitant price for a chance at expansion. More moderate leaders are apt to become defenders of the status quo when they receive significant concessions. Of course the value of these concessions to the status quo power may be high enough to justify resistance and even war, but the demands are not always the tip of an iceberg. To use the more common metaphor, the appetite does not always grow with the eating."[22]

As I shall argue later, cases of successful appeasement can be found. But even if they could not, this would not in itself prove the futility of the strategy. Defenders of deterrence have recently argued that, contrary to claims made by critics, most deterrence failures can be attributed mainly to improper implementation of a deterrent policy, rather than to flaws in the underlying model of state behavior on which the policy is based.[23] While this dispute remains unresolved, it offers an important lesson to those who would reject appeasement because of its failures, without investigating their causes. Failed attempts at appeasement must be scrutinized in order to determine whether the outcome was primarily the result of policy mistakes—which could presumably be remedied by policymakers—or the consequence of erroneous assumptions made by appeasement about the nature of states and of their interactions.

There is also only minimal evidence to support the second major criticism of appeasement: that by undermining a state's credibility, it renders later attempts at deterrence futile. Glenn Snyder and Paul Diesing, in their study of crisis bargaining, found that states did not generally base expectations regarding others' behavior on their past actions.[24] Paul Huth and Bruce Russett similarly concluded that, in terms of what makes deterrence work, "the defender's past behavior in crises seems to make no systematic difference."[25]

In a more recent study of immediate-extended deterrence, Huth identified eight cases in which a prior confrontation between the potential attacker and the defender had ended with the defender suffering a put-down or diplomatic defeat. The defender succeeded in deterring the potential attacker in only two of these cases, failing in the other six. This success rate of 25 percent compared poorly with the overall deterrence success rate of nearly 60 percent in the 58 cases examined by Huth and suggested that the defender's credibility had in fact been damaged by his previous crisis behavior. Indeed, on the basis of his statistical analysis, Huth concluded that by backing down in the previous confrontation, the defender had reduced his chances of deterrence success by 42 percent.[26]

Huth's findings appear to substantiate the conventional wisdom regarding appeasement, but they are far from conclusive. First, although his data suggest that conciliation makes deterrence more difficult than it would otherwise be, they do not support the more extreme belief that appeasement makes deterrence impossible. Indeed, as noted above, in two of the eight cases examined by Huth in which a state sought to deter an adversary after conciliating this same opponent in a previous encounter, the state succeeded. Probabilistic laws generated from the aggregate analysis of a large number of cases may tell us something about the effect of appeasement on deterrence in general. They cannot, however, tell us anything about the effect of appeasement on deterrence in a given situation. In particular, they cannot explain why concessions may have a harmful, even fatal, impact in certain cases and not in others.

Second, Huth's study did not address the impact of appeasement on general—as opposed to immediate—deterrence. While his data indicate that past concessions may hamper efforts at deterrence once some act of aggression has been threatened, they are silent as to whether concessions may help to prevent the issuance of such threats, thereby averting future immediate-deterrence confrontations.[27]

Perhaps most crucially, Huth concluded that the prospects for successful deterrence were reduced not only if a state had backed down in a previous confrontation with its adversary. They were also diminished—by 32 percent—if in that encounter the state had adopted an unyielding posture and forced its opponent into a diplomatic defeat. This suggests that appeasement is not significantly worse from the standpoint of future efforts at deterrence than its principal alternative: a deterrent or compellent policy. And it casts doubt upon the claim that reputation for weakness and lack of credibility play an important role in producing deterrence failures. As Jonathan Mercer has written, "If a history of prevailing *or* backing down prompts a challenge, then a state's reputation cannot be the cause of these outcomes."[28] Similarly, from his reexamination of Huth's data and methodology, James Fearon has concluded that "the data do not provide significant support for the hypothesis . . . that being highly conciliatory leads the challenger to discredit the defender's threats in subsequent crises." According to Fearon, only the fact that a previous crisis occurred, rather than the adoption in that crisis of a particular strategy by the defender, is a predictor of immediate deterrence failure.[29]

Mercer's *Reputation and International Politics* represents the first systematic analysis of the formation and effects of states' international reputations. Drawing on theory from social psychology, Mercer hypothesizes that a state will attribute desirable behavior by its adversary to situational imperatives or constraints rather than the adversary's disposition. For example, "the adversary yielded in the confrontation because he was forced to do so by circumstances, not because he lacked resolve." Because reputation is based upon (perceived) disposition, only a dispositional explanation can lead a state to confer a reputation on another. Desirable behavior by an adversary, since it is attributed to situation and not disposition, will not result in a reputation being conferred. It follows that appeasement—which is in most cases likely to be regarded as desirable behavior by one's opponent—should not cause a state to acquire a reputation for irresolution and should not undermine its credibility. Mercer's analysis of historical cases generally confirms his hypothesis. He finds, contrary to the conventional wisdom, that commitments are independent, not interdependent: "Decision-makers do not consistently use another state's past behavior . . . to predict that state's behavior."[30] Crucially, he concludes, "Adversaries rarely get reputations for lacking resolve."[31]

Although the absence of evidence for the traditional critique—and the evidence offered by Mercer against it—warrant, by themselves, a reconsideration of appeasement, there exists another, perhaps equally compelling, reason to undertake the task. It is the problems associated with the alternative to appeasement, threat-based influence strategies, and particularly with deterrence.

One of the reasons deterrence has often seemed preferable to appeasement is that it is widely regarded as being less expensive.[32] Inducements, after all, require one to concede something, presumably something of value—national territory in perhaps the most extreme case. Threats on the other hand, do not require one to sacrifice anything up front. Thus, even if appeasement could be as successful as deterrence in preventing an adversary's hostile action, threats would still be the preferred mode of influence.

There are, however, serious difficulties with this notion. Deterrent threats, even when they work, are hardly costless. General deterrence in particular may require an extensive commitment of human and material resources over a considerable period of time. A state may, in some cases, feel obliged to resort to military action in order to maintain its reputation for firmness. The Vietnam War, fought, as was the war in Korea, partly for the symbolic purpose of demonstrating American resolve, cost tens of thousands of lives and caused great social upheaval.[33] During the Cold War, the United States and the Soviet Union spent literally trillions of dollars for the purpose of deterring one another. Although the effects of defense spending have been hotly debated, there is substantial evidence that the investment of resources in military rather than civilian production has damaged the American economy.[34] Influential analysts have contended that America's refusal to abandon some of her overseas commitments is hastening the decline of the United States as a great power.[35] And there exists an almost remarkable consensus among policymakers and scholars that excessive military expenditures played a major role in the dramatic deterioration and eventual collapse of the Soviet economy. Given the fact that deterrence can be exceedingly expensive, the possibility that under some circumstances appeasement would be a less costly option surely exists. Indeed, as we shall see, British appeasement of the United States around the turn of the century was prompted in considerable part by the (accurate) perception that concessions were the less expensive alternative.[36]

Beyond this, and more importantly, there is a growing body of evidence to suggest that deterrent threats work less often than commonly believed. Huth's study found that efforts at immediate-extended deterrence failed in roughly 40 percent of the cases, and his critics have claimed that this may, for methodological reasons, understate the true rate of failure.[37] The causes of deterrence failure are varied. More traditional rational-model theorists, including Huth, emphasize such factors as threats that are not credible and military balances favoring the potential attacker, while psychological theorists, among them Lebow and Stein, stress elements such as domestic and international insecurities that cause leaders to act aggressively even when threats are credible and military balances unfavorable.[38] In any event, deterrence is hardly failure-proof; the conditions for successful deterrence may often be difficult or even impossible to fulfill.

Given the less than overwhelming evidence for its supposed futility and the acknowledged problems with its alternatives, a reappraisal of appeasement as a diplomatic strategy is clearly in order. Unlike deterrence or compellence (coercive diplomacy), however, appeasement has received little attention from political scientists and other students of international politics.[39] A few scholars, it should be noted, have considered the efficacy of a policy of concessions. David Baldwin, in his essay, "The Power of Positive Sanctions," argued that rewards and promises could sometimes induce states to modify their behavior.[40] But this piece, while suggestive, was not an empirical study. More recently, Russell Leng and Hugh Wheeler examined the effectiveness of what they termed an "appeasing strategy" in the resolution of international crises.[41] They found that such an approach was rarely, if ever, successful; it scored lower than any of the half dozen or so other strategies also examined. However, the way in which Leng and Wheeler defined policy outcomes virtually guaranteed this result. The authors characterized as a failure any case in which a given strategy led to either war or diplomatic defeat. But appeasement in a crisis may be essentially a policy of diplomatic defeat undertaken in the hope of easing tensions and averting war. Leng and Wheeler's definition thus borders on the tautological. Moreover, if preventing war is the ultimate objective of the strategy, only the outbreak of war constitutes its failure. Reinterpreting Leng and Wheeler's data according to this standard, it appears that appeasement actually succeeded in five of the six cases in which it was attempted—a success rate of better than 80 percent.

For Leng and Wheeler, appeasement represents one value of an independent variable—bargaining strategy—that helps to explain their dependent variable: crisis outcome. In much the same way, Huth treats prior conciliation of an adversary as a causal factor helping to explain deterrence success or failure. Importantly, these scholars do not seek to account for the success or failure of appeasement *itself*. Indeed, relatively little effort has been made to identify conditions under which a conciliatory policy will succeed or fail.[42] Even historians treating the most famous case—Anglo-French efforts to accommodate Germany during the 1930s—have devoted themselves to explaining why appeasement was pursued while ignoring almost entirely the question of why it did not work.[43] Thus this study seeks to fill, at least in part, what must be regarded as a significant gap in the international relations literature.

TOWARD A THEORY OF APPEASEMENT

Cases examined in subsequent chapters of this book confirm the observation made by Gilpin, Jervis, and others that appeasement *can* work.[44] Inducements can remove the causes of tension between states without prompting further demands or overt acts of aggression. Of course, appeasement can also fail. What is needed, then, is a theory to explain why appeasement succeeded or failed in certain historical cases, to predict with some degree of accuracy its prospects in future situations, and to provide policymakers with guidance regarding both the appropriateness of the policy and its proper implementation.

DEFINING APPEASEMENT

The first step in developing a theory of appeasement is to define the term itself. Unfortunately, as we have noted, the word "appeasement" has been used widely and almost indiscriminately for symbolic and partisan political purposes. Moreover, even among students of international politics there exists no consensus as to its precise meaning. What is a policy of appeasement, properly defined?

According to Gordon Craig and Alexander George, in the language of classical European diplomacy, "appeasement" referred to "the reduction of tension between [two states] by the methodical removal of the principal causes of conflict and disagreement between them."[45] It was a more ambitious undertaking than, for example, detente, which sought to reduce hostility without resolving its underlying causes, or entente, which attempted to settle only a limited range of issues. Ideally, appeasement (sometimes accompanied by alliance), represented the culmination of a process of tension-reduction, which began with detente and progressed through rapprochement and entente before reaching its final stage.[46]

As a stage, perhaps the highest stage, of tension-reduction between states, appeasement could only be the result of policies aimed at its achievement. While policies of appeasement could be, and sometimes were, pursued by both parties to a conflict, typically one side took the lead in initiating the settlement process and made the greater sacrifices. During the nineteenth and early twentieth centuries, this role of "appeaser" was played most consistently by the government of Great Britain. In fact, historian Paul Kennedy has traced the development of a "tradition of appeasement" among British statesmen from the 1860s to the 1930s.[47]

As Kennedy notes, prior to Munich, appeasement—"the policy of settling international (or, for that matter, domestic) quarrels by admitting and satisfying grievances through rational negotiation and compromise, thereby avoiding the resort to an armed conflict which would be expensive, bloody, and possibly very dangerous"—was widely regarded as being "constructive, positive, honourable." It was, in short, a policy of which one could be proud rather than a policy of which one had to be ashamed.[48]

The catastrophic failure of appeasement during the 1920s and 1930s, however, changed the meaning of the term, and especially its connotation.[49] Appeasement was no longer simply defined according to its ends (the reduction of tension, the avoidance of conflict) or its means (the satisfaction of grievances via concession and/or compromise). Rather, judgments—invariably unfavorable—were added regarding the efficacy, and often the morality, of the policy. Thus, states *Webster's,* to appease is "to conciliate or buy off (a potential aggressor) by political or economic concessions [usually] *at the sacrifice of principles.*"[50] In one of the most important books on postwar U.S. foreign policy, Hans Morgenthau defined appeasement as "a *politically unwise* negotiated settlement that misjudges the interests and power involved," adding, "We speak of appeasement when a nation surrenders one of its vital interests without obtaining anything worth while in return."[51]

Confronted by the dramatic shift in definitions of appeasement, some students of international politics have employed the term in both its prewar and its postwar meanings. In their 1950 volume, *International Relations in the Age of the Conflict between Dictatorship and Democracy,* Robert Strausz-Hupé and Stefan Possony defined appeasement as "any policy designed to alleviate grievances through compromise and concession that otherwise may lead to war." Praising this approach, the authors wrote, "Although appeasement is merely a method and can, like any method, be used clumsily and inappropriately, it is a method of adaptation that is indispensable and recurrent in any foreign policy." Later, however, they condemned what they referred to as "appeasement in the proper sense" (where concessions were not reciprocated), noting "the futility of such a policy."[52]

Given the semantic confusion to which "appeasement" is susceptible, and its frequent use—and misuse—as a term of derogation, perhaps the word itself should be abandoned, in favor of some more neutral term like "conciliation" or "accommodation." Such action seems undesirable, however, given the prominent place of "appeasement" in the lexicon of classical diplomacy, as well as the futility of attempting to remove it from contemporary political discourse. Instead, it would appear preferable to define the term as specifically as possible, and to return it to something approximating its traditional meaning, free from the negative connotations with which it has been more recently burdened.[53] That is what this study seeks to do.

This study defines appeasement as *the policy of reducing tensions with one's adversary by removing the causes of conflict and disagreement*. Several aspects of this definition should be emphasized. First, appeasement is not incompatible with compromise, reciprocity, and mutual accommodation. It does not require that one make unilateral concessions. It does, however, imply that a state pursuing a policy of appeasement will usually take the initiative in offering inducements and will ultimately make greater sacrifices than its opponent. Second, nothing in this definition excludes the possibility, or the desirability, of combining appeasement with deterrent threats in a mixed influence strategy. In the pursuit of certain objectives—for example, the prevention of war—appeasement can be viewed as an alternative to deterrence, but also as a potential complement to it.[54] Third, the definition of appeasement offered here does not specify the extent to which the appeaser aims to reduce tensions with its adversary nor the ultimate objective the reduction in tensions is intended to achieve. As I shall argue, appeasement may be put to a variety of purposes. Finally, this definition of appeasement says nothing about the morality or immorality of the policy, nor about its ultimate success or failure.

OBJECTIVES OF APPEASEMENT

Appeasement, as it has been defined here, is a policy of tension-reduction. However, this definition specifies neither the degree to which tensions are to be reduced nor the policy's ultimate objective. In fact, states may engage in appeasement for a variety of reasons. An objective-based typology of appeasement policies thus seems essential to any study of this subject.

Cases examined later in this volume suggest that at the most fundamental level appeasement policies differ from one another along two dimensions: (1) the time horizon to which they apply (short term versus long term), and (2) whether they seek to maintain or to alter the international status quo. These same characteristics have traditionally been employed by students of international politics to differentiate among threat-based influence strategies. A difference in time horizon, of course, underlies the distinction between immediate and general deterrence, while whether a state is attempting to preserve or to change the international status quo constitutes the basis for distinguishing between deterrence and compellence (or coercive diplomacy).[55] By combining them, one can generate a simple four-fold typology of appeasement objectives, as shown in Table 1.

Table 1. A Typology of Appeasement Objectives		
	Short Term	**Long Term**
Maintenance of Status Quo	Crisis Resolution	Crisis Prevention
Alteration of Status Quo	Limited Political Trade	Friendship/Alliance

As a short-term strategy for maintaining the international status quo, appeasement may be a policy of *crisis resolution*. Confronted by an adversary threatening it or another area to which it is committed, a state may try to avert conflict by meeting some or all of its opponent's demands. This was the goal of Anglo-French concessions to Germany at Munich, of the 1898 French retreat from Fashoda in the face of British threats, and of the Soviet Union's acquiescence to American demands in withdrawing its nuclear missiles from Cuba, to name just several examples.[56]

Appeasement that seeks to maintain the status quo over the long term may aim at *crisis prevention*. Because crisis resolution is often problematic, a state that truly wishes to avoid conflict is not likely to be satisfied with trying to cope with crises as they arise. Rather, it will prefer to forestall the outbreak of potentially explosive disputes. Certain British attempts to appease the United States around the turn of the century had this objective. So did the Nixon-Kissinger efforts at detente with the Soviet Union.

As a strategy hoping to effect a short-term alteration of the international status quo, appeasement seeks a *limited political trade*. In return for its concessions, the appeaser expects some specific form of reciprocation on the part of its adversary. The effort in the early 1990s by the Clinton administration to induce North Korea to abandon its nuclear weapons program is an excellent example of this form of appeasement. So, too, is Willy Brandt's policy of Ostpolitik directed at the German Democratic Republic, and its sponsor, the Soviet Union, during the late 1960s and early 1970s.

Finally, appeasement that aims to achieve a long-term alteration of the international status quo may be characterized as a policy of *friendship* and/or *alliance*. By reducing tensions with an adversary, the appeaser attempts to fundamentally change the nature of its relationship with that country, securing good will and cooperation on matters of common concern. Britain's appeasement of the United States was ultimately of this type; so, too, was French appeasement of Great Britain in the aftermath of the 1898 Fashoda Crisis. Some efforts at appeasement, of course, do not fit neatly into one or another of these categories. Indeed, policies of appeasement often have both a minimum goal (e.g., crisis resolution) and a maximum goal (e.g., reconciliation or alliance).

Regardless of their objective(s), appeasement policies are undertaken for the preservation and advancement of what states—or more properly, decision makers within them—perceive to be their interests. States wish to resolve crises, prevent crises, and obtain friends and allies for a wide variety of reasons, which are not always easy to categorize. Some of these may be rooted in the economic, political, cultural, or military relationships between them and their adversaries. A state may, for example, want to avoid conflict with an opponent for whom it feels an ideological or cultural affinity. It may wish to protect important financial or commercial connections. It may fear military defeat or devastation in the event of war. Other reasons may derive from perceived imperatives of the international system, especially the need to confront threats, immediate or longer term, to national security. Historically, the preservation of a favorable balance of power has been a principal aim of appeasing states, including the preeminent conciliator, Great Britain. Indeed, as Paul Schroeder has written, from the middle of the nineteenth century to the 1930s, Britain's "policy of appeasement was essentially the same as the policy (supposed or so-called) of maintaining the balance of power in Europe."[57]

HOW APPEASEMENT REDUCES TENSIONS

Appeasement aims to reduce tensions with an adversary by removing the causes of conflict and disagreement. But what is the process by which this tension reduction is supposed to occur? Cases examined in this study indicate that policymakers attempting appeasement have seen the strategy as operating through at least four distinct mechanisms.

The first of these is *satiation*—satisfying the hunger of a greedy, expansionist state. This is, of course, the popular view of appeasement, and of the best-known example of the policy: the effort by Britain and France to conciliate Nazi Germany during the 1930s. Interestingly, however, in their approach to Hitler, French and British policymakers did not employ inducements solely, and in the early years of the policy not even mainly, for the purpose of satiation. Besides satiation, they also had three other purposes in mind. One of these was *reassurance*—increasing an insecure state's confidence in the safety of its international and/or domestic position. Another was *socialization*—an effort to inculcate cooperative norms of behavior into an "uncivilized" state or leader and, thereby, hopefully bringing it into the role of a responsible, legitimate actor in the existing international system. Although it is convenient and often useful to think of satiation, reassurance, and socialization as being directed at a unitary, monolithic state, in fact each of these mechanisms operates, in the final analysis, on individuals and groups of individuals within the state. Thus, in confronting Germany, British policymakers also sought to achieve appeasement via a fourth mechanism: *manipulation of the political balance within the adversary*—weakening the proponents of a hostile, aggressive policy and strengthening the advocates of cooperation. Policies of appeasement pursued by other governments in other contexts—especially American policy toward the Soviet Union during the 1940s and the Bush administration's approach to Iraq under Saddam Hussein—contained elements of each of these approaches.

Recently, scholars, particularly Richard Ned Lebow and Janice Gross Stein, have begun to investigate the prospects for reassuring an insecure adversary. Most of this work has consisted of: developing a critique of the theory of deterrence, outlining an alternative "reassurance model," and identifying and illustrating with historical examples a number of specific reassurance policies.[58] To date, however, detailed empirical analyses of cases of successful and unsuccessful reassurance remain few and far between. Still less attention has been paid by students of international politics to the possibilities of reforming so-called "rogue" states or leaders. One study of the subject, by Robert Litwak, is now currently underway.[59]

The three primary mechanisms of tension reduction—satiation, reassurance, and socialization—imply, of course, different causes of conflict and disagreement among states and different reasons for hostility on the part of one's opponent. In this sense, appeasement, unlike deterrence, does not rely upon a particular theory of motivation. For this reason, it may hold greater attraction for policymakers uncertain as to the underlying sources of an adversary's behavior.

METHODOLOGY

In working toward a theory of appeasement, this study relies primarily upon what Alexander George has called the method of "structured, focused comparison."[60] This technique, a refined version of the so-called "comparative method," requires the researcher to undertake a detailed examination of a small number of cases.[61] The same set of questions is asked of each of the cases, allowing the identification of crucial similarities and differences among them. The object of the process is the development of "contingent generalizations"—statements regarding conditions, or sets of conditions, under which certain outcomes are likely to occur.[62]

The theory-building utility of this approach, which has become increasingly popular in recent years, has been the subject of some debate. Proponents of deductive theory have criticized empirical generalizations as deficient in several respects.[63] First, such generalizations are not parsimonious, since they usually incorporate a multiplicity of variables. Second, they are typological rather than universalistic; hence they do not provide either a comprehensive explanation for a phenomenon (e.g., deterrence failure) or a general prescription for policymakers to follow. Third, because they are empirical rather than logical, they are by nature incapable of generating counterintuitive hypotheses or "theoretical surprises."

In addition, contingent generalizations are held to suffer from weaknesses of the comparative case study method from which they are derived. Because only a few cases are considered, one's results cannot be viewed with the same degree of confidence as those from large-n, statistical studies. Moreover, key variables tend to be operationalized less precisely than in formal, quantitative analyses. As a result, comparative methodologies often cannot provide conclusive empirical verification of theoretical propositions.[64]

Advocates of the comparative case study approach note that deductive methods and statistical testing techniques confront obstacles to successful theory-building that are equally formidable.[65] More importantly, the alleged deficiencies of contingent generalizations, while real, are hardly fatal, and are compensated for by certain advantages. The inability to produce counterintuitive hypotheses, for example, is offset by a closer approximation to historical reality—a better empirical fit—which is regarded by some theorists as more crucial than theoretical surprise. A less parsimonious explanation, which takes into account a greater number of variables, is often a more accurate explanation, and is therefore capable of generating better predictions. For similar reasons, a typological theory, which identifies different causal patterns for the same phenomenon, is much more likely to provide useful guidance to policymakers than a universalistic theory that prescribes the same course of action under every set of circumstances.[66]

Even the method's critics admit that "well-designed case-study tests may not be decisive, but they can be highly enlightening and strongly persuasive."[67] Comparative analyses, unlike large-n, statistical analyses, are sensitive to the unique characteristics of specific cases. More importantly, because they require the detailed examination of individual case histories, they are ideally suited to the identification of causal variables and of the relationships among these variables. Comparative case studies can thus play an especially useful role in the development of theoretical propositions and in the building of theories.[68]

QUESTIONS ON APPEASEMENT

The method of structured, focused comparison requires that the researcher pose the same series of questions to each of the historical cases being considered.[69] In the case of appeasement, which has been the subject of relatively little scholarly investigation, specific, well-developed theoretical propositions are lacking. However, some fairly general questions may be deduced from the logic according to which an appeasement policy is presumed to operate. Others may be derived from the conventional critique of appeasement, or from theories of international politics that seem to bear upon the issue. Still others may arise during the course of examining cases of appeasement themselves.

What questions should be asked in pursuit of a theory of appeasement? As noted previously, policies of appeasement may be employed in a variety of situations for a variety of reasons. Before engaging in a detailed examination of any case of attempted appeasement it would seem necessary to inquire as to why the policy was undertaken. Hence we must ask:

Question 1: What objective(s) did policymakers in the appeasing state seek in pursuing a policy of appeasement vis-à-vis the adversary?

It is worth emphasizing that policymakers in the appeasing state— and their counterparts in the adversary's government—are unlikely to be of a single mind. Differences of opinion regarding the objectives of appeasement, and issues raised by each of the questions that follow, are discussed in the case studies. In any event, once policymakers in a state have decided to employ a policy of appeasement, for whatever purpose, they must implement it. Appeasement, as it has been defined here, involves making concessions designed to satisfy at least some of an adversary's grievances. An obvious question, therefore, is:

> Question 2: What concessions did policymakers in the appeasing state offer to their adversary?

The very logic by which a policy of appeasement is supposed to operate suggests that the perception of concessions by the adversary's decision makers will be a critical factor—even *the* critical factor—in determining whether appeasement succeeds or fails. Hence:

> Question 3: How did the adversary's decision makers perceive the concessions offered by the appeasing state?

Here we will want to know not only the extent to which concessions were perceived as satisfying the adversary's grievances, but also the degree to which they were viewed as a sign of weakness and an invitation to additional demands or further aggressive behavior. More importantly, we will want to understand *why* the adversary's decision makers perceived the concessions the way they did. To gain such an understanding we must ask:

> Question 4: What factors accounted for the perception of the appeasing state's concessions by the adversary's decision makers?

In seeking an answer to this question, we must cast a broad net, for we do not want to exclude from our consideration any important variable. At the same time, however, the international relations literature can provide us with some guidance regarding the most potentially fruitful areas of investigation. In particular, writings on the causes of cooperation among states suggest that two basic types of factors are likely to affect an adversary's perception of concessions. "Structural factors" are those rooted in the nature of the adversary, in the bilateral relationship between the adversary and the appeasing state, and in the international environment in which the attempt at appeasement takes place. They may include the adversary's motives and objectives, the degree to which it is risk-acceptant or risk-averse, the importance it attaches to various interests, the economic, political, military, and ideological relations between the adversary and the appeaser, and the presence or absence of diplomatic or strategic constraints on the adversary's behavior. By contrast, "process factors" have to do with the way in which a policy of appeasement is implemented. Much of the literature on international cooperation suggests, for example, that so-called "strategies of reciprocity"—GRIT, Tit-for-Tat, Firm-but-Flexible—are superior to purely accommodative strategies in eliciting cooperative behavior.[70] Similarly, scholars have argued that concessions are most likely to be effective when coupled with a resolute deterrence posture in a policy of "generosity from strength."[71] Still other studies have suggested that appeasing states may influence their adversary's perception of concessions in a desired manner by presenting them as being motivated by factors other than weakness, such as "justice" or "principle."[72]

Depending upon how they view the appeasing state's concessions, the adversary's decision makers may respond in several ways. First, they may modify their behavior and/or attitude so that the objectives of the appeasing state are met. Second, they may alter their behavior and/or attitude in ways that fulfill some but not all of the appeasing state's aims. Third, they may decline to change their attitude and/or behavior, perhaps even acting directly contrary to the wishes of the appeasing state. Fourth, they may attempt to bargain or negotiate in order to secure better terms. Hence we ask:

Question 5: What was the response, if any, of the adversary's decision makers to concessions offered by the appeasing state?

Unless the adversary's response is seen by policymakers in the appeasing state as fulfilling all of their objectives, these policymakers will be themselves confronted with the need to make a critical decision. At the most fundamental level, they must choose between continuing the policy of appeasement and attempting to obtain a more favorable response, or abandoning it in favor of some alternative. Two final questions are:

Question 6: How did policymakers in the appeasing state perceive the adversary's response to their concessions?

Question 7: What decision(s) regarding the continuation of their appeasement policy did policymakers in the appeasing state make on the basis of their perception of the adversary's response?

If policymakers in the appeasing state elect to maintain a policy of appeasement, question 7 logically returns one to question 2. Indeed, as the case studies will make clear, efforts at appeasement frequently involve an iterative process of concession and response (i.e. bargaining); thus in a single case a researcher must ask the same series of questions over and over again. Although this complicates the investigator's task, it is not without benefit. Since each iteration of the appeasement process in effect represents a distinct case, the sample of cases becomes larger when "sub-cases" or "cases-within-cases" are taken into account. As a result, the researcher's findings may be considered somewhat more conclusive than would otherwise be true.

SELECTION OF CASES

The cases for any structured, focused comparison must be selected with some care. In a study of appeasement, the researcher should, insofar as possible, include historical examples reflecting the range of objectives appeasement policies may be intended to achieve, as well as the diversity of their outcomes. Comparisons among cases with disparate outcomes are, of course, strengthened if the cases resemble one another in other respects, while comparisons among cases with similar outcomes are enhanced if the cases otherwise differ.

Unfortunately, appeasement, perhaps in part because of its reputation, has not been employed by states as frequently as more coercive strategies. One study of "accommodation" identified only thirty-five instances of the phenomenon between 339 B.C. and 1949.[73] Researchers in the Correlates of War Project estimated that in the roughly six hundred militarized interstate disputes that occurred from 1816 to 1985, appeasement—as they defined it—"occurred in fewer than thirty cases."[74]

Because of the relative infrequency with which the policy has been pursued, and the fact that in some instances diplomatic documentation and other evidence needed for a reasonably thorough investigation is lacking, the selection of cases for this study was not a simple task. Nevertheless, it did prove possible to identify a number of cases which could be adequately researched and which, for the most part, fulfilled the requirements of a structured, focused comparison. These cases are:

1. Great Britain's appeasement of the United States from 1895 to about 1905, reflected especially in British concessions on the Venezuelan

boundary issue, the question of the Central American canal, and the dispute over the border between Canada and Alaska.

2. Great Britain's attempted appeasement of Germany during the 1930s, represented not only by the Munich Agreement, but also by prior efforts to conciliate Germany with territorial and economic concessions.

3. Great Britain's and the United States' attempted appeasement of the Soviet Union during the mid-1940s, reflected mainly in concessions made regarding the disposition of territory and the composition of governments in Central and Eastern Europe following World War II.

4. The United States' attempted appeasement of Iraq from 1989 to 1990, represented by concessions made to the government of Iraqi president Saddam Hussein by the Bush administration.

5. The United States' appeasement of North Korea from 1988 to 1994, represented by its effort to persuade the North Korean government to abandon its nuclear weapons program in return for nuclear reactors and other political and economic inducements.

APPEASEMENT AND ENGAGEMENT

Unlike "appeasement," the term "engagement" pervades contemporary U.S. diplomatic discourse. The official national security policy of the Clinton administration is "engagement and enlargement" of the zone of market-capitalist, liberal-democratic states.[75] Engagement is Washington's current policy toward China and, to a lesser extent, Vietnam and other countries. It has also been advocated by certain analysts as the best approach to dealing with Fidel Castro's Cuba.[76] What is engagement, and what is the connection, if any, between engagement and appeasement?

The Clinton administration formally articulated its vision of engagement in *A National Security Strategy of Engagement and Enlargement,* published in 1996. Throughout much of this document, the policy is defined in broad, grand-strategic terms. Engagement is essentially a synonym for involvement overseas, the opposite of disengagement or isolation. Its components include maintaining strong defense capabilities, combating the proliferation of weapons of mass destruction, fighting drug trafficking, participating in peacekeeping operations, and increasing American access to foreign markets. At the level of grand strategy, engagement calls for active, multifaceted U.S. involvement abroad in order to ensure that America's economic, ideological, and security interests are protected and advanced.[77] This is not, however, how most analysts and practitioners of contemporary U.S. foreign policy tend to think of engagement.

Engagement, as typically conceived, is not a global national security strategy, but an approach to dealing with a specific state (or states) exhibiting hostile or otherwise undesirable behavior. In this more common sense of the term, "engagement" is often contrasted with "containment." Rather than confronting one's opponent through economic sanctions or even military threats, engagement involves establishing or enhancing contacts, communication, and exchanges, especially in the commercial realm.[78] This notion of engagement is articulated in those portions of *A National Security Strategy of Engagement and Enlargement* in which the document discusses China and certain other countries, and is the basis of America's current China policy. In fact, however, it predates the Clinton presidency. U.S. administrations from Nixon to Reagan pursued engagement with respect to South Africa and the practice of apartheid. The Bush administration did so in its approach to China before and after the shooting of pro-democracy demonstrators in Tienanmen Square.[79]

Various types of engagement—comprehensive, constructive, conditional, coercive—have been employed or advocated, but they share the same basic objectives: (1) to integrate the adversary into the international system, with its institutions, legal rules, and norms; (2) to maintain open channels for cooperation in areas of mutual interest; and (3) to gain leverage in order to influence the adversary's domestic and/or international behavior.[80] Often, as with China, for example, the hope is that engagement will lead to liberalization of the target state's economy and, in turn, to liberalization and democratization of its political system.

Critics of engagement—and there are many—consider it "a modern form of appeasement."[81] Their insinuation that engagement is therefore doomed to fail can be disputed, but as a matter of definition they have a point. Appeasement and engagement share a number of attributes. Both are nonconfrontational approaches to dealing with an adversary. Each hopes eventually to produce a relaxation of tensions with the opponent and some modification of its internal and/or external behavior. Each relies, in part, on the offering of inducements. Each sees some role for socialization or learning on the part of the adversary, as well as the potential value of reassurance.

Appeasement and engagement are not identical. Appeasement can be a strategy with short-run aims, while engagement almost necessarily implies a lengthy process and a distant time horizon. More importantly, engagement is a broader, more wide-ranging approach to dealing with an opponent. It places greater emphasis on cooperation on matters of mutual interest, enmeshing the adversary in a web of commercial connections, rules, and institutions, on the development of increased leverage, and on shaping the long-term evolution of the adversary's economic and/or political system. Appeasement tends to be somewhat narrower in scope, relying more heavily on inducements to remove the causes of conflict and reduce tensions.

Nevertheless, appeasement and engagement are similar, and the two strategies overlap in certain respects. Several of the cases of appeasement examined in this volume contained elements of engagement, and could perhaps be interpreted by some as examples of the latter rather than of the former. It may, in fact, be appropriate to think of appeasement as a subcategory of engagement. For these reasons, this work on appeasement is intended to be of interest to scholars who study engagement and of relevance to practitioners of foreign policy who must decide whether and how to pursue such a strategy.

2

BRITISH APPEASEMENT
OF THE UNITED STATES,
1896–1903

> In Anglo-American relations . . . a policy of one-sided concession
> . . . was the wise policy. It led to the settlement of all Anglo-
> American differences, to friendship and finally to alliance.
> J.A.S. Grenville, *Lord Salisbury and Foreign Policy*

> British ministries from Salisbury to Asquith made important
> concessions of substance and form to the United States. These
> statesmen gained not alliance nor even true reciprocity, but the
> elimination of grounds of conflict, occasional and essentially
> "platonic" or negative support in world politics, and above all a
> transformation of American attitudes which would pay immense
> dividends after 1914.
> Bradford Perkins, *The Great Rapprochement*

Britain's conciliation of the United States around the turn of the century
is widely regarded as the preeminent example of a successful appeasement policy.[1] Under increasing diplomatic and military pressure from
America, the British government submitted to arbitration its dispute with
Venezuela over the border between that country and British Guiana, acceded to American claims regarding the boundary between Alaska and
the Canadian Yukon, and agreed to abandon the Clayton-Bulwer Treaty
of 1850, allowing the United States to construct and fortify a Central
American canal. These concessions not only averted a potential conflict,

but laid the foundation for a complete reorientation of the Anglo-American diplomatic relationship.[2] Britain and the United States, adversaries since the time of American independence, became firm friends and in 1917 fought together as allies in the First World War.

BRITAIN'S APPEASEMENT POLICY, 1896–1903

After the War of 1812, relations between Great Britain and the United States remained less than amicable. In the 1830s and 1840s hostilities nearly broke out over disputed boundaries in Maine and Oregon. The 1860s and 1870s saw American resentment at perceived British support for the Confederacy during the American Civil War and the *Alabama* claims controversy. Subsequent differences over fishing rights and the taking of fur seals in the Bering Sea also caused considerable acrimony.[3] Although British leaders were willing to negotiate and compromise on such issues when they arose, they felt little sense of urgency. Disagreements with the United States, while distasteful, could not compare in importance to those with Britain's European rivals. A prominent American statesman later reminisced that Englishmen of the time considered the United States a "negligible quantity" in international affairs.[4] His comment, though something of an exaggeration, was not entirely off the mark.

Beginning in 1895, however, the government of the United States issued a series of challenges to British interests and authority that could not safely be ignored. The first and most important of these involved a longstanding quarrel between Great Britain and Venezuela over the boundary between the latter country and the colony of British Guiana. In July 1895, at the direction of President Grover Cleveland, the American secretary of state, Richard Olney, dispatched a message to London inviting Great Britain to submit the matter to international arbitration. To justify America's intervention, Olney cited the Monroe Doctrine, which, he claimed, had come to be recognized as international law.[5]

The British prime minister, Lord Salisbury, rejected the American position, denying the legality of the Monroe Doctrine and asserting that the United States had no right to interpose itself in the dispute.[6] Earlier American requests to arbitrate the issue had been rebuffed, and the United States had never pursued the subject with any vigor. Cleveland, however, was serious. In a message to Congress on 17 December, he requested the appropriation of funds allowing him to appoint a commission to investigate and report upon the boundary between Venezuela and British Guiana.

Once the report had been accepted, warned Cleveland, it would "be the duty of the United States to resist, by every means in its power, as a willful aggression upon its rights and interests, the appropriation by Great Britain of any lands or the exercise of governmental jurisdiction over any territory which, after investigation, we have determined of right belongs to Venezuela."[7] In a fit of jingoistic fervor, and backed by popular sentiment, Congress approved the president's request.

Initially, the British government determined to resist U.S. efforts to intervene. Events, however, quickly forced a reversal of this policy. The most important of these were the Jameson Raid in South Africa and the subsequent publication of the Kruger Telegram, in which the German emperor, Wilhelm II, expressed his sympathy for the Boers.[8] In light of the volatile European situation, becoming embroiled with the United States suddenly seemed most unwise. Although Salisbury wished to maintain a resolute opposition to American demands, he could not carry the cabinet. By 11 January the British government had decided to retreat.[9] Negotiations quickly ensued, and in little more than a year, Great Britain and Venezuela reached an agreement submitting their dispute to arbitration. At about the same time, Britain declared its acceptance of the Monroe Doctrine. On 11 February 1896, Arthur Balfour, first lord of the Treasury and later prime minister, told the House of Commons that "in the disputes between successive English Governments and Venezuela there never has been, and there is not now, the slightest intention on the part of this country to violate what is the substance and the essence of the Monroe doctrine . . . a principle of policy which both they [the United States] and we cherish."[10]

Britain's course was now set. For reasons that will be discussed below, appeasing the United States quickly became a principal aim of British statesmen, who thus continued their conciliatory policy when two additional issues threatened to disrupt Anglo-American relations.

The first of these concerned the construction of a canal through the isthmus of Central America.[11] Since 1880, it had been the stated policy of the U.S. government to build and control such a waterway. As America's overseas trade expanded, and the United States began to develop a large and powerful fleet, the commercial and military incentives for its construction became increasingly strong. Only Great Britain stood in the way. Under the terms of the Clayton-Bulwer Treaty of 1850, the United States was prohibited from single-handedly digging a canal, from fortifying it, or from exercising exclusive control over it. Unless Britain were willing to renounce its treaty rights, the United States could not legally proceed. And the British government, knowing that a passage through the Central American isthmus would operate to the strategic benefit of the United States and to its own detriment, had little interest in seeing one built.

By 1898, American sentiment favoring the construction of an isthmian canal—regardless of Britain's attitude—reached a fever pitch. Bills to study possible routes were introduced in both houses of Congress, and in January 1899 debate began on legislation authorizing a canal through Nicaragua, in direct violation of the Clayton-Bulwer Treaty.

Confronted with the threat of America's unilateral abrogation of the Clayton-Bulwer Pact, the British government again elected to retreat. In February 1900, the British ambassador, Lord Pauncefote, and the American secretary of state, John Hay, signed an agreement permitting the United States to build and operate an isthmian canal. This accord, however, was not acceptable to the Senate, nor to much of American public opinion, for two main reasons. First, it did not abrogate the hated Clayton-Bulwer Treaty. More importantly, it did not allow the United States to fortify the canal, a serious deficiency in the event of war. As a result, the Senate refused to ratify the agreement in its original form, voting favorably on it only after attaching several amendments.

British officials, affronted by the Senate's changes, declined to accept the amended treaty. But unwilling to provoke a confrontation, London entered into a new round of negotiations. In November 1901, Britain and the United States concluded a second Hay-Pauncefote Treaty. This agreement met the American objections to the previous pact. The Clayton-Bulwer Treaty was explicitly superceded, and the United States obtained the right not only to build and operate, but also to fortify, a Central American canal.

The Hay-Pauncefote Treaty, which effectively ceded maritime supremacy in the Western Hemisphere to the United States, ended any realistic hope Britain might have had of successfully resisting American demands on the one remaining bone of contention in Anglo-American relations: a controversy over the boundary between Alaska and the Yukon Territory of Canada.[12] Although a border had been established by Anglo-Russian treaty in 1825, the terms of the agreement were vague. When, in 1896, gold was discovered in the Klondike region, the Canadian government advanced an interpretation of the treaty that would have extended Canadian territory through parts of the Alaskan panhandle all the way to the coast, providing access to the goldfields from the sea. The United States, unwilling to see the panhandle thus divided, refused to accept the Canadian claim, and tensions began to mount. A temporary settlement was reached in 1899, but the continued flow of miners into the disputed territory heightened the danger that hostilities might break out at any time. By 1902, the situation had become so volatile that the American president, Theodore Roosevelt, dispatched eight hundred cavalry troops to the area in an effort to maintain order.

In January 1903, after considerable negotiation, Great Britain and the United States concluded the Hay-Herbert Treaty. The agreement provided for the Alaskan boundary question to be adjudicated by a panel of six "impartial jurists of repute," three of whom would be appointed by the American president and three by the British government. Roosevelt, who had long since determined that the Canadian claim was "an outrage pure and simple," refused to take any chances.[13] Violating not only the spirit but the letter of the Hay-Herbert Pact, he selected for the tribunal men who were neither impartial nor jurists, and who, he could be confident, would vote to uphold the American claim.[14]

The British government, which had appointed to the commission two Canadians and the chief justice of England, Lord Alverstone, was justifiably distressed by Roosevelt's selections. Despite howls of protest from Canada, however, Britain decided to proceed, and the panel convened in London. When it became clear that the Canadian representatives were committed to upholding their country's claim, a deadlock appeared likely. But Lord Alverstone, in one final British concession, tipped the scales by siding with the United States. Although the Alaskan panhandle was narrowed somewhat by the tribunal's verdict, America's most important contention, that its control of the coastline should extend uninterrupted, was sustained by a vote of four to two.

With the resolution of the Alaskan boundary dispute, British appeasement of the United States had reached its conclusion. The last serious bone of contention had been removed from the Anglo-American diplomatic agenda, and relations between the two countries became increasingly close and cordial. In 1905, Theodore Roosevelt wrote to Arthur Lee, former British naval attaché and civil lord of the Admiralty, "You need not ever be troubled by the nightmare of a possible contest between the two great English-speaking peoples. I believe that is practically impossible now, and that it will grow entirely so as the years go by. In keeping ready for possible war I never even take into account a war with

England. I treat it as out of the question."[15] His sentiment was widely shared on both sides of the Atlantic.

BRITISH OBJECTIVES AND CALCULATIONS

The British government embarked upon its policy of appeasement in January 1896 with the short-term aim of resolving the crisis over the Venezuelan boundary. However, British statesmen quickly adopted a more ambitious, long-term goal: the amelioration of American hostility and the establishment of a stable, cooperative, Anglo-American relationship. Although their principal concern in both the short and long term was to avoid war with America, they were also eager to secure the fiscal and strategic benefits associated with the elimination of the United States as a potential adversary.

The desirability—even necessity—of avoiding war with the United States stemmed from a variety of factors. In the first place, it seemed doubtful that such a war could be won. On land, an American invasion of Canada was virtually certain, and British leaders did not believe that Canada could be defended.[16] Sir John Ardagh, the director of military intelligence, noted in 1897 that in the event of hostilities with America, British and Canadian troops might score some early successes, but "We should eventually be swept out of the country by mere superiority of numbers, and Canada would be overrun and occupied. . . . a land war on the American Continent would be perhaps the most hazardous military enterprise that we could possibly be driven to engage in."[17]

Nor did the prospects of naval success appear much brighter. True, the Royal Navy was far superior to the American fleet. However, the latter had grown rapidly and become a formidable force. The American Navy, which in 1890 contained not a single battleship, by 1905 had twenty-four built or under construction, and by 1906 was the second most powerful fleet in the world.[18] A decisive naval victory, by which British planners had long hoped to overcome their losses on land, could now be achieved only by devoting a substantial portion of Britain's maritime power to dealing with the Americans.

Given the international situation, this simply could not be done. At the end of the nineteenth century, Britain faced serious threats to its home and imperial security.[19] German colonial ambitions menaced British interests in Africa. There was friction with Russia over Turkey, Persia, and Afghanistan, and, as the railway from Orenburg to Tashkent approached completion, British leaders began to fear a Russian advance on India, the jewel in their imperial crown. In North Africa and Southeast Asia, colonial disputes with France, Russia's ally, seemed ready to flare into conflict. When the Venezuelan Boundary Crisis erupted, as Arthur Marder has written, "Britain stood completely isolated. . . . Her position was scarcely endurable. France, Russia, Turkey, Germany, and the United States were openly hostile."[20] Concerned that other enemies would take advantage if Britain diverted naval forces to the Western Hemisphere, the cabinet felt unable "to take even precautionary measures" against the United States. The Admiralty refused "to contemplate the possibility of strengthening British squadrons in American waters."[21]

In 1898, Germany, at the instigation of Kaiser Wilhelm II and the head of the imperial naval ministry, Alfred von Tirpitz, began a program of naval construction so ambitious that it menaced British naval supremacy. The following year, Britain found itself fighting a difficult and bloody war in South Africa, in which the other European powers seemed likely to intervene. Although no such intervention occurred and relations with France soon began to improve, Britain's strategic position remained precarious. Under the circumstances, sending the bulk of the fleet across the Atlantic to engage the Americans was just too dangerous. An Admiralty memorandum captured perfectly Britain's plight:

> Centuries of triumphant conflict with her European rivals have left Great Britain the double legacy of world-wide Empire and of a jealousy (of which we had a sad glimpse during the South African War) which would render it hazardous indeed to denude our home waters of the battle squadrons, which stand between our own land and foreign invasion.
>
> America, it seems, can employ every ship she possesses in the Western Atlantic, but the conditions under which England could employ her whole naval force in such a distant locality are hardly conceivable. . . .
>
> It appears, then, that however unwelcome, the conclusion is inevitable that, in the event of an occurrence so much to be deprecated as the rupture of friendly relations with the United States, the position of Canada is one of extreme danger, and, so far as the navy is concerned, any effective assistance would be exceedingly difficult. . . .
>
> Generally, the more carefully this problem is considered,

the more tremendous do the difficulties which would confront Great Britain in a war with the United States appear. It may be hoped that the policy of the British Government will ever be to use all possible means to avoid such a war.[22]

If the strategic consequences of conflict with America were unacceptable, the likely economic repercussions were scarcely more palatable. Britain depended heavily on the United States for her supplies of cotton and foodstuffs. Between 1896 and 1905, about three-quarters of all the raw cotton used in British textile mills came from the United States. From 1897 to 1901, Britain obtained nearly 60 percent of her imports of wheat and wheat flour from America, a figure representing almost half of total British consumption.[23] If war with the United States were to occur, some analysts predicted that British textile mills would be shut down and large parts of the population would starve.[24] The government itself was not immune from such concerns. In 1897 the House of Commons unanimously passed a resolution stating "That in the opinion of this House, the dependence of the United Kingdom on foreign imports for the necessities of life, and the consequences that might arise therefrom in the event of war, demands the serious attention of Her Majesty's Government."[25] Several years later, the War Office observed that should hostilities with the United States break out, not only would trade with that country be suspended, but shipments of Canadian and Argentine grains might be cut off by American military and naval action. It warned that "such a condition of affairs might result in our being compelled to sue for peace on humiliating terms."[26]

Finally, there was the "psychological" cost of having to go to war with one's racial kin. Many of Britain's political leaders espoused the belief that Englishmen and Americans were but two branches of a single Anglo-Saxon race.[27] Arthur Balfour spoke for millions of his countrymen when, in 1896, during the crisis over the Venezuelan boundary, he declared, "The idea of war with the United States carries with it some of the unnatural horror of a civil war. . . . The time will come, the time must come, when someone, some statesman of authority . . . will lay down the doctrine that between English-speaking peoples war is impossible."[28]

The costs of an Anglo-American war, daunting enough in the abstract, loomed even larger when Britons considered what was really at stake in their disputes with the United States. Some territory of British Guiana might be lost to Venezuela in arbitration, but this was hardly cru-

cial.[29] The contested land along Canada's border with Alaska was important from the standpoint of Canadian pride, but little else. The *Spectator*, in
support of the government's decision to concede this issue, noted that
some matters might be worth fighting over, but asked rhetorically, "can it
be said that the dispossessing of the Americans from the disputed territory in Alaska in order to assert the rights of Canada would have been
worth while?"[30] American control over the projected isthmian canal might
adversely affect Britain's strategic position in time of war, but as the foreign secretary, Lansdowne, reminded the cabinet, it was irrelevant who
built and fortified the canal. Control of the canal in wartime would rest
with the country capable of establishing naval superiority in the region,
something Britain could not do.[31] Further resistance on this issue meant
that the British government would be seeking to preserve a right it could
no longer hope to exercise.

There was, of course, the chance that British statesmen could avoid
war with the United States by adopting a deterrent rather than a conciliatory policy. Salisbury vigorously advocated such an approach on the
Venezuelan boundary question. Convinced that Cleveland's appointment
of a commission to study the issue was a delaying tactic designed to save
face, the prime minister believed the Americans would eventually back
down, a view with which the British ambassador in Washington, Lord
Pauncefote, concurred.[32] However, this course of action was judged too
risky by other British leaders, who were less certain that the United States
could be deterred.

To most British observers, the Americans appeared strongly committed to their aims. Cleveland's message on the Venezuelan issue, and the
initial popular and congressional enthusiasm with which it had been
greeted, seemed evidence of this. Similarly, bellicose statements in the
halls of Congress and in the press left little doubt that America was determined to have her isthmian canal. Reporting on congressional delibera-
tions, the British ambassador wrote to Salisbury in 1899 that "public
sentiment is firmly set upon the construction of the Canal *at whatever cost*
as a national duty."[33] In 1900, the new foreign secretary, Lansdowne, expressed his fear "that public opinion in the United States runs so high in
favour of an American canal . . . that we shall be unable to stem the tide."
If Britain did not accept America's conditions for a settlement of the
issue, "it seems probable that Congress will pass a Bill . . . virtually abrogating the Clayton-Bulwer Treaty."[34]

British leaders were no more sanguine about American intentions regarding the border between Alaska and the Canadian Yukon. President Theodore Roosevelt sent a steady stream of letters to American diplomats, requesting that they warn London of the dire consequences that would follow Britain's refusal to yield. In one such missive, Roosevelt wrote, "I wish it distinctly understood, not only that there will be no arbitration of the matter, but that in my message to Congress I shall take a position which will prevent any possibility of arbitration hereafter; a position, I am inclined to believe, which will render it necessary for Congress to give me the authority to run the line as we claim it, by our own people, without any further regard to the attitude of England and Canada."[35] According to a prominent historian, Roosevelt "was ready to fight rather than give up the Alaskan panhandle."[36] Whether or not this was true, the British had ample reason to believe it.

Britain's deterrent problems were compounded by the fact that many Americans found implausible the notion that Britain might actually go to war against the United States. Reporting on the prospects for a favorable resolution of the Venezuelan boundary question, the American ambassador to London informed the secretary of state in 1896 that England had "her hands very full in other quarters of the globe" and that consequently "the United States is the last nation on earth with whom the British people or their rulers desire to quarrel."[37] With regard to the Central American canal, Massachusetts senator Henry Cabot Lodge wrote to U.S. diplomat Henry White that "England does not care enough about it to go to war to prevent our building it, and it would be ruinous if she did make war on us."[38] Official and popular skepticism about Britain's willingness to fight over the Alaskan boundary issue was also widespread.

On the whole, then, deterrence was problematic. If a deterrent policy were attempted, and failed, the British government would then be confronted with two options. One of these, war, had already been ruled out. The only alternative was to do nothing, to allow Britain's bluff to be called. This might, however, be more damaging to Britain's reputation, and more likely to encourage future aggression by her opponents, than concessions made in negotiated settlements. Secretary of State John Hay wrote to Joseph Choate, the U.S. ambassador, that if Britain refused to grant the United States permission to construct a Central American canal, Washington would proceed to do so anyway, and Britain's weakness would be exposed.[39] Henry Cabot Lodge likewise suggested that it would be better for Britain to accede formally to American demands than to push the United States into unilaterally abrogating its treaty commitments.[40]

Even if British statesmen had believed that the United States could be deterred—which they did not—there remained compelling long-term reasons to attempt a more conciliatory approach. The first was the fiscal savings that could be realized by eliminating America as a potential enemy. Deterrence was, to put it mildly, exceedingly expensive, and it was doubtful that Britain could afford the expenditures required to sustain such a policy against the United States for an extended period of time. As noted previously, the American fleet of battleships had expanded from zero in 1890 to twenty-four in 1905; by 1906, the U.S. navy was the second most powerful in the world.[41] Faced with more pressing threats to her imperial and even home security from France, Russia, and Germany, Britain's army and navy estimates were already rising dramatically. It was during precisely this era, too, that education and a variety of other social programs, strongly desired by the public, laid greater and greater claim to government funds.[42] Thus, as Paul Kennedy has argued, "The simplistic remedy of increasing the defence budget until Britain's navy and army were capable of satisfying all the demands which were placed upon them was financially impossible."[43] Even had Britain's other adversaries been magically eliminated, it might have been unable to keep pace with the United States, whose resources were far superior. In 1901, Selborne, first lord of the Admiralty, warned that "if the Americans choose to pay for what they can easily afford, they can gradually build up a navy, fully as large and then larger than ours." He added, "I am not sure they will not do it."[44]

More important to Britain than the financial benefits of American friendship were the strategic advantages. Confronted with an increasingly menacing international environment that made it impossible to maintain the policy of "splendid isolation," to which they had been committed, at least theoretically, for many decades, British leaders began to cast about for friends that might enable them to preserve their most important interests. For reasons of geography, race, and ideology, the United States, despite its long tradition of anglophobia, seemed better suited to this role than any other power. For the most part, British policymakers did not expect the positive military and diplomatic cooperation characteristic of an alliance. Instead, they had the essentially negative goal of removing the United States from the list of Britain's enemies so that scarce resources could be employed elsewhere. The culmination of this policy occurred between 1904 and 1906, when, with American friendship secured, the British government reorganized its fleet, ending its permanent naval presence in the Western Hemisphere so that its forces could be concentrated in waters nearer the British Isles.[45]

In the end, British policymakers achieved all for which they hoped. American attitudes toward Britain, both public and official, improved dramatically. The British government was able to remove the United States from its list of potential adversaries and to count upon American support in international affairs, even to the point of active military cooperation in 1917. An explanation of Britain's success must begin with an examination of American motives and objectives.

U.S. MOTIVES AND OBJECTIVES

Cases examined later in this study reveal the virtual impossibility of appeasing an adversary bent on war. Fortunately for Great Britain, American demands were not motivated by the desire to provoke an armed conflict. Even the dispute over the Venezuelan boundary, in which American policy was arguably most belligerent, was not what Richard Ned Lebow has called a "justification of hostility crisis"—a pretext for war.[46] In fact, had the British not backed down, it is uncertain whether conflict would have occurred. Cleveland's message, despite its bellicosity, was something short of an ultimatum. In particular, it did not call for the United States to take action until the commission appointed by Cleveland to investigate the issue had finished its report—a process that might take months—and the president had accepted it, which he could always refuse to do. Moreover, as we shall see later, there were powerful segments of the American public that had strong reasons for wishing to avoid conflict with England, and sentiment to this effect began to emerge early in the Venezuelan Crisis, even before British concessions had been made.

Although the United States was not a country desirous of war, it was in some sense what Charles Glaser has termed a "greedy" power, that is, a state seeking to achieve nonsecurity objectives.[47] Most of the nineteenth century had been devoted to the extension of American control across the North American continent in the pursuit of what many Americans considered to be their "manifest destiny." Beginning about 1880, the United States moved more aggressively to acquire overseas naval bases and coaling stations in an effort to protect and advance its commercial interests. Hawaii and parts of Samoa became American possessions. At the very end of the century, the United States fought a war with Spain, seizing Cuba and the Philippine Islands in the process.

Despite this record, however, the United States had only limited territorial ambitions. The Philippines, at first a popular acquisition, soon lost their appeal. In 1907, President Theodore Roosevelt noted that the American people "think that they are of no value, and I am bound to say that in the physical sense I don't see where they are of any value to us or where they are likely to be of any value."[48] One historian of the period has noted that American expansionism was marked by an "essential continentalism" which "set limits upon its aspirations . . . even the most grandiose of expansionists hesitated to project their visions beyond the bounds of the western hemisphere."[49] Given this, it is not surprising that by 1902 or 1903, the imperialist fever unleashed by the war with Spain had run its course and a firm "anti-colonial consensus" again reigned within the American establishment.[50]

The demand on the part of the United States for the right to build and fortify an isthmian canal, as well as the right to disputed territory in Alaska must, of course, be regarded as expansionist, nonsecurity objectives. But even within the Western Hemisphere, America's territorial aims were not very extensive. Beyond the canal and the Alaskan boundary, in fact, it is possible to regard them as almost nonexistent insofar as British interests were concerned. American sentiment favoring the forcible annexation of Canada had, for example, virtually disappeared by the end of the nineteenth century. The American demand in the Venezuelan boundary dispute was not, strictly speaking, territorial at all. Olney's letter to the British government regarding the matter asked only that Britain submit the question to international arbitration, a purely procedural point. Cleveland's address similarly offered no judgment on the substantive issue of the relative validity of the British and Venezuelan positions. Indeed, when the arbitral panel finally rendered a decision that upheld the British claim almost completely, the United States was perfectly satisfied.

America's most important nonsecurity objective vis-à-vis Great Britain was not territorial acquisition, but status. Because the United States was a relative latecomer to the world stage, turn-of-the-century Americans seemed to have something of an inferiority complex, which was reflected in a burning desire to have their country recognized as an important member of the international community. William Dunning has noted that during this period, "Pride of strength and of achievement became particularly demonstrative in the United States. . . . Through press and pulpit and platform was revealed a consuming sense of power and a deep craving to make it felt, and to extort recognition of it from other peoples."[51] This wish was by far the strongest with respect to Britain, presumably a consequence of America's origins as part of the British Empire. H.C. Allen has noted that Anglo-American relations of the time bore a striking resemblance to those between parent and child.[52] It is certainly true that many Americans were exceedingly sensitive to any unfavorable comparison between themselves and their mother country. Cecil Spring-Rice of the British diplomatic service, a strong advocate of Anglo-American friendship, despaired in 1895 as American agitation over Venezuela reached a climax:

> The jealousy of England is so acute that nothing we can do will do the slightest good. Suppose we are civil to their naval officers—still, our ships are larger and more numerous. Suppose we entertain their Ambassador—the English lord on the continent is still a greater personage than the American patriot, etc., etc. Then there is the question of international marriages. It is a most irritating thing for instance, that a beautiful and wealthy girl like Miss Leiter goes abroad to marry. The fact is that as long as we exist and talk English we shall be hated here.[53]

As events subsequently proved, Spring-Rice was too pessimistic, but his letter supports the contention that what the United States really wanted from Britain was recognition of its stature as a nation. Americans wished their country to be seen as Britain's equal, and some were prepared to fight if the requisite British gestures were not forthcoming. It is in this light that one can understand Richard Olney's boastful declaration that "the United States is practically sovereign on this continent, and its fiat is law upon the subjects to which it confines its interposition," words that sound only too much like the bragging of an insecure adolescent uncertain of his position in life.[54] And it is in this light that one can comprehend why Olney and Cleveland were so incensed when the British prime minister, Lord Salisbury, refused their invitation to arbitrate the Venezuelan issue in a letter that could only be described as condescending. Many Americans, it is safe to say, agreed with Senator William Stewart, who responded to this perceived slight by proclaiming on the floor of the Senate that "War is a great calamity; but it is nothing to the sacrifice of honor," and declaring that "I want American manhood asserted."[55]

Although nonsecurity objectives—territory, status—were partly responsible for the American challenge to Britain, for the United States the most powerful motive was security. Americans had scant fear of a British attack on the United States itself, but they were exceedingly nervous about what they believed to be Britain's imperial aspirations in Latin America, which they had long considered an American sphere of influence. Since the pronouncement in 1823 of the Monroe Doctrine, which proscribed European colonial activity in the Western Hemisphere, Latin American markets had become increasingly valuable to the United States as an outlet for exports. There was little sense that the United States needed to exclude others from these markets. America's proximity to them would presumably allow it to prevail over its competitors in a free and open system. There was, however, the danger that one or another of the European powers, alarmed by the increasing success of American exports, would seek to establish exclusive control, denying access to American goods.[56]

Many Americans strongly suspected the British government of harboring such designs. Thomas Bayard, the American ambassador in London, wrote in January 1896, at the height of the Venezuelan Crisis, that there prevailed in the United States "the fear that there was an indefinite plan of British occupation in the heart of America, involving a purpose of extensive domination originating in private possessions, and backed up by imperial force in the end."[57] Much of this apprehension flowed from a well-orchestrated propaganda campaign conducted on behalf of the Venezuelan government by William L. Scruggs, a former American diplomat.[58] In October 1894, Scruggs published an inflammatory pamphlet, *British Aggressions in Venezuela, Or the Monroe Doctrine on Trial.* Citing British attempts to gain a commercial foothold at the mouth of the Orinoco River, Scruggs warned that "the navigable outlet of the Orinoco is the key to more than a quarter of the whole continent" and that its control by Great Britain "could hardly fail, in the course of a few decades, to work radical changes in the commercial relations and political institutions of at least three of the South American republics."[59]

Scruggs's effort had a profound effect upon popular and official opinion. As Grenville and Young have noted, implicit in Olney's July letter to the British government was the notion that "British pretensions in Latin America menaced the United States."[60] Others were considerably more explicit. Joseph Wheeler, a U.S. congressman from Alabama, wrote in the November 1895 issue of the *North American Review* that if Britain refused to submit the Venezuelan question to arbitration, "it will show conclusively that England has decided to dispute the right of the United States to maintain the doctrine laid down by President Monroe in 1823. It will also prove that Great Britain has determined by force to extend her colonies in America, and we cannot be too prompt in meeting and resenting any such purpose."[61] The *Atlanta Constitution* worried that "if we do not wake up very soon, England will have all of Central and South America under her control, and the United States will be forced back into the ranks of the third and fourth class commercial powers."[62] And Massachusetts senator Henry Cabot Lodge declared:

> The practical result of England's aggressions in Venezuela is plain enough. They are directed to securing the control of the Orinoco, the great river system of Northern South America, and also of the rich mining district of the Yuruari. All that England has done has been a direct violation of the Monroe doctrine, and she has increased and quickened her aggressions in proportion as the United States have appeared indifferent. The time has come for decisive action. The United States must either maintain the Monroe doctrine and treat its infringement as an act of hostility or abandon it. If Great Britain is to be permitted to occupy the ports of Nicaragua and, still worse, take the territory of Venezuela, there is nothing to prevent her taking the whole of Venezuela or any other South American state. If Great Britain can do this with impunity, France and Germany will do it also. . . . It is not too late to peacefully but firmly put an end to these territorial aggressions of Great Britain and to enforce the Monroe doctrine so that no other power will be disposed to infringe upon it. But immediate action is necessary. . . . The supremacy of the Monroe doctrine should be established and at once—peaceably if we can, forcibly if we must.[63]

This examination of American motives reveals several points which bear upon the outcome of the case. First, because it was not a country desirous of war, the United States was in principle capable of being appeased. Second, America's nonsecurity objectives were quite limited, and many Americans, while they suspected British intentions, did not regard British hostility as a foregone conclusion. For these reasons, the United States could be conciliated with fairly modest concessions, which it was well within the power of the British government to make. Finally, because, America's challenges to Britain were rooted mainly in a sense of insecurity, a strategy of appeasement aimed primarily at reassurance was clearly required.

BRITAIN'S APPEASEMENT STRATEGY

A central conclusion of this work is that there exists no single, best approach to appeasement. Rather, different adversaries in different sets of circumstances call for different appeasement strategies. Britain's strategy of appeasement was, in hindsight, almost ideally suited for dealing with the United States. It was, moreover, carried out in a highly effective manner.

In seeking to appease the United States, the British government employed a pure inducement strategy. British leaders did not require reciprocity from the American government as a condition for further concessions. Although they initially sought to link negotiations on the isthmian canal and Alaskan boundary questions—receiving a favorable settlement on one in return for concessions on the other—they quickly backed down when the United States refused to agree.[64] As Bradford Perkins has written, "In hard diplomatic coin, the Americans took but they did not give."[65]

Nor did the British government make any real attempt to mix concessions with deterrent threats. On the contrary, British statesmen scrupulously avoided doing anything that might antagonize the United States. On several occasions, this led them to suffer, in silence, American behavior that was boorish and offensive. When, for example, the American Senate failed to ratify the first Hay-Pauncefote Treaty without radically amending it, the British government refused to take offense, but instead quickly agreed to a second treaty that met almost all of the Senate's objections. When President Theodore Roosevelt attempted to "stack" the commission charged with resolving the Alaskan boundary question by appointing representatives who had prejudged the issue, Britain not only raised no complaint, but averted a potential deadlock by instructing its representative, Lord Alverstone, to side with the United States.

Given the fact that America's principal motive in challenging Britain was its sense of insecurity and the need for reassurance, a pure inducement strategy was almost certainly the proper one. Requiring reciprocity or employing a mixed strategy of positive and negative sanctions might have diluted the reassuring impact of British concessions to such an extent that the United States would not have been appeased. Although Britain eventually capitulated on the isthmian canal issue, its initial attempt to link the resolution of this question to a favorable settlement of the Alaskan boundary dispute had an adverse effect on American opinion, including the attitude of Theodore Roosevelt. Indeed, Britain's reluctance to concede may have contributed to the president's doubts about British intentions and helped to provoke his belligerent stance on the Alaskan matter. According to Bradford Perkins, "Recent events connected with the isthmian question made [Roosevelt] wonder if England was really as friendly as she pretended to be; Alaska would provide a good test, since the right was so clearly on America's side."[66]

In part because their effect was not negated by deterrent threats or demands for reciprocity, British concessions addressed fully and directly the substance of American aims, as well as the motives that underlay them. Resolution of the isthmian canal and Alaskan boundary questions satisfied America's nonsecurity objectives, while Britain's decision to submit the Venezuelan boundary dispute to arbitration greatly reduced America's sense of insecurity. To reinforce the message that their intentions were benign, British statesmen also formally recognized the Monroe Doctrine and engaged in what can best be described as a public relations campaign aimed at influencing American opinion. This campaign, although resented by a few in England who complained about their government's "over-strained eulogium" of American statesmen and the "fatuous courting of their goodwill,"[67] was an undeniable success. In 1905, George Harvey informed his English readers in the *Nineteenth Century* that "genuine friendliness of the American people has been won. . . . we have come to believe that the English people tell the truth when they say they want to be our friends."[68]

One of the principal criticisms of appeasement is that it is viewed by the target of the policy as a sign of weakness and an invitation to further aggression. A pure inducement strategy should be especially susceptible to this problem, because it does not employ deterrent threats and/or an insistence on reciprocity in order to discourage such an interpretation. It is interesting to note, therefore, that British concessions to the United States did not encounter this difficulty. Although at least one British paper worried that "perpetual surrender only means further demands, and either more concession or an aggravation of ill-feeling as a result of unexpected resistance," its fears proved unfounded.[69] While Britain, in fact, conceded her position on a succession of issues between 1896 and 1903, every one of these predated her initial retreat in the Venezuelan boundary dispute. It is difficult to argue that capitulation on one matter elicited harsher demands on another. There is no evidence of such a connection in the minds of Americans; on the contrary, they explicitly rejected the notion that British concessions could be seen as a sign of weakness. The *Philadelphia Press* wrote in January 1896 of the horror expressed by Britons at the prospect of war with the United States, noting that "No American has dreamed of attributing this to cowardice."[70] The dominant theme—that England had acted on the basis of principle and simply done the right thing—was reflected by the *New York Tribune* a few months later when it said that Englishmen had found it "not difficult to make concessions when the concessions were in the line of equity and honor."[71]

Why did Britain's pure inducement strategy not elicit further demands or additional bellicose behavior by the United States? One explanation is that the British government framed its concessions as a matter of principle rather than a surrender to naked threats. Lord Salisbury, in announcing his cabinet's decision to submit the Venezuelan dispute to arbitration, acknowledged that "the United States has some right, as we have, to show an interest in the welfare of a neighbouring people."[72] A more persuasive explanation, however, lies in the nature of American motives and objectives. As noted above, America's challenges to Britain were motivated more by a sense of insecurity than a desire for gain. The United States, seeking evidence of British good will, framed its disputes with Britain as tests of British intentions, not as tests of British capabilities or resolve. When concessions were made, they were interpreted by Americans in the context of this preexisting framework. The strength or weakness of the British government was simply not at issue.

Although American motives meant that Britain's appeasement strategy would not be very risky, the way in which the policy was carried out reduced the risk still further. None of the concessions made to the United States involved Britain's vital interests. None substantially impaired the ability of Britain to defend itself or its empire against further acts of American aggression, should they occur.

Moreover, in making concessions sequentially, over a period of time, British statesmen were able to test the effectiveness of their strategy before proceeding further. Almost from the beginning, they possessed strong and convincing evidence that their conciliatory approach was working. There began during the Venezuelan Boundary Crisis a dramatic shift in

American attitudes toward Britain, when initial enthusiasm for Cleveland's belligerent position dissipated as many Americans contemplated the implications of an Anglo-American war. This shift was solidified by Britain's concessions and by a growing recognition, in the United States, that the British people overwhelmingly abhorred the idea of conflict with America. It gathered additional momentum with the conclusion, in 1897, of the Olney-Pauncefote Arbitration Treaty (which the Senate refused to ratify) and, the following year, Britain's benevolent attitude during the Spanish-American War.[73] In 1898, the British ambassador to the United States reported that Americans were demonstrating "the most exuberant affection for England and 'Britishers' in general."[74] Another diplomat in Washington echoed this statement, writing that "unanimous, or almost unanimous friendliness to England is now manifested by the Press throughout the length and breadth of the country." The prevailing sentiment was so strong, he claimed, that it "bid fair to pass the bound of moderation in as great degree as the dislike and distrust of yesterday."[75]

A corresponding change in official opinion was also apparent. A long list of leading Americans, including Henry Cabot Lodge, John Hay, Alfred Thayer Mahan, and Theodore Roosevelt, declared their affinity for Britain. Even Richard Olney, whose belligerent note had precipitated the Venezuelan Boundary Crisis, changed his tune. In a speech at Harvard College, Olney told his audience that America should renounce her habitual policy of isolation in international affairs and begin cooperating with England, her "best friend."[76]

Despite American bellicosity on the isthmian canal and Alaskan boundary issues, then, a general trend seemed clear to British leaders. American hostility to England was being effaced, and prospects for a complete relaxation of Anglo-American tensions were becoming increasingly bright. If Britain maintained her course, and was not distracted by occasionally offensive and boorish American diplomatic behavior, her policy might well succeed.

AMERICAN RECEPTIVITY TO BRITISH CONCESSIONS

American motives and the nature of British policy are probably sufficient, in themselves, to explain the success of Britain's appeasement policy. It is important to note, however, that there also existed strong incentives for the United States to remain on cordial terms with Great Britain, incentives that help to account for the receptivity of Americans to British concessions.

Some Americans found themselves drawn toward Britain for geostrategic reasons, out of a growing sense of hemispheric insecurity. Spain was one menace here, but the real threat was seen as coming from Germany. As early as 1896 the American consul-general in Berlin had warned that "the United States must be prepared for an 'aggressive' colonial policy in Germany and this aggression points towards South America."[77] American distrust of German aims, fueled by the rapid growth of the German navy, economic competition, and a series of incidents in Samoa, the Philippines, and Venezuela, spread quickly. By 1902, the British ambassador in Washington was reporting that "suspicion of the German Emperor's designs in the Caribbean Sea is shared by the Administration, the press, and the public alike."[78]

Friendship with Great Britain appeared to be one means of gaining protection from the German threat. Theodore Roosevelt appreciated the fact that British neutrality, if nothing more, would be useful in resisting German aggression. Thus, although he favored building a Central American canal, and later pressured Britain on the Alaskan boundary issue, the soon-to-be president warned in 1901 that "we should be exceedingly cautious about embroiling ourselves with England, from whom we have not the least little particle of danger to fear in any way or shape; while the only power which may be a menace to us in anything like the immediate future is Germany."[79] Brooks Adams, a highly regarded and influential public intellectual, adopted an even stronger position, declaring that "England is essential to the United States, in the face of the enemies who fear and hate us, and who, but for her, would already have fleets upon our shores."[80]

Many Americans had additional reasons to favor cordial relations with Great Britain. Some had as their rationale the close and lucrative economic relationship between the two nations. Britain was easily America's most important export market. During the decade from 1896 to 1905, more than 40 percent of American goods shipped abroad went to England. British purchases of wheat and cotton were especially vital; almost one-quarter of America's annual cotton crop was sold to England, and about 15 percent of the yearly wheat harvest.[81] As one American observer noted at the time, for the United States "a quarrel with Great Britain would be disastrous. If her ports were closed to us, we should lose our principal customer, not only for our surplus cotton, but for our surplus breadstuffs. To the farmers of our prairie States and to the planters of our Southern States, such an obstruction to the export of their staples would mean catastrophe."[82]

Beyond this, Great Britain was America's leading source of foreign capital. In 1899, British investors held about $2.5 billion in American stocks and bonds, roughly 75 percent of all American securities in foreign hands.[83] The dependence of the American market on British funds was demonstrated in dramatic fashion by the Venezuelan boundary episode. Following President Cleveland's bellicose address to Congress on the issue, British financiers began to sell their American holdings, precipitating a crash. Five firms failed, losses of $170 million were recorded, and interest rates climbed as high as 80 percent.[84] Railway stocks, dominated by British investors, plummeted in value. Within a week's time, the price of railway issues had dropped as much as $16.75 per share.[85] This crisis, which was attributed to the threat of Anglo-American war, helped spark a growing clamor for peace. Wrote the British ambassador, "The extraordinary state of excitement into which the Congress of the United States and the whole country were thrown by the warlike message of the President . . . has given way . . . to consternation at the financial panic which it caused."[86]

Finally, growing numbers of Americans desired friendly relations with Britain because they viewed Englishmen as racial kin. A belief in Anglo-Saxon unity, grounded in a shared language, religion, history, and political ideology, led many to feel that a war with Britain would be civil or even fratricidal. Such sentiments catalyzed under the impact of the Venezuelan boundary crisis, and quickly came to exert considerable influence among America's leaders. John Hay, secretary of state under McKinley and Roosevelt, Capt. Alfred Thayer Mahan, the most prominent of America's naval and military experts, and Theodore Roosevelt, who ironically was of Dutch descent, were but three of the most important figures who professed to be guided by Anglo-Saxonist feelings.[87]

It may be wondered whether these geopolitical, economic, and racial-cultural incentives for Anglo-American amity might have been sufficient to cause the United States to drop its challenge to British interests had Britain stood firm. In others words, perhaps London's policy of appeasement was not a necessary cause of improved relations between Great Britain and the United States. One cannot prove otherwise, but given the strength of American motives, security and nonsecurity, this seems doubtful. While Britain might have achieved its minimum aim—avoiding war with the United States—without seeking to remove the causes of American hostility, it is hard to see how the more ambitious goals of British policy—friendship and cooperation in the strategic realm—could have been attained. At the turn of the century, American attitudes toward Britain stood at something of a crossroads. That there had been substantial improvement since the days of American independence was evident. Yet lurking just beneath the surface the traditional anglophobia remained. A tough, uncompromising policy of resistance would probably have produced a recrudescence of this ill feeling, rendering significant Anglo-American cooperation impossible. As Lionel Gelber has written, "What the British Government abandoned might only have been held at the cost of Anglo-American goodwill; what they secured was the possibility of endowing it with fresh strength."[88] Indeed, it is conceivable that had British leaders refused to accommodate the United States, the consequences for Britain could have been disastrous. Henry Cabot Lodge, a central figure in Anglo-American relations of the period, reminisced some years later that if the issues dividing the two countries had not been satisfactorily resolved, "the attitude of the United States toward England would have been of such a character as to have embarrassed us most seriously when the great war of 1914 broke out."[89]

CONCLUSION

Britain's conciliation of the United States suggests one set of conditions under which appeasement can succeed in achieving both a short-term aim of crisis resolution and a long-term aim of friendly, cooperative relations: (1) the adversary is motivated primarily by insecurity and the need for reassurance, and its nonsecurity aims are quite limited; (2) a pure inducement strategy is employed, so that the reassuring effects of concessions are not diluted by threats or by demands for reciprocity; (3) concessions are made incrementally; initial concessions do not affect adversely the ability of the appeaser to defend its interests, and further concessions are made only on the basis of evidence that the strategy is working; (4) concessions effectively address the adversary's immediate demands and underlying motives; and (5) there exist significant incentives for the adversary to remain on good terms with the appeaser, so that once the adversary's central aims have been met it is constrained from issuing further demands or engaging in further aggressive behavior. Unfortunately, several of these conditions did not prevail in the next case to be examined: British efforts to appease Nazi Germany during the 1930s.

3

British Appeasement of Germany, 1936–1939

> The fundamental reason for the failure of appeasement was that
> Hitler's goals lay far beyond the limits of reasonable
> accommodation that the appeasers were prepared to contemplate.
> J.L. Richardson, "New Perspectives on Appeasement"

> The essence of Chamberlain's tragedy was that, having pursued a
> course that revealed the nature of Nazi policy, he refused to
> recognize that reality.
> Williamson Murray,
> *The Change in the European Balance of Power*

The failed attempt by Great Britain, along with France, to conciliate Nazi Germany during the late 1930s forms the basis for much of the conventional wisdom regarding appeasement. However, a good deal of what is commonly supposed to be true of this case is in fact myth. The British government did not, for example, pursue a policy of unilateral concessions toward Germany. On the contrary, in seeking to relax tensions with their adversary, British statesmen consistently demanded reciprocation by the German government as a condition for agreement. Even at Munich, the British prime minister, Neville Chamberlain, procured a written promise from Adolf Hitler that further changes in the European territorial status quo would not be forcibly imposed. Nor was Chamberlain a naive babe-in-the-woods who invariably accepted at face value his enemy's pledges of good behavior. Rather, he, like many British officials, was sometimes intensely suspicious of the German chancellor's intentions, and he pursued a conciliatory policy in part because he saw it as the only chance—albeit a slim one—of avoiding war.[1] Hitler, in turn, did not perceive Anglo-French concessions as unambiguous signs of irresolution and weakness. For him, surprisingly enough, the outcome of the Munich Conference was a bitter diplomatic defeat.

Because much of what is popularly believed about the Anglo-French efforts to appease Germany is of dubious validity, the "lessons of the 1930s" are called into question. One thing, however, remains manifestly true: the policy did not succeed. Even if appeasement did not actually encourage Hitler to commit further acts of aggression, it failed to satisfy him and thereby preserve peace and stability in Europe.

THE ROOTS OF BRITISH POLICY

Adolf Hitler became chancellor of Germany in January 1933. The following October, he abruptly and unexpectedly withdrew the country from participation in disarmament negotiations being held in Geneva and from the League of Nations. In February 1934, Britain's Defence Requirements Committee identified Germany as the country's principal enemy over the long term.[2] This view was shared in the Foreign Office, where Sir Robert Vansittart, the permanent under-secretary, wrote a long memorandum in support of the committee's position, citing, among other things, Germany's aggressive rhetoric, her rearmament program, and the propaganda with which her schoolchildren were being indoctrinated.[3] In an earlier memorandum, Vansittart had already offered a highly pessimistic view of German intentions in Eastern and Central Europe. With remarkable prescience, the under-secretary wrote of Germany's demand for the annexation of Austria: "The seriousness of the challenge can only be realised if it is seen not as an isolated case, in which this country has no direct interest, but as the first of a series of challenges, each one of which will carry with it a nearer threat to this country, culminating in the demand for a navy and a colonial empire."[4] Since Britain was the world's preeminent imperial power, and since the security of the British Empire and the island nation itself rested upon control of the seas, the menace posed by Germany's apparent ambitions was only too evident.

There were those in Britain who favored meeting the German threat by rearming and/or securing allies in order to confront Germany with a resolute deterrent posture. Ironically, Neville Chamberlain, chancellor of the exchequer in the Baldwin cabinet, was a leading advocate of (limited) rearmament during the mid-1930s. Chamberlain wrote in his diary in 1934, "[Force] is the only thing Germans understand. . . . What does not satisfy me is that we do not shape our foreign policy accordingly."[5] Three years later, the Chiefs of Staff composed a memorandum in which they stated what should have been obvious to British policymakers: that efforts "to gain the support of potential allies" would greatly improve Britain's strategic position.[6]

Rearmament and resistance to German demands were not, however, the approach adopted by the British government. The principal reason was that such a strategy envisaged the possibility of going to war, should Germany refuse to be deterred. In the 1930s, with memories of the First World War still fresh, this was an eventuality few in Britain were prepared to contemplate. Moreover, even if war did not occur, rearmament on the scale required to block German ambitions over the long term would be financially ruinous. The public was generally opposed,[7] as were the Dominions.[8] The Soviet Union was judged untrustworthy as a potential ally, and British leaders believed no help could be expected from the United States, which had declined to join the League of Nations and retreated into its habitual isolation.[9] Considering the number and strength of the arguments against confronting Germany, it is easy to see why the British government pursued a policy of appeasement. Indeed, in hindsight, it would have been remarkable had the cabinet adopted a different strategy. As Paul Schroeder has written:

> If one begins to tot up all the plausible motivations for appeasement—fear and horror of another war, Britain's state of military unpreparedness, fear for the British economy and the Empire, the unprepared state of public opinion, the isolationism of the Dominions and the United States, lack of confidence in France, lack of interest in Central Europe, failure to understand Hitler and Nazism, fear and distrust of the Soviet Union and Communism, the absence of a viable alternative presented either by the Conservative opposition or Labour, and more—one sees that these are far more than enough to explain it. It was massively overdetermined; any other policy in 1938 would have been an astounding, almost inexplicable divergence from the norm.[10]

Given the ultimate failure of appeasement, it is worth noting that in the mid-1930s there were reasons to believe—or at least to hope—that the outcome would be otherwise. The policy had produced positive results with Britain's enemies in the past. Concessions to the United States during the 1890s had led to a dramatic improvement in relations, and a willingness to compromise had been crucial to the achievement of ententes with both France and Russia in the first decade of the century.

Moreover, although Germany was obviously an expansionist power, the extent of her ambitions was by no means clear. When the prime minister, Stanley Baldwin, told his private secretary in April 1934, "We don't know what Germany really intends," he expressed a sense of confusion shared by many in Britain.[11] Although Hitler's book *Mein Kampf* was available, few Englishmen had read it; those who had found it difficult to imagine that anyone could seriously contemplate the program of conquest outlined therein. Many people, including Nevile Henderson, Britain's ambassador to Berlin from April 1937 until the outbreak of war, were convinced that Germany's objectives in Europe were limited to the recovery of territories lost during the First World War or to incorporation into the *Reich* of all ethnic Germans. Once these aspirations—which were widely regarded as legitimate expressions of the desire for national self-determination—were fulfilled, Germany "would settle down" and become "territorially contented."[12]

If the extent of German aims was unclear, the motives driving policy in Berlin were equally murky. Was Germany's belligerent behavior evidence of avarice or insecurity (or both)? Did the country's geopolitical ambitions—however far they might extend—represent a malignant quest for domination, or a more benign effort to deal with continuing economic weakness? Unlike Vansittart, many Britons thought it was the latter. According to Bernd Jürgen-Wendt, "From the British point of view National Socialism was essentially a product of the impoverishment of the German masses and the collapse of the German economic system in the wake of the First World War and the World Depression. Political aggression, demands for *Lebensraum* and militaristic one-upmanship in foreign affairs . . . were essentially attributed to economic causes."[13] Some British leaders, Chamberlain among them, felt that German aggressiveness stemmed more from the insecurity of the Nazi regime, a function of Germany's precarious economic position and the threat of domestic unrest it was likely to produce, than from the desire for territorial aggrandizement *per se*. R.J. Overy writes that "The rise of economic nationalism in Germany, following on the serious credit crisis of 1930–3, inclined British politicians to view the German economy even before 1933 as a fragile structure, highly susceptible to financial and trading problems, faced all the time with serious economic difficulties, which might bring social discontent. It was this situation that prompted the onset of economic appeasement. Western statesmen assumed that if Hitler were granted economic concessions, he could be brought to the conference table to work out a general European settlement. 'Might not,' asked Chamberlain, 'a great improvement in Germany's economic situation result in her becoming quieter and less interested in political adventures?'"[14]

British leaders were also not entirely certain who was in charge of German policy. As early as 1933, the thesis emerged that there existed two groups within the German leadership that were contending for influence with Hitler.[15] The "extremists," principally Joseph Goebbels, the minister of propaganda; Heinrich Himmler, chief of the SS; and Joachim von Ribbentrop, the foreign minister, were judged to be hostile to England. Against them were arrayed the "moderates": Hjalmar Schacht, head of the Reichsbank and minister of economics; Baron Konstantin von Neurath, Ribbentrop's predecessor as foreign minister; and Gen. Werner von Blomberg, war minister and chief of the *Reichswehr*. This latter group later came to include Hermann Göring, the head of the Luftwaffe, and Walther Funk, Schacht's successor as minister of economics and head of the Reichsbank. The moderates, it was widely believed, desired good political and economic relations with Britain. If they could be cultivated, and their influence with Hitler strengthened, a conciliatory policy might well succeed. Economic appeasement—the offering of financial and commercial benefits, including colonies, to Germany—was in part an attempt to bolster the moderates and undermine the extremists' arguments for the necessity of German expansion.[16] Chamberlain wrote in April 1937:

> The present rulers of Germany and Italy have been organising their nations systematically for war: but they justify these measures to their people on the ground that they are surrounded by enemies and that they have no alternative means of self-preservation. For there are sections in both countries which are anxious to restore good international relations and thereby alleviate the economic difficulties with which these countries are faced.[17]

Since Germany's motives and the ultimate objectives of German policy were ambiguous, and since the political and economic case against rearmament was so compelling, it appears reasonable, even in hindsight, for the British government to have adopted a conciliatory approach, subject to two basic conditions: (1) that the policy would proceed cautiously and with a view toward ascertaining the prospects for success; and (2) that if and when strong evidence emerged that the policy could not succeed it would be abandoned. The second condition implied a third: (3) that Britain would maintain the capacity to adopt an alternative strategy—e.g., deterrence—if the need arose. Unfortunately, as the policy of appeasement evolved, these conditions were not fulfilled.

PASSIVE APPEASEMENT, 1935–1936

Exactly when the British government can be said to have embarked upon its policy of appeasement is open to debate. The first important concessions to the Nazi regime, however, came in March 1935, when Germany announced the existence of an air force and then, a week later, the reintroduction of universal conscription and plans for a German army of twelve corps and thirty-six divisions—all in blatant violation of the Treaty of Versailles. A year later, German troops reentered the Rhineland. Although the French were apparently ready to march, the British government was not, and no action was taken.

This exercise in what George Lanyi has called "passive appeasement"—attempting to meet an adversary's demands by acquiescing to its aggressive behavior—had as its objective nothing more than the avoidance of war in the immediate short term.[18] Few in Britain thought that rearmament and the remilitarization of the Rhineland represented the full scope of German ambitions; few anticipated a lasting improvement in relations with Germany as a consequence of Anglo-French passivity. Indeed, the events of 1935 and 1936 only reinforced existing concerns about German behavior. Shortly before he became prime minister, Chamberlain dispatched a letter to Henry Morgenthau, the American treasury secretary, warning of this menace:

> The fierce propaganda against other nations . . . the intensity and persistence of German military preparations, together with the many acts of the German Government in violation of treaties, cynically justified on the ground that unilateral action

was the quickest way of getting what they wanted, have inspired all her neighbours with a profound uneasiness. Even these islands, which could be reached in less than an hour from German territory by an air force equipped with hundreds of tons of bombs cannot be exempt from anxiety.

The motive for this aggressiveness on the part of Germany appears to arise from her desire to make herself so strong that no one will venture to withstand whatever demands she may make whether for European or colonial territory.

With this intention in her heart she is not likely to agree to any disarmament which would defeat her purpose. The only consideration which would influence her to a contrary decision would be the conviction that her efforts to secure superiority of force were doomed to failure by reason of the superior force which would meet her if she attempted aggression.[19]

THE QUEST FOR A GENERAL SETTLEMENT

If Germany's actions in 1935 and 1936 heightened British apprehension, they did not conclusively resolve the question of Germany's ultimate ambitions. In late 1936, in fact, there seemed good reason to believe that German policy might be turned in a more pacific direction. In August, while on a visit to Paris, Schacht, president of the Reichsbank and one of the so-called "moderates," suggested to the French premier, Leon Blum, the possibility of an arrangement whereby Germany, in return for colonial and other economic concessions, would adopt a more cooperative policy on the European continent. While nothing of substance emerged from this encounter, the French and British governments were sufficiently encouraged to pursue the matter further.

In January 1937, therefore, Chamberlain and Anthony Eden, the foreign secretary, decided to explore more fully the prospects for a "general settlement" along the lines proposed by Schacht.[20] Sir Frederick Leith-Ross, the government's principal economic adviser, was instructed to speak with Schacht in an effort to ascertain precisely what contributions to such a settlement Germany was prepared to make. Eden's formal instructions to Leith-Ross show clearly that the British government did not contemplate making unilateral concessions. Wrote Eden, "If Schacht's ideas are to form the basis of further discussion, it is essential that they should envisage *political* undertakings and assurances on the part of Germany." These must not, he said, be "merely 'eyewash,'" but must be "outward and visible signs" of "a definite change of political orientation in Germany." Among the undertakings to be required of Germany were the following: "(a) Entry of Germany into a new Locarno; (b) Abandonment of the policy of economic self-sufficiency and its corollary of territorial expansion; (c) Establishment of neighbourly relations with Czechoslovakia. (In this case a treaty of non-aggression would not be enough; a treaty of non-interference would be necessary.) (d) Readiness to consider means for putting a stop to the present armaments race. (e) Germany's return to the League."[21]

On 2 February 1937, Leith-Ross met with Schacht, who strongly implied that, in exchange for colonial and other economic concessions, all the political conditions demanded by Britain could be fulfilled.[22] But British officials remained doubtful, a feeling that was strengthened by an 11 February conversation between Lord Halifax, acting foreign secretary, and Ribbentrop, the German ambassador in London, who insisted that Germany's colonies must be returned to her without any *quid pro quo*.[23] Nevertheless, they decided to proceed. On 27 April, a message was dispatched to the French government, expressing British skepticism regarding Schacht's authority to conduct negotiations, but arguing that no opportunity to stabilize the European situation, however slight, should be missed. Noting that Schacht seemed to envisage a "comprehensive settlement covering, on the one hand, certain economic and financial concessions to Germany, the most important of which related to the transfer of colonies; and, on the other hand, the acceptance by Germany of the political desiderata of the French and United Kingdom Governments," the British government then laid out what it believed to be the appropriate desiderata. They were virtually identical to those contained in Eden's instructions to Leith-Ross: "(a) The conclusion of a treaty or treaties of non-aggression and guarantee for Western Europe to replace the Treaty of Locarno; (b) Measures by Germany, in treaty form or otherwise, which will satisfy the Governments of Central and Eastern Europe with regard to Germany's intention to respect the territorial integrity and sovereign independence of all Central and Eastern European States. . . . (c) The return of Germany to the League of Nations. . . . (d) An international arrangement for the limitation of armaments."[24]

French leaders agreed in principle with the British approach and suggested that a planned visit by Schacht to Paris in May be used as the occasion for further exploration of the subject. Like the British, however, they were decidedly pessimistic about the prospects for a settlement. Their pessimism proved justified, for the May visit produced nothing. Schacht was unwilling to discuss political issues at all, and it soon became apparent that he had no authority to negotiate on behalf of the German government.

There the matter rested until November 1937, when Lord Halifax paid a visit to Germany, meeting with Hitler and other German leaders. His purpose, he told the German chancellor, "was to discover in what ways an opportunity could be made for a comprehensive and open discussion of all questions of interest to both parties."[25] He reiterated, however, the British government's position that the question of colonies "could only be broached as a part of a general settlement by means of which quiet and security might be established in Europe."[26] Hitler was not interested in such a bargain. He explained that Germany would ultimately have the colonial question resolved to her satisfaction, if not through a "reasonable solution," then through "the free play of forces." In the event that the latter should become necessary, "What Germany would take in the way of colonies . . . could not be foretold."[27]

The British cabinet was becoming thoroughly discouraged. Eden noted that "Germany clearly did not now wish to connect Central Europe with the Colonial question. It was important to realise this for if the Cabinet's attitude was, as his was, that Colonial concessions could only be contemplated in return for a general settlement, this was clearly not Germany's view. He did not say that on this account the attempt should not be made, but the difficulties should be realised."[28]

After some discussion with the French, the British government decided to make one final attempt to get Hitler to agree to "a colonial settlement at the price of being a good European."[29] In March 1938, the ambassador to Berlin, Nevile Henderson, presented Hitler with a specific proposal for a "new regime of colonial administration" in tropical Africa. Within a given zone, the colonial powers would surrender their League of Nations mandates. While each would alone be responsible for administering its territories, it would be asked to accept certain principles of colonial administration, including demilitarization, freedom of trade and communications, and provisions relating to the treatment of native peoples. Germany would be awarded some territory to administer and would be given a seat on a commission established to oversee the new regime.[30]

Henderson, whose instructions from Eden and Halifax had repeated the list of British desiderata, made it plain that colonial concessions would come at a price.[31] His purpose, he told Hitler, was to ascertain two things: "first, whether Germany was prepared in principle to participate in a new colonial regime as provided for by the British proposal, and second, what contribution she would be prepared to make to the general peace and security of Europe."[32]

Hitler's response to this inquiry was entirely unsatisfactory. He said that the "simplest and most natural way" to resolve the colonial question was to return the former German colonies to Germany. But, in any event, he "did not consider the colonial problem ripe for settlement as yet." He would "wait quietly for 4, 6, 8, or 10 years. Perhaps by that time a change of mind would have occurred in Paris and London, and they would understand that the best solution was to return to Germany her rightful property."[33] Hitler was not interested in disarmament proposals nor a return to the League of Nations. Most ominously, he warned Henderson that "Concerning Central Europe, it should be noted that Germany would not tolerate any interference by third powers in the settlement of her relations with kindred countries or with countries having large German elements in their population."[34]

From his conversation with the chancellor, Henderson drew the obvious conclusion: that Hitler was not prepared to "tie his hands in Central Europe" in return for colonial concessions.[35] He believed, further, that Hitler was determined to move against Austria and Czechoslovakia, and that in any attempt to stop him, "only force will be effective."[36] Germany's annexation of Austria the following week proved that he was right.

THE PIECEMEAL APPROACH

After the annexation of Austria, British statesmen abandoned their efforts to obtain a comprehensive settlement with Germany. While they remained hopeful that such an arrangement might ultimately be achieved, it was now clear that this could not be negotiated in a single agreement. British officials therefore embarked upon an incremental, "piecemeal" approach to appeasement.[37] In the economic realm, this meant continuing talks on trade and financial issues, with the hope of gradually weaning Germany from her autarkic economic policy and reintegrating her into the European and world economy. As the British government was well aware,

Germany's stated goal of autarky implied considerable territorial expansion. If she could be convinced to renounce this objective, her aggressive appetite might be curbed.

In the more important political realm, the piecemeal approach to appeasement meant that Britain would seek to achieve, on a case-by-case basis, solutions to the outstanding territorial problems of Europe. Britain had never been rigidly committed to upholding the European status quo. Halifax told Hitler in November 1937 that "certain changes in the European system could probably not be avoided in the long run. The British," he said, "did not believe that the *status quo* had to be maintained under all circumstances. Among the questions in which changes would probably be made sooner or later were Danzig, Austria, and Czechoslovakia. England was only interested in seeing that such changes were brought about by peaceful development."[38]

Britain's acceptance of the *Anschluß* with Austria, which could in some sense be regarded as "peaceful," was the first manifestation of this new approach. It reached its high point in the Munich Agreement of September 1938, whereby Britain and France, after a summer-long period of rising tensions and fear of imminent war, surrendered the Sudetenland region of Czechoslovakia to Germany. The political dimension of what may be called "appeasement in parts" was jettisoned by the British cabinet in March of 1939, when, following the German invasion and seizure of the remainder of Czechoslovakia, the government issued its guarantee to Poland.[39] The economic portion of the strategy was, however, pursued throughout the summer of 1939 and was in fact abandoned only upon the outbreak of war.

German Aims and British Concessions

The failure of Britain's attempt to negotiate a general settlement with Germany is explained most fundamentally by the fact that the concessions offered by Great Britain and France did not meet—or even address—Germany's most important objectives, which lay in Europe. Chamberlain and his colleagues recognized, of course, that Germany had ambitions on the continent. However, as noted above, they believed that German policy was being driven in considerable part by short-term economic difficulties: unemployment, tight credit, high foreign debt, and declining trade.[40] If this were true, the best way to moderate German behavior was to offer colonial and other economic concessions that would bolster Germany's economy. Anthony Eden, the foreign secretary, argued in early 1936:

> The poverty of Nazi Germany, measured in that country's dwindling export trade and increase of unemployment, may be expected to have the same effect as in Italy, and to encourage a dictator to launch his people on some foreign venture as the only means that remain to him to distract their attention from the failure of his policy at home. Our purpose being to avoid war, it should follow that we should be wise to do everything in our power to assist Germany's economic recovery, thereby easing the strain upon the German rulers, and making an outbreak less likely.[41]

The British government was partly right: German ambitions on the European continent did have an economic basis.[42] But policymakers in London were mistaken in their belief that it was a short-term economic "crisis" and the possibility of popular revolt that concerned Hitler. Although Germany had faced significant economic problems early in the decade, there was no economic crisis in the late 1930s, nor was one perceived by Hitler and his closest advisers. Much of the information received by London regarding Germany's alleged economic difficulties was simply inaccurate. It came from "circles within Germany, or exiles, hostile to Hitler, who had their own motives for painting a bleak picture" of the situation.[43]

Hitler's focus, contrary to what the British cabinet believed, was on Germany's long-term economic prospects. The führer was convinced that his country had economic needs that must ultimately be met through territorial expansion. These needs, as he saw it, were two. The first was food to feed a growing German population. The second was the raw materials needed to fuel the German economy and military. Hitler rejected the liberal economic doctrines of Adam Smith, on which British policy was founded, believing that commercial exchange as a method of acquiring food and resources was inherently unreliable and a potential source of weakness in time of war. He wrote in 1928: "World trade, world economy, tourist traffic, etc., etc., are all transient means for securing a nation's sustenance. . . . The increase of population can be balanced only through an increase, that is an enlargement, of living space."[44] In 1934, he noted that "Our dependence on foreign trade . . . would condemn us eternally to the position of a politically dependent nation."[45]

Hitler conceived of international politics as a Darwinian "struggle for existence" in which only the fittest nations would survive.[46] In this world, trade was more a danger than a benefit; self-sufficiency or autarky was required to render a state invulnerable. Given the limitations of the country's resource base, including its agricultural land, autarky for Germany implied territorial expansion. And this expansion, in the chancellor's mind, had to come in Europe. Only in Europe could Hitler fulfill his wish to unite, within a single state, all ethnic Germans. As he wrote in the opening paragraphs of *Mein Kampf,* "Common blood belongs in a common Reich."[47] More crucially, only Europe could provide the living space needed to support the growing German population. "For Germany," claimed Hitler, "the only possibility of carrying out a sound territorial policy [is] to be found in the acquisition of new soil in Europe proper. Colonies cannot serve this purpose, since they do not appear suitable for settlement with Europeans on a large scale."[48] Colonies were equally inadequate as a source of raw materials, since shipments from them were subject to disruption by enemy naval forces.

Over the longer term, Hitler hoped to use German economic and political domination of Europe as a springboard to world power. Establishment of a colonial empire in Africa and a strong naval presence in the Atlantic would allow Germany to take its rightful place alongside Britain, Japan, and the United States, and would prepare Germany for a final showdown with America.[49] Although this plan envisaged the eventual acquisition of colonies, it did not make them a short-term priority. The expansion and consolidation of German power in Europe had to come first. Once this had been accomplished, then colonies could be obtained. If they were surrendered by Britain and the other imperial powers, fine. If not, Germany would simply seize them.

Because he viewed expansion in Europe as critical, and because he believed that Germany could eventually take what she wanted in the colonial field, Britain's offer of colonial concessions, in return for which Germany would renounce her continental ambitions, held no attraction for Hitler. Göring put it well when he told Henderson in March of 1938, "If you offered us the whole of Africa we would not accept it as the price of Austria."[50] According to the field marshal, Germany would be willing to reach an understanding with Britain on one basis only: German recognition of British overseas interests and the maintenance of her Empire in exchange for British recognition of Germany's "preponderating influence in Central Europe."[51]

This proposal was, of course, exactly the reverse of the settlement being advocated by the British government. It was, moreover, a proposal London could, for strategic reasons, never accept. British policymakers had long believed that the security of Britain and its empire depended on preventing a single European power from dominating the continent. Such a power, enjoying the vast material and human resources of Europe and freed from the necessity of preparing to defend itself on land, would be capable of building a navy sufficient to challenge British supremacy on the seas.[52] Because Britain's offer of colonial concessions was aimed at blocking German expansion on the continent—the very thing the Germans were determined to achieve—no general accommodation was possible.

The piecemeal approach to appeasement, which recognized the need for some adjustment in the European status quo, failed for two basic reasons. First, Hitler's objectives with respect to European territorial expansion went far beyond the limited aim of self-determination for German-speaking peoples that the appeasers were prepared to accept. Although the full extent of his ambitions was never clearly articulated, in his so-called "second" or "secret" book, published after his death, he wrote that living space comprising "an additional 500,000 square kilometers in Europe" would have to be acquired.[53] The territories inhabited by ethnic Germans did not, of course, total more than a small fraction of this amount.

More importantly, by 1938 Hitler had become determined to achieve his territorial objectives not by coercion or intimidation but through the actual use of force. Why this was so can only be speculated upon. Perhaps, remembering his experience in World War I, he desired to recapture the feelings of comradeship and service in a common cause he had shared with his fellow soldiers. Or perhaps his Social Darwinist worldview led him to seek armed conflict as a true test of his—and Germany's—mettle. Many of his early speeches in particular support the conclusion of one historian that Hitler saw "violent conflict between warring peoples" as "the highest and ideal form of life for states," and that he believed it "corresponded absolutely to the plan of creation."[54]

Whatever the reason for it, Hitler's desire for war meant that he and Germany were ultimately unappeasable. The relaxation of tensions sought by his opponents was the opposite of what he desired. Indeed, as we shall see, by the time of the Munich Conference, he viewed concessions by his enemies not as diplomatic victories, but rather as unwelcome obstacles to the realization of his true objective.

THE ABSENCE OF CONSTRAINTS ON GERMAN POLICY

That the inducements offered by Britain and France fell so far short of fulfilling German aims may provide a sufficient explanation for the failure of appeasement in this case. Still, the proposed Anglo-French concessions were not insignificant, and, had Hitler accepted them, Germany's economic and geopolitical position would have been markedly improved. In retrospect, it is of course evident that Germany would have been much better served by agreeing to Britain's colonial bargain than by entering into a war which resulted not merely in defeat, but the loss of territory and partition.

Hitler's refusal to acquiesce in the reduction of tensions desired by Britain and France flowed in part from the absence of compelling reasons for him to do so. Unlike the turn-of-the-century United States, which possessed significant incentives to accept British inducements, Germany lacked major constraints on its international behavior.

German leaders did not feel the need to cooperate with Britain for strategic reasons. As Weinberg has noted, by 1937 "Germany was unquestionably the most powerful country in Europe."[55] She was threatened militarily by none of the major powers. France, her traditional continental enemy, was defense-minded and too beset by internal strife to pose a danger. Relations with Benito Mussolini's Italy were good. Even prior to the conclusion of the Rome-Berlin Axis, joint intervention in the Spanish Civil War had provided a framework for cooperation between the German and Italian dictators. The Soviet Union, with which Germany concluded the now-infamous Molotov-Ribbentrop nonaggression pact in August 1939, had for several years been signaling its desire for an agreement. The United States, isolationist and half a world away, certainly posed no danger. With respect to Britain itself, only in naval power did Germany face any disadvantage. On land and in the air, German capabilities significantly outstripped those of the British. By September 1939, Germany's military advantage over Britain (even in combination with France) was sufficient to cause Hitler to discount the threat of Anglo-French intervention in support of Poland.[56]

Nor, in contrast to their American counterparts of four decades before, did German leaders perceive economic incentives to accept British concessions and cooperate in a reduction of tensions. It is true that Germany was potentially vulnerable to a disruption of trade in the event of war. Murray writes that in the 1930s "German resources of every strategic raw material except coal ... were at best insufficient, and in most cases simply did not exist. Even Germany's agricultural production could not meet her needs."[57] Should Britain, with its powerful navy, impose a blockade, the country would face strangulation.[58]

Rather than viewing economic dependence as an argument for avoiding conflict with Britain, however, Hitler and his associates regarded it as necessitating a policy of expansion, the ultimate objective of which was self-sufficiency.[59] As far as the German leader was concerned, the solution to Germany's excessive reliance on foreign sources of raw materials was "not greater industrialization and foreign trade, but conquest of vast territories in eastern Europe."[60] In September 1936, he noted, "If we had at our disposal the Urals, with their incalculable wealth of raw materials, and the forests of Siberia, and if the unending wheat-fields of the Ukraine lay within Germany, our country would swim in plenty."[61] Declared Hitler, "National independence, and independence on the political level, depend as much on autarky as on military power."[62]

Finally, the Nazi leadership faced little or no domestic pressure to pursue amicable relations with Britain. Weinberg notes that by 1937, "the National Socialist regime was firmly in control. The other political parties had disappeared, independent political and other organizations were practically nonexistent, and a system of mass propaganda and indoctrination was reinforced by censorship and secret police."[63] The army, which constituted the only real potential challenge to Nazi dominance, was generally supportive. Although many officers doubted whether Germany was adequately prepared to fight Britain at the time of the Munich Conference, they did not oppose war on principle, and after Munich, which seemed to confirm the superiority of Hitler's judgment, opposition within the army melted away.

BRITAIN'S NONRESPONSE TO SIGNS OF FAILURE

As noted earlier, Britain's appeasement policy was predicated on two assumptions, which, as British leaders recognized, might or might not be true. The first was that Germany's ambitions on the continent of Europe were limited, the second that "moderates" in the German government might ultimately exercise a decisive, and pacific, influence on German policy.

It is difficult to identify a specific point at which these assumptions were proved false. Indeed, it could be argued that the fact that Germany's continental ambitions exceeded mere self-determination for ethnic Germans was not conclusively established until the occupation of Prague in March 1939, while the impotence of German moderates was not definitively revealed until Göring failed to dissuade Hitler from invading Poland the following September.

At the same time, however, it must be admitted that an overwhelming preponderance of evidence pointed toward the ultimate futility of appeasement well before these dates. The attempt at a general settlement had gone nowhere, and Hitler had repeatedly emphasized his unwillingness to tie his hands in Europe, even in return for significant colonial concessions. There were such strong similarities between the program of expansion detailed in *Mein Kampf* and Germany's behavior that as early as 1936 members of the House of Commons suggested that the book was serving as a blueprint for German policy, a not unreasonable conclusion.[64] Moreover, most of the "moderates" on whom Britain pinned her hopes—Blomberg, Schacht, and Neurath—were gradually removed from office and replaced by "extremists" such as Ribbentrop.

"Anti-appeasers" like Churchill naturally recognized such things, but it is important to understand that those who favored a conciliatory policy also appreciated the weight of the evidence against their position. Expressions of skepticism and discouragement regarding the prospects for appeasement appear with great frequency in diary entries, diplomatic correspondence, and cabinet minutes, as do comments about the aggressive, untrustworthy, fanatical nature of Hitler and his regime. Yet despite this, the British cabinet abandoned the idea of territorial concessions only in March 1939 and pursued a conciliatory policy in the economic realm throughout the summer of that year.

The reason for this appears in retrospect quite simple: the policy of the British government was dominated by wishful thinking. There was, in fact, an almost astonishing discrepancy between what British leaders increasingly came to know in their minds—that Germany could not be appeased—and what they continued to hope in their hearts—that it could. In this conflict between hope and evidence, hope prevailed as the chief source of belief, especially for the prime minister. As William Rock has written, "For Chamberlain the dividing line between hope and belief was so indistinguishable as to be practically non-existent. Though he may on occasion have believed the worst, he so ardently hoped for the best that the two became inseparably intertwined."[65]

In part, the wishful thinking of the British government was a reflection of Neville Chamberlain's conviction that he had the unique capacity to deal with Hitler (and Mussolini) man-to-man. According to Rock, "Chamberlain seemed to believe that there was an affinity between himself and the dictators entirely denied to other men. He could not believe that he could not influence them by his patience, understanding, and reasonableness."[66] The prime minister lacked a warm and charming personality; he had few if any genuine personal friends. But he had great faith in his ability to establish close, working, businesslike relations with others, and thereby to gain their trust and convince them to modify their behavior. Plan Z, Chamberlain's scheme to negotiate personally with the German chancellor, which (in modified form) was realized in his visits to Berchtesgaden, Godesberg, and Munich, was a reflection of this faith.[67] Falsely, Chamberlain believed that his meetings with Hitler had succeeded: Hitler "had been most favourably impressed," he had "won Hitler's goodwill" and had "established an influence over [the German chancellor], who 'trusted him' and was willing to work with him."[68] Only the occupation of Prague in March of 1939 finally shattered the British leader's perception of "the special relationship he believed he had established with Hitler," a relationship in which he "had placed considerable trust."[69]

The wishful thinking of the British government was also a function of the increasingly powerful belief that there was simply no alternative to conciliation. To abandon appeasement meant not only fighting a war, but fighting a war for which Britain was woefully unprepared and which she might even lose. If the use of force to stop German aggression was politically and economically difficult in the mid-1930s, by the late 1930s (when it was perhaps politically possible) it had become militarily problematic. As Alan Alexandroff and Richard Rosecrance ask, "If Britain and France could not realistically oppose the extension of German power in Eastern Europe, what could they do but appease?"[70] This suggests that one of the greatest failures of British policy in the 1930s was the premature foreclosure of Britain's options. Whatever the financial implications of rearmament, whatever the public opposition, it was foolish for the British government to place itself in a position from which appeasement could not be abandoned in favor of deterrence should the evidence indicate that such a move was required.[71] This is not to argue that deterrence would have succeeded in restraining Hitler; probably it would not. But it might have done so, and in any event, adoption of such a policy at an earlier stage would have put Britain in a far more favorable position when war actually broke out.

Appeasement and the Failure of Deterrence in Poland

British appeasement of Nazi Germany during the 1930s has been criticized not only because it did not pacify Hitler, but because it caused deterrence to fail in 1939. The German government, it is argued, viewed Anglo-French concessions as signs of weakness and irresolution. Encouraged by his success at Munich, Hitler issued new demands on Poland, threatening that country with attack. When France and Britain declared their intention to intervene, the German chancellor refused to believe them. As Paul Huth writes, "British weakness in the Czech crisis convinced Hitler that the British guarantee was likely to be a bluff."[72] His miscalculation led him to invade Poland and was a principal cause of World War II.

Much of the evidence regarding the German view of the Anglo-French commitment to Poland does not, however, support this interpretation. The German diplomats, the record shows, were virtually unanimous in their belief that Britain and France would intervene on behalf of Poland. The German embassy in London reported again and again that the British guarantee to Poland would be fulfilled. In July 1939, the ambassador, Herbert von Dirksen, noted a "decisive difference between Britain's mood in the autumn of 1938 and now," that the British people felt "'We must not put up with any more of this. Our honour is at stake; we must fight; the Government must not give way.'"[73] On 18 August, he submitted a "Memorandum on Britain's Probable Attitude in the Event of a German–Polish Conflict," in which he argued: "Should Germany, from military considerations of any kind—e.g. in order to forestall a Polish attack believed to be imminent—feel herself forced to take military action against Poland, the fact would have to be reckoned with that Britain would come to Poland's aid. It is also unlikely that Britain would remain neutral if, in such a war with Germany, Poland were very soon defeated."[74] And on 25 August, the embassy reported to the Foreign Ministry that "The fulfilment of the guarantee to Poland has become a point of honour which is no longer even questioned."[75] Corroborating information was received in Berlin from other sources, including the press director of the Landesgruppe for Great Britain of the Auslandsorganisation and the German naval attaché.[76]

This intelligence convinced Ernst von Weizsäcker, the state secretary in the Foreign Ministry, that Britain and France were not making idle threats. On 23 August, he warned Hitler that "the English were captives of their policy. They were not logical or systematic, but were governed by emotion. They were in the grip of a psychosis—drunk, as it were. What they were doing had no tactical purpose. When Chamberlain issued the call to arms he would have the entire Parliament behind him."[77] Two days later, he noted prophetically, "I am of the opinion that the Italians will back out and that the Western Powers will intervene, the most unfavorable circumstances in which Germany could fight."[78]

Weizsäcker's assessment appears to have been shared by others within the German leadership. Göring, at Nuremberg, maintained that "After the guarantee I held an English declaration of war inevitable."[79] Given the circumstances of his testimony, this statement must be taken with a grain of salt, but it is supported by some corroborating evidence. In a July conversation with Swedish businessman and self-styled diplomat Birger Dahlerus, Göring said that he realized "Great Britain was not bluffing but was prepared to fight."[80] The head of the Luftwaffe apparently continued to hold this view. At a 27 August meeting with Ribbentrop and Rudolf Hess, Hitler's close adviser, Göring "merely nodded" as Fritz Hesse, the German press attaché in London, told the group that "only a complete withdrawal on the part of Germany would make it possible to avoid a war." Hesse noted that both Ribbentrop and Hess informed him that their views on the subject conformed to his own.[81]

There is, then, considerable evidence that the credibility of Britain's promise to defend Poland was not damaged beyond repair by British appeasement. Despite London's efforts at conciliation, German diplomats and some of Hitler's closest political advisers were convinced that if Germany invaded Poland, Britain and France would intervene.[82]

It remains to consider the attitude of Adolf Hitler himself. The claim that the German leader did not believe Britain and France would come to the aid of Poland has been based largely upon statements he made in August 1939. The most important of these are contained in two addresses by Hitler to high-ranking military officers at Obersalzberg. In a meeting on 14 August, and again on 22 August, Hitler warned his audience that the two Western Powers might respond to a German attack on Poland. He argued, however, that this response would amount to nothing more than a recalling of ambassadors, or perhaps a blockade.[83]

Critics of appeasement have contended that Hitler's expressions of doubt regarding the likelihood of military intervention by Britain and France flowed from his belief, formed especially during the Munich Crisis, that leaders of the two countries lacked the resolve to carry out their threats. At the meeting of 14 August, Hitler told his audience that "The men I got to know in Munich are not the kind that start a new World War."[84] One source reports him saying eight days later: "I experienced those poor worms Daladier and Chamberlain in Munich. They will be too cowardly to attack."[85]

On the surface, Hitler's remarks certainly seem to suggest that he regarded the threat of Anglo-French military intervention as less than credible. But the evidence is not as conclusive as it might seem. First, it is difficult to know whether to take the statements at face value. It is conceivable that they represented Hitler's true beliefs, but other interpretations are equally plausible. In his addresses, the German chancellor cited an extensive catalogue of reasons why Britain and France would not intervene. Ranging from an unfavorable military balance to the absence of formal treaty commitments to British efforts to restrain the Poles from doing anything that might be construed as provocative, the list is sufficiently long to make one wonder, as Shakespeare's Queen Gertrude once did, whether perhaps the protest was a bit excessive.[86] Who was Hitler trying to convince? One possibility, discussed further below, was himself. The other was his military leadership, easily the most cautious element in the German decision-making hierarchy. Skeptical of the prospects for success against the Western Powers and fearful of the consequences of defeat, the German officers clearly needed some reassurance. Thus, as one historian has written, the arguments that Hitler "advanced to his hesitant and anxious generals for the improbability of a British intervention may be interpreted as an attempt to win the skeptics over to the venture, as well as a justification to attack quickly and in a 'lightning action' achieve a fait accompli."[87]

More serious questions about Hitler's alleged doubts regarding the willingness of Britain and France to carry out their threats are raised by various reports suggesting that the chancellor did in fact believe the Western Powers would intervene. As Josef Henke notes, by July 1939 a number of persons with close connections to Hitler, "including Burckhardt, Weizsäcker, Henderson, Dirksen, and the French chargé d'affaires in Berlin, held the view that the German leader no longer harbored any doubts about the genuineness of England's intention to help Poland under any circumstances."[88] On 20 August, according to Henke, Hesse told Sir Horace Wilson that "Hitler knows full well that if war should break out between Germany and Poland Great Britain will be in it."[89]

Hitler's statements at Obersalzberg do not, then, prove that he found the threats of Anglo-French military action incredible. The most one can say is that the German chancellor's opinion on the matter is unclear. It is possible, perhaps likely, that it varied according to the occasion and his mood. But there is a still more fundamental problem with the conventional wisdom linking appeasement to the invasion of Poland: the further evolution of Hitler's views after 22 August, the date of the second Obersalzberg meeting. By 1 September, he was convinced of the likelihood of intervention, a fact even some critics of Munich do not dispute.[90]

Three events appear to have contributed to this change. The first was the delivery, on 23 August, of a personal letter from Neville Chamberlain to Hitler in which the British prime minister warned that the conclusion of the anticipated Nazi-Soviet nonaggression pact "cannot alter Great Britain's obligation to Poland, which His Majesty's Government have stated in public repeatedly and plainly and which they are determined to fulfil."[91] Noted Alfred Jodl, operations chief of the Armed Forces High Command, "the Führer is no longer entirely certain that England is not serious this time. He does not want a conflict with England."[92] The second, and most important, was the embodiment, on 25 August, of the informal British guarantee in a formal Anglo-Polish defense treaty. The impact of this agreement, which came only two days after the conclusion of the Nazi-Soviet pact, an event that Hitler expected would result in the fall of the Chamberlain government and abandonment of the guarantee to Poland,[93] was strengthened by a third occurrence: the notification—also on 25 August—by Italy that it was not prepared to fight as Germany's ally.[94] Although Britain's decision to enter into an alliance with Poland was unrelated to the Italian declaration, the German chancellor saw a clear connection. In a telephone conversation with Wilhelm Keitel, chief of the Armed Forces High Command, Hitler complained, "There's absolutely no doubt that London has realised by now that Italy won't go along with us. Now Britain's attitude towards us will stiffen—now they will back up Poland to the hilt."[95]

By 25 August, Hitler appears to have become convinced that Britain would honor her guarantee to Poland. In order to avert British intervention, he abruptly and unexpectedly cancelled orders to begin Operation White, scheduled for the following day.[96] Working to recover his nerve, he asked Mussolini to "try to achieve the pinning down of Anglo-French forces by active propaganda and suitable military demonstrations," adding "I do not shrink from solving the Eastern question even at the risk of complications in the West."[97] On 26 August, he expressed his willingness to fight a two-front war,[98] and by 31 August, he had decided to launch his attack regardless of the inevitable Anglo-French reaction.[99] It is interesting, and surely instructive, that Hitler's "Directive No. 1 for the Conduct of War," issued on 31 August, deals extensively, and almost exclusively, with the German military's response to a counterattack by the Western Powers.[100]

Even if one continues to take the view that Hitler found the threat of Anglo-French military intervention incredible, there is little evidence that a perceived lack of resolve on the part of Britain and France was responsible. The report of Hitler's comment of 22 August that Chamberlain and French Premier Edouard Daladier were "too cowardly to attack" is based on third-hand information and is not confirmed by any of the three principal accounts of that meeting.[101] His brief reference on 14 August to "the men I got to know in Munich" seems, in the context of his lengthy speech, little more than a passing remark.

It is probable that any doubts harbored by Hitler regarding the willingness of Britain and France to carry out their threats reflected his own wishful thinking rather than his analysis of past diplomatic encounters. Students of perception typically distinguish between two sources of misperception: "cognitive bias"—seeing what one expects to see, often based on previous experience—and "motivated bias"—seeing what one would like to see.[102] The claim that Hitler wrongly perceived Britain's commitment to Poland as a result of appeasement identifies cognitive bias as the source of his misperception: he expected the British to back down because they had done so before. There is, however, evidence to suggest motivated bias as a more likely explanation.[103]

Hitler, it may be argued, viewed Anglo-French intervention as unlikely because he did not want it to occur. Walther Hofer has noted that the German chancellor was "able to believe quite firmly that an event that did not fit into his plans would not take place."[104] In an effort to confirm his beliefs, Hitler and his sycophantic advisers tried to ensure that information that conflicted with them would not reach his eyes and ears. Thus, for example, he recalled his ambassadors from their posts during times of crisis and refused to read diplomatic reports that did not correspond to what he already "knew" to be true.[105] In May 1939, the German foreign minister, Ribbentrop, declared with respect to the Polish question: "England will never dare to oppose him [Hitler] because she would be defeated and lose her empire, while France, if she should become involved, would bleed to death at the West Wall. If I hear that any official expresses a contrary opinion, I will personally shoot him in his office and be responsible to the Führer for my action."[106] Such a policy seems more consistent with beliefs that are motivated rather than cognitive in origin. So, too, does Hitler's 1 September outburst in a meeting with Birger Dahlerus. According to the Swedish businessman, the German leader expressed again his willingness to negotiate a settlement with Britain. But, he warned, if the British should decide to intervene on behalf of Poland, they would "live to repent their folly." Becoming increasingly agitated the more he thought about this prospect, Hitler began to gesticulate wildly and shouted his determination to battle England for as long as she wished—a year, two years, even three years. Finally, having worked himself into an utter frenzy, he exploded, "And if it is necessary, I will fight for ten years."[107] This tantrum, which erupted two days prior to Britain's declaration of war, suggests that the German chancellor desperately wished to avoid a conflict with the Western Powers and that he was deeply frustrated at the failure of his efforts to secure their neutrality.

Hitler's encounter with Chamberlain and Daladier at Munich lies at the heart of the conventional wisdom linking appeasement to the failure of deterrence in 1939. The notion that the Munich Conference, by casting doubts upon the credibility of the subsequent Anglo-French commitment to Poland, encouraged Germany's invasion of that country, rests logically upon the assumption that Hitler viewed the outcome of his meetings with the French and British leaders as a great diplomatic victory in which his determination triumphed over their weakness and irresolution.

In fact, however, a preponderance of evidence suggests that Hitler regarded Munich as a crushing defeat, one in which he abandoned his true objective—war—in the face of Anglo-French intransigence. In mid-September 1938, the German chancellor told the Hungarian prime minister and foreign minister that "action by the Army would provide the only satisfactory solution" to the Czech situation. "There was, however, a danger of the Czechs submitting to every demand."[108] Echoing his führer's sentiments, Ribbentrop informed Gen. Rudolf Schmundt, Hitler's military aide, that from the perspective of the German government, Czechoslovakia's acquiescence to German demands was the worst thing that could happen.[109] Of course, pressed by Britain and France, the Czechs did submit, and Hitler lost his pretext for an attack.[110]

The Munich Conference is often regarded as a case of unadulterated appeasement, but it is more complex than that. The conference itself was the third in a series of meetings between the German chancellor and the British prime minister to discuss the Czechoslovakian situation. At the first, held in Berchtesgaden on 15 September, Hitler presented his substantive demand: the cession of the Sudetenland to Germany.[111] After discussion with the cabinet and with the French government, Chamberlain then met with Hitler in Bad Godesberg on 22 and 23 September. Having secured approval for the cession of the Sudetenland on the basis of the principle of self-determination, the British prime minister found himself confronted with a new set of procedural demands: the evacuation of German-speaking regions of Czechoslovakia must begin on 26 September and be completed within two days; occupation by German troops would take place immediately. Hitler expressed his willingness to hold a plebiscite in those areas where the ethnic mix was open to question, and he magnanimously agreed, when Chamberlain noted his displeasure with these demands, to put off the evacuation and occupation until 1 October.[112]

The French and British governments considered Hitler's new demands and determined to reject them.[113] On 26 September, Halifax, the foreign secretary, issued a statement to the press: "During the last week Mr. Chamberlain has tried with the German Chancellor to find the way of settling peacefully the Czechoslovak question. It is still possible to do so by negotiations. The German claim to the transfer of the Sudeten areas has already been conceded by the French, British and Czechoslovak Governments, but if in spite of all efforts made by the British Prime Minister a German attack is made upon Czechoslovakia the imminent result must be that France will be bound to come to her assistance, and Great Britain and Russia will certainly stand by France."[114] Sir Horace Wilson was dispatched to convey this message directly to Berlin.[115] In a stormy session on 27 September, the British envoy told Hitler that if France chose to fulfill her obligation to defend Czechoslovakia, as she had stated she would, Britain would offer her complete support. Reinforced by his government's public statements and by the mobilization of the Royal Navy, Wilson's words had the desired effect. Records of the meeting indicate the German chancellor's appreciation of the fact that an attack on Czechoslovakia would result in general war.[116]

In retrospect, the Munich Agreement of 29 September 1938 appears to differ only marginally from Hitler's Godesberg demands. It extended the date for German occupation of the Sudetenland from 1 October to 10 October, and called for an international commission to establish the terms under which the occupation should take place, a provision the Germans later ignored.[117] Nevertheless, members of the British government believed an important principle—that territorial changes should be negotiated rather than forcibly imposed—had been maintained.[118] Although Britain and France were prepared to appease Hitler by ceding him the Sudetenland, their policy of preventing him from acquiring it by force was mainly one of deterrence. And in the end, Hitler was deterred.[119] Confronted with the certainty of Anglo-French intervention, an acute lack of enthusiasm among the German public, opposition within the military, and Mussolini's urging that a peaceful solution be found, along with acquiescence to his substantive demands, Hitler decided to postpone his attack.[120]

Given the German chancellor's desire for military action, it is hardly surprising that he began almost immediately to regret his decision. His disappointment—even outrage—at the results of Munich was recorded by those who observed it. André François-Poncet, the French ambassador in Berlin, noted that Hitler "did not at all believe that he had, at Munich, achieved a success. He felt, on the contrary, that he had renounced his original objective, that he had compromised and capitulated. As after the invasion of Austria, he regretted having been a coward. He believed himself, or wanted to believe himself, cheated, fooled by British artifice, frustrated in the proper object of his ambition, which was to seize Prague."[121] Otto Dietrich, a member of Hitler's entourage, reported that within minutes of Chamberlain's departure from Munich, Hitler "made remarks bitterly accusing the British Prime Minister of having come only 'in order to trick and cheat' him."[122]

Having once retreated, Hitler was determined not to do so again. His greatest fear during the Polish crisis was not that Britain and France would intervene, but that they would again broker some kind of agreement, which he would be unable to reject.[123] On 15 August, the Ministry of Propaganda issued instructions to the press: "Nothing was feared more than a new Munich, a new 'conference psychosis,' and every compromise solution had for that reason to be ignored as unacceptable."[124] A week later, at Obersalzberg, Hitler told the assembled officers, "I am afraid only that at the last moment some S.O.B. will present me with a plan for mediation."[125] Hitler's momentary vacillation on 25 August, when he learned of the signing of the Anglo-Polish treaty and of his abandonment by the Italians, only served to increase his resolve once he had recovered his nerve. The world's leading historian of Nazi foreign policy concludes:

Hitler conducted his foreign policy in 1939 under the personal trauma of Munich. He had shrunk from war then—and attributed such cowardice to everyone else—so he would not be cheated once again of the war he had always intended. Just as his anger at having been deprived of war in 1938 made him all the more determined to have it in 1939, so his postponement of the attack on 25 August left him all the firmer in an almost hysterical fixation to attack a few days later. He would not back off again.[126]

In sum, Munich contributed to the failure of deterrence in 1939, but not in the way usually supposed. Rather than convincing Hitler that his enemies were spineless, the conference led him to believe they were determined to thwart his aims. More important, Munich caused him to doubt his own qualities as a leader, convincing him that he had to prevail in the confrontation over Poland.

Although British appeasement of Nazi Germany does not appear to have undermined deterrence by producing the "psychological effect"— i.e. a reputation for irresolution—emphasized in the traditional critique of the policy, there is some evidence for the damaging impact of a "material effect." If one construes British appeasement broadly, taking it to include not merely the offering of economic and territorial concessions but also restraint in the building of armaments, then it appears that the strategy may have encouraged Germany to attack Poland in September 1939. Hitler's argument at the two August meetings in Obersalzberg for the unlikelihood of an Anglo-French military response rested not upon his analysis of the character of French and British leaders, but on his assessment of the military situation. He noted that Britain's naval construction program for 1938 had not been completed and that there would be little or no strengthening of the Royal Navy before 1941 or 1942. He stated that London's position on land was equally poor; a maximum of three divisions could be sent to the continent. And Britain was vulnerable from the air. Her air defenses were rudimentary and her air force was only a third the size of the Luftwaffe. After reviewing Britain's position, Hitler concluded, "It thus appears to me out of the question that a responsible English statesman would in this situation accept for England the risk of a war."[127] Alexandroff and Rosecrance have written that deterrence failed in 1939 because Britain and France, which had long-term military superiority over Germany, did not possess the means to aid Poland effectively in the short run. Because the Germans had a short-term time horizon, the Anglo-French deterrence strategy was doomed.[128] Appeasement, to the extent it contributed to the weakness of British and French military capabilities, was partly responsible for this failure.

CONCLUSION

The futile efforts of the Western Powers to conciliate Germany during the 1930s offer several "lessons" for theorists and policymakers. Most importantly, it needs to be recognized that some adversaries are fundamentally unappeasable, either because their demands are so extreme that they simply cannot be met, or because they actually desire war. In the latter case, of course, concessions are regarded as nuisances to the extent that they deprive a state of its pretext for aggression. It follows from this that in formulating policy, it is essential to know one's adversary, and—in the event that the adversary's objectives are unclear—to proceed cautiously until greater evidence on this score has been obtained. The British, in fact, did rather well in this regard, initially offering concessions only in the colonial realm—where their interests were not vital—and then only on the basis of considerable reciprocity. The tragedy of British diplomacy was not that appeasement was tried and failed, for there was, at least initially, some reason to believe that it might succeed. Rather, the tragedy was, as Murray has noted, that the British government continued to pursue appeasement well after there existed overwhelming evidence that it would not work, in large part because there appeared to be no acceptable alternative policy.

4

ANGLO-AMERICAN
APPEASEMENT OF THE
SOVIET UNION, 1941–1945

We have seen that a policy of appeasement toward the Soviet
Union has failed dismally, just as it failed toward Hitler at Munich.
                              Arthur Bliss Lane, *I Saw Poland Betrayed*

The Axis powers were defeated, a chance for democracy was
preserved, and [Roosevelt] got far more than the twenty-five years
of peace he once said he hoped to ensure. Whatever his errors, he
deserves kudos for both his efforts and his results: He succeeded in
his search for victory.
                                            Edward Moore Bennett,
                          Franklin D. Roosevelt and the Search for Victory

Observers of international affairs in Britain and the United States during
the mid-1940s detected a strong resemblance between Anglo-American
policy toward the Soviet Union and the British approach to Nazi Germany in the previous decade. This was especially true in the aftermath of
the February 1945 meeting of Winston Churchill, Franklin D. Roosevelt,
and Josef Stalin in the Crimean city of Yalta. References to the Yalta
Conference as "an eastern Munich" or "a second Munich" appeared in the
American and British presses; so did the word "appeasement."[1] The *San
Francisco Examiner* laid it out quite neatly: "For Czechoslovakia, substitute Poland, Lithuania, Latvia, and Estonia; for Munich, substitute Yalta; for

Chamberlain, substitute Churchill; for Hitler, substitute Stalin."[2] Rather than being offended by the comparison, Churchill apparently recognized and appreciated the irony of his role in conciliating the Soviet Union. Harold Nicolson recorded in his diary that the British prime minister was "as amused as I am that the warmongers of the Munich period have now become the appeasers."[3]

The agreements at Yalta—and Anglo-American policy toward the Soviet Union as a whole—engendered considerable controversy.[4] Opponents claimed that concessions, particularly those regarding the territory and government of Poland, were "indefensible" and gained the Western Allies nothing.[5] Advocates argued that Anglo-American concessions were required because the United States and Britain lacked the capacity to resist Soviet demands. Eugene Lyons regarded the agreement at Yalta as "an act of appeasement that history will rank with those compounded by Chamberlain and Daladier in Munich," but he believed it was justified as an "unavoidable act of military necessity."[6] Churchill and Roosevelt, in this view, got the best deal they could, even if it was not a very good one.

For the past fifty years, professional students of American foreign relations have been similarly divided. Critics of Franklin Roosevelt—usually conservative, and often associated with the orthodox school of Cold War historians—have argued that the Anglo-American approach toward the Soviet Union was fundamentally misguided and that only a strong deterrent stance, backed by threats of military action, could have succeeded in checking Soviet expansion. Defenders of the president—generally liberal—have countered that a policy of firmness would likely not have worked and that in any event the United States and Britain were in no position politically or militarily to adopt such a strategy. American policy, they suggest, was clear-sighted and realistic, if ultimately unsuccessful. Oddly, the radical revisionists have, like the members of the orthodox school, found American policy deficient, but because of what they see as its excessive belligerence rather than its overly accommodating character.[7]

At best, then, for most of the Cold War, Anglo-American policy toward the Soviet Union during the years 1941–1945 was regarded as an unavoidable failure. It is true that appeasement did not achieve certain of its objectives, including the establishment of democratic regimes in Central Europe and the maintenance of cooperation with Moscow into the postwar period. But these were not the only aims pursued by American and British policymakers. Early in the war, Washington and London were concerned mainly with ensuring continued Soviet participation in the fight against Germany and with guarding against the possibility of Moscow concluding a separate peace with Berlin. After 1943, when this danger had passed, two new objectives gained ascendancy, especially in the mind of Franklin Roosevelt, the American president. The first of these was to gain Soviet entry into the war against Japan, so that the war in the Pacific might be shortened and American casualties limited. The second was to obtain Soviet agreement to a plan for an international organization that would be responsible for maintaining peace in the postwar world. There was, in addition, a rarely stated but almost universally understood aim, which was ultimately perhaps the most important of all: avoidance of a new war against the Soviet Union.

Measured against these objectives, Anglo-American policy appears to have been more successful. Moscow did not conclude a separate peace with Berlin. The Soviets entered the war against Japan, though by that time the Truman administration, in possession of the atomic bomb, had decided it would be preferable if they did not. Stalin agreed, after protracted and difficult negotiations, to Soviet participation in the United Nations. And, finally, open conflict with the Soviet Union was averted, although a Cold War—involving clashes in various parts of the world—did ensue. That these goals, plus others, could have been achieved via a different policy has sometimes been suggested, but the weight of evidence suggests otherwise.

Preventing a Separate Peace, 1941–1943

The United States adopted a conciliatory policy with respect to the Soviet Union soon after Germany's invasion of Soviet territory in June of 1941. When American officials met to consider extending Lend-Lease aid to Moscow, diplomat and presidential adviser William Bullitt and others encouraged Roosevelt to offer assistance only on the condition that Stalin renounce, in writing, the territorial gains made by the Soviet Union since the conclusion of the infamous Nazi-Soviet Nonaggression Pact roughly two years before. Roosevelt, however, demurred. One reason, according to Bullitt, was that FDR believed the Soviet leader's word had little value: "although there was no doubt that Stalin would make such promises, there was equally little doubt that Stalin would break the promises as soon as it might suit him to break them."[8]

A more fundamental reason, however, was Roosevelt's fear that any outright rejection of Russia's territorial claims might weaken the Soviets' determination to resist Hitler and encourage Stalin to seek a separate peace with Germany.[9] This concern was shared by the British government. Indeed, by February 1942, Churchill and his colleagues were prepared to accede formally to Soviet demands in Eastern and Central Europe as the price for a treaty of mutual defense.[10] These demands, which had been presented to Foreign Secretary Anthony Eden during a visit to Moscow the previous December, called for British recognition of Russia's annexation of the Baltic states, parts of Finland and Rumania, and eastern Poland to the Curzon line—in short, for the restoration of the Soviet Union's pre-1941 borders. Churchill requested that the American government join with London in agreeing to these terms. Roosevelt, however, recognized that ratifying territorial acquisitions made by the Soviet Union following the conclusion of the hated Nazi-Soviet Nonaggression Pact was inconsistent with the stated goals of the Atlantic Charter. Fearing such action might undermine popular and congressional support for the war effort, he advocated postponing a decision, a position the British reluctantly accepted.[11]

The "consensus in Washington and London that [Stalin] might sue for a separate peace with Germany" influenced Anglo-American policy for the next several years.[12] It led, in June 1942, to the promise to open a second front in Europe that same year—a promise that was not kept, with unfortunate consequences for Soviet perceptions of Anglo-American trustworthiness. In January 1943, concern over Russian morale and fears that Stalin "felt out of the picture" caused Roosevelt to inform the Joint Chiefs that he intended to tell Stalin of America's commitment to Germany's unconditional surrender.[13] Historian and long-time diplomat George Kennan has written that, until 1944, worry that the Soviets might abandon the war effort was the single most important reason for American conciliation of the Soviet Union.[14]

The Soviet Union did not, of course, conclude a separate peace with Germany. Whether it would have done so in the absence of an accommodating policy on the part of the Western Powers must remain an open question, at least until archival material to resolve the issue becomes available. In view of the cynical violation of the 1939 nonaggression treaty represented by the Nazi invasion, it seems unlikely that Stalin would have been eager to enter into yet another agreement with Hitler. At the same time, from the perspective of policymakers in Washington and London, this was hardly a guarantee. The Bolsheviks had, after all, concluded the Treaty of Brest-Litovsk in order to extricate themselves from the First World War, leaving the burden of fighting the Germans to the Western Allies. In September 1941, the British cabinet received a message from Moscow that led members to believe that Stalin was considering a similar move.[15] Recently uncovered evidence suggests—though not conclusively—that in November, when German troops had nearly reached Moscow, Stalin did in fact offer Hitler parts of Poland, the Ukraine, and the Baltic states in return for a cessation of hostilities. However, the German chancellor, presumably confident of victory, declined.[16] In any event, given the ambiguity of Soviet intentions and the critical importance to the United States and especially to Britain of Russia's continued participation in the war against Germany, it is difficult to criticize American and British policymakers for adopting a policy of appeasement.

SEEKING SOVIET COOPERATION IN THE PACIFIC WAR AND POSTWAR COLLECTIVE SECURITY, 1943–1945

Anglo-American concern over the possibility of a second Treaty of Brest-Litovsk eventually receded. This was particularly true as Soviet military fortunes improved, beginning with the crucial victory at Stalingrad in January and February of 1943. In November of that year, Averell Harriman, the U.S. ambassador to Moscow, wrote to FDR that in his judgment the Soviets were bent on the "complete destruction" of Nazism and Hitler; a separate peace was therefore unlikely.[17] However, by this time, additional reasons for pursuing a policy of appeasement had emerged.

The first of these was the need to secure the participation of the Soviet Union in the war against Japan. An August 1943 memo from Maj. Gen. J.H. Burns to Roosevelt adviser Harry Hopkins quoted from "a very high level" military document:

> The most important factor the United States has to consider in relation to Russia is the prosecution of the war in the Pacific. With Russia as an ally in the war against Japan, the war can be terminated in less time and less expense in life and resources than if the reverse were the case. Should the war in the Pacific have to be carried on with an unfriendly or a negative attitude on the part of Russia, the difficulties will be immeasurably increased and operations might become abortive.[18]

The Joint Chiefs of Staff, and especially Army Chief George C. Marshall, noted the urgency of the matter on numerous occasions. A memorandum of September 1944 stated "that every effort should be made to bring the U.S.S.R. into the war against Japan at the earliest practicable date."[19] Military leaders envisioned Soviet participation as having three main objectives: "defeat of the Japanese forces in Manchuria, air operations against Japan proper in collaboration with U.S. air forces based in eastern Siberia, and maximum interference with Japanese sea traffic between Japan and the mainland of Asia."[20]

In February 1945, the American and British combined chiefs of staff recommended to Roosevelt and Churchill "that the planning date for the end of the war against Japan should be set at 18 months after the defeat of Germany." They estimated that Germany might not be defeated until the end of the year, putting the conclusion of the Pacific War as late as the middle of 1947.[21] It is important to emphasize that this projection was based on the assumption of Soviet participation in the war effort. There was no attempt to predict the length of the war without such participation, but it would certainly have been much longer. Henry Stimson's account of the anticipated difficulties facing Allied forces suggests just how crucial Soviet assistance appeared to American military planners:

> As we understood it in July [1945], there was a very strong possibility that the Japanese Government might determine upon resistance to the end, in all the areas of the Far East under its control. In such an event the Allies would be faced with the enormous task of destroying an armed force of five million men and five thousand suicide aircraft, belonging to a race which had already amply demonstrated its ability to fight literally to the death.
>
> The strategic plans of our armed forces for the defeat of Japan, as they stood in July, had been prepared without reliance upon the atomic bomb, which had not yet been tested in New Mexico. We were planning an intensified sea and air blockade, and greatly intensified strategic air bombing, through the summer and early fall, to be followed on November 1 by an invasion of the southern island of Kyushu. This would be followed in turn by an invasion of the main island of Honshu in the spring of 1946. The total U.S. military and naval force

involved in this grand design was of the order of 5,000,000 men; if all those indirectly concerned are included, it was larger still. . . .

We estimated that if we should be forced to carry this plan to its conclusion, the major fighting would not end until the latter part of 1946, at the earliest. I was informed that such operations might be expected to cost over a million casualties to American forces alone.[22]

The second major consideration driving American policy from 1943 onward was the desire to ensure the cooperation of the Soviet Union in postwar collective security. Roosevelt believed strongly that this was essential if peace were to be maintained. Refusal of the Soviets to cooperate would not only be damaging in itself, but might also lead the United States to retreat into its own habitual isolation, as had happened following the First World War. The president's plan, therefore, was to enlist the Soviet Union as a participant in an international organization, through which the victorious allied powers would collaborate in policing the globe.[23] This so-called "great design" was outlined most fully in an essay, "Roosevelt's World Blueprint," authored by Forrest Davis, which appeared in the *Saturday Evening Post* and which was approved by the White House prior to its publication.[24]

To achieve these ends, the American government continued its policy of conciliation, occasionally against the wishes of its British counterpart. In August 1944, Churchill, angered by the Soviets' failure to assist the Polish underground during the Warsaw uprising and concerned with Britain's obligation to Poland under the terms of the Anglo-Polish defense treaty of August 1939, suggested sending a message to Stalin informing the Soviet leader of the intent, on the part of Britain and the United States, to send American planes to the relief of the embattled Polish fighters, after which they would land at Soviet airfields for refueling.[25] In view of the fact that Stalin had already refused requests by London and Washington to use Soviet airfields for this purpose, Roosevelt rejected the proposal as too confrontational. On 26 August, he wrote to Churchill:

In consideration of Stalin's present attitude in regard to relief of the Polish underground in Warsaw as expressed in his messages to you and to me, and his definite refusal to permit the use by us of Soviet airfields for that purpose, and in view of current American conversations in regard to the subsequent use of other Soviet bases, I do not consider it advantageous to the long-range general war prospect for me to join with you in the proposed message to U. J.[26]

The most important—and the most controversial—Anglo-American concessions to the Soviet Union were made at two wartime meetings of the Allied leaders. In November 1943, at Teheran, Churchill conveyed to Stalin his readiness to see Poland's borders shifted several hundred miles to the west.[27] The eastern boundary would generally follow the so-called Curzon line, giving the Soviet Union virtually all the territory it had acquired under the terms of the Molotov-Ribbentrop pact of September 1939. The western border would be set at the Oder River, compensating Poland for its lost lands in the east and contributing to the dismemberment of Germany, a further Soviet objective. With a presidential election, in which Polish-American voters might well play a crucial role, looming less than a year away, Roosevelt regarded the issue as politically explosive. Reluctant to discuss the plan and unwilling to commit himself to it in writing, he nevertheless gave his oral assent.[28]

The conference at Yalta, which took place in February 1945, represented the culmination of the Anglo-American policy of appeasement. Discussions at Yalta covered a variety of subjects and resulted in a number of agreements.[29] The Soviets made some concessions. They accepted the voting formula proposed by the United States for the United Nations Security Council and abandoned their demand for U.N. membership for each of the Soviet Union's sixteen republics. Instead Moscow would settle for three seats in the General Assembly: for Russia, the Ukraine, and Byelorussia. Stalin informed Roosevelt that he would have no objection to the United States being given the same special consideration.

The Soviets also acquiesced to French membership on the Control Council for postwar Germany, accepted changes in the language of agreements pertaining to the composition of the Polish and Yugoslav governments, and gave ground on the issue of German reparations. Still, the Western Powers must be regarded as having made the greater concessions.[30] In the Far East, they acceded to Russian demands for the port of Sakhalin and the islands adjacent thereto, for the Kurile Islands, and for the restoration of a naval base at Port Arthur. With respect to Poland's borders, the informal agreement reached at Teheran was largely reaffirmed.

A modified version of the Curzon line was established as the eastern boundary. The western boundary was left to a peace conference to determine, but it was agreed that Poland would realize "substantial accessions of territory in the north and west."[31]

The most important concession by the Western Powers at Yalta was their acceptance of a formula for establishing a postwar Polish government that made it likely Poland would be nondemocratic and dominated by the Soviet Union. The agreement left the existing pro-Soviet Provisional Government of the Lublin Poles in firm control of the country, requiring only that this government should "be reorganized on a broader democratic basis with the inclusion of democratic leaders from Poland itself and from Poles abroad."[32] For the British, who had gone to war to defend Poland and had steadfastly recognized the government-in-exile as the legitimate Polish leadership, this was a bitter pill to swallow, though irritation at the London Poles' utter unwillingness to compromise made sacrificing them somewhat less painful. Roosevelt appreciated Britain's position, but, as he had reminded Churchill on a previous occasion, "Our primary concern is . . . the essential unity [of the Allies] which was so successfully established at Moscow and Teheran."[33] To maintain this unity, the president acceded to an agreement that placed Polish independence and the prospects for democracy at the mercy of the Soviet Union. Told by his chief of staff, Admiral Leahy, that the language was "so elastic that the Russians can stretch it all the way from Yalta to Washington without ever technically breaking it," Roosevelt replied, "I know, Bill—I know it. But it's the best I can do for Poland at this time."[34]

American concessions reflected the fact that, in the final analysis, U.S. policymakers regarded cooperation with the Soviet Union as more important than self-determination for the Poles and other peoples threatened by the expansion of Soviet influence. In January 1945, a month before the Yalta conference opened, John Hickerson, deputy director of the State Department's Office of European Affairs, composed a memo in which he commented on suggestions that the United States ratify Soviet acquisitions of territory in Eastern and Central Europe. Wrote Hickerson:

> We must have the support of the Soviet Union to defeat Germany. We sorely need the Soviet Union in the war against Japan when the war in Europe is over. The importance of these two things can be reckoned in terms of American lives. We must have the cooperation of the Soviet Union to orga-

nize the peace. There are certain things in connection with the foregoing proposals which are repugnant to me personally, but I am prepared to urge their adoption to obtain the cooperation of the Soviet Union in winning the war and organizing the peace.[35]

Roosevelt shared these sentiments. If he were forced to choose between cooperation with the Soviet Union and an independent, democratic Poland, the Poles would be sacrificed.[36] With characteristic optimism, however, the president hoped that these apparently incompatible objectives could be reconciled through Soviet participation in an international organization. He and his advisers believed that Soviet demands in Europe were motivated mainly by Moscow's fear of foreign invasion. If the United States could draw the Soviets into a collective security organization that would afford them protection, the Soviets might well abandon many of their demands. In a February 1943 memo, Elbridge Durbrow, a State Department expert on Europe, suggested "that if a workable plan of collective security was set up in Europe and throughout the world the Soviet Union would not have any fears of attack from the west and therefore would not have any need to obtain strategic areas on its western frontiers and that since the Soviet Union had no reasonable right to demand additional territory per se, it might be persuaded to drop its claims to these areas of eastern Europe."[37] The following September, the State Department's Advisory Committee on Postwar Foreign Policy offered much the same argument: "If the Soviet Union comes to an agreement with Great Britain and the United States for participation in a general system of collective security, it would be more likely to respect the independence of East European nations and to permit the existence of normal relations between them and other powers."[38] Roosevelt's own thinking has been described by Undersecretary of State Sumner Welles:

> It might be impossible to obtain the kind of agreement on future settlements in Eastern Europe, in the Near East, or even in the Far East, that would represent one hundred per cent of what the President regarded as equitable or desirable. But if a United Nations organization could be created, in which the Soviet Union and the United States would jointly participate and through which a rule of law rather than a rule of force could gradually be evolved, that would provide the best op-

portunity later to correct such inequities as might exist when the peace settlements were first entered into.[39]

AVOIDING WAR WITH THE SOVIET UNION

The belief that membership in a postwar security organization would moderate, or even reverse, the expansionist thrust of Soviet foreign policy was not, it must be noted, universally shared. As early as 1943, certain officials in Washington began urging the adoption of a much more aggressive strategy designed to prevent Soviet territorial gains.[40] In January of that year, William Bullitt wrote to Roosevelt: "We shall never again have as much influence on Great Britain and the Soviet Union as we have today. Today they are dependent on us for their lives. We are the lady bountiful. They are the beggars. . . . There is only one guarantee that the Red Army will not cross into Europe—the prior arrival of American and British armies in the eastern frontiers of Europe."[41]

By the middle of 1944, other American diplomats had become so skeptical about the prospects for long-term cooperation with the Soviets that they, too, argued for the abandonment of America's conciliatory stance, even at the risk of alienating Moscow.[42] In September, Averell Harriman wrote to Harry Hopkins that relations with the Soviet Union had deteriorated markedly in the previous two months. The Soviets were becoming increasingly demanding and were using the "strength and prestige of the Red Army" to force the Western Allies "to accept all Soviet policies." The ambassador concluded:

> I am convinced that we can divert this trend but only if we materially change our policy toward the Soviet Government. I have evidence that they have misinterpreted our generous attitude toward them as a sign of weakness, and acceptance of their policies. Time has come when we must make clear what we expect of them as the price of our good will. Unless we take issue with the present policy there is every indication the Soviet Union will become a world bully wherever their [sic] interests are involved.[43]

In a briefing paper that same month the State Department offered a similar argument. Noting that recent Soviet behavior had been "far from encouraging" with regard to the prospects for postwar cooperation, the report remarked on the "danger that the Soviet Government may mistake friendliness for weakness." In the view of the State Department, "A greater degree of firmness in our attitude and policy toward the Soviet Union would avoid more serious difficulties in the future and would place our relations with it on a firmer foundation."[44]

Roosevelt was not oblivious to these concerns, and he recognized the arguments in favor of a less accommodating approach. The officially inspired 1943 article, "What Really Happened at Teheran," by Forrest Davis, acknowledged that the policy of conciliation carried certain risks. Asked Davis, "Suppose that Stalin, in spite of all concessions, should prove unappeasable, determined to pursue his own policy regardless of the west? What assurance does the Roosevelt approach hold that he may not capture all Poland, Finland, the Balkans, and even Germany from within, as was the case with the Baltic states, once his armies occupy those countries and recognize his own Moscow-dominated undergrounds?"[45] The answer, as Davis admitted—and Roosevelt knew—was none.

Toward the end of his life, Roosevelt himself became increasingly doubtful about the efficacy of his conciliatory policy. In a September 1944 conversation with Austrian Archduke Otto, the president termed Stalin "untrustworthy" and "deceitful." He was even more "bitterly critical" of other Soviet leaders. The Austrian royal concluded that Roosevelt was "afraid of the Communists and wants to do everything he can to contain Russia's power—naturally short of war."[46] There are other indications that in the months before his death, Roosevelt was planning "to stiffen his approach" toward the Soviet Union.[47]

Whether or not Roosevelt was really considering a strategy of "containment" like that of the Truman administration, under his leadership the United States never adopted such a confrontational policy. This was in part a reflection of the ambiguous nature of the evidence regarding Soviet motives and objectives. While advocates of a hardline policy could point to what they saw as Moscow's increasingly belligerent behavior, proponents of continued conciliation thought they detected a certain measure of cooperation and restraint. In his memoirs, William Leahy argued that the violations of the Yalta accords committed by the Soviets in the spring and summer of 1945 could not have been predicted from their previous behavior. The Soviet Union, he noted, had not made a separate peace with Germany, had abided by the terms of every military agreement that had been concluded during the war, and had been accommodating on several of the issues decided at the conference.[48] Moreover, Stalin had dissolved the Comintern, suggesting to some that the Soviets were abandoning their commitment to the exportation of socialist revolution.

Because the evidence regarding Soviet intentions was less than clear-cut, Roosevelt was able to interpret it in ways consistent with his innate optimism and belief in his own personal powers of persuasion. In his bitter critique of Roosevelt's policy, "How We Won the War and Lost the Peace," William Bullitt described a conversation with the president in which he tried to convince him of the Soviets' malign motives and the impossibility of cooperating with them. At the end, Roosevelt told his former adviser, "Bill, I don't dispute your facts, they are accurate. I don't dispute the logic of your reasoning. I just have a hunch that Stalin is not that kind of man. Harry [Hopkins] says he's not and that he doesn't want anything but security for his country, and I think that if I give him everything I possibly can and ask nothing from him in return, *noblesse oblige,* he won't try to annex anything and will work with me for a world of democracy and peace."[49]

Roosevelt, like Chamberlain before him, believed that he—and only he—possessed the ability to establish a personal relationship with a dictator that would lead to an alteration in his enemy's behavior. In FDR's case, this meant not simply developing the capacity to "do business," but cultivating a kind of friendship with the Soviet leader. He wrote to Churchill on one occasion that "I think I can personally handle Stalin better than either your Foreign Office or my State Department. Stalin hates the guts of all your people. He thinks he likes me better, and I hope that he will continue to do so."[50] Reflecting a view widely held among historians, Keith Eubank has written that Roosevelt had an "arrogant confidence in his ability to persuade people to change their minds. He believed that his unique ability to charm people into accepting his point of view would work with Joseph Stalin."[51]

Roosevelt's faith in his powers of persuasion, the ambiguous nature of the evidence regarding Soviet motives, and the president's rosy interpretation of this evidence, were each partly responsible for his administration's rejection of a more aggressive policy of resistance. More important, however, was the fact that Roosevelt—and others in the American government—saw no real alternative to conciliation because they were ultimately unwilling to contemplate going to war with the Soviet Union over Poland or other portions of Eastern and Central Europe.

Avoidance of armed conflict with the Soviet Union was in fact the objective which underlay virtually all of American diplomacy in the latter stages of the Second World War. So fundamental was it that it was often left unstated, or was mentioned only in passing, as though no one could possibly take issue with it. War with the Soviet Union would, of course, dash all hopes for the achievement of either of Roosevelt's principal aims: Soviet participation in the fight against Japan and the maintenance of Anglo-Soviet-American cooperation in the postwar world. However, additional reasons for the reluctance of American policymakers to consider war with the Soviet Union also existed. The first of these was the attitude of the American public, which, as the State Department knew from reports it was compiling, had no stomach for a battle with the Soviets. Indeed, as Lynn Davis notes, "Following the defeat of Germany, strong domestic pressures developed for the removal of United States troops from Europe and the demobilization of the army."[52] Roosevelt's statement to Stalin at Yalta that he did not think he could "obtain support in Congress and throughout the country" for "the maintenance of an appreciable American force in Europe," indicates that such pressures existed even before the end of the war in Europe.[53] Americans had become accustomed to viewing the Soviets not just as allies but as friends, a perception encouraged by U.S. government propaganda stressing the similarity of the Soviet and American political and economic systems. A policy that suddenly reversed direction would have encountered heavy, perhaps insurmountable opposition.

A second major reason for the unwillingness of the American government to adopt a hardline policy that might lead to a Soviet-American war was the near impossibility of prosecuting such a war effectively. In the summer of 1943, William Bullitt advocated establishing an Anglo-American military line in Eastern Europe to block Soviet expansion westward. The State Department's European Division rejected the idea, noting that the War Department regarded it as "sheer military fantasy . . . the United States and the United Kingdom are not in a position successfully to oppose the Soviet Union in Eastern Europe if Germany is defeated."[54]

Others agreed. In a long letter to Secretary of State Cordell Hull in May 1944, Adm. William Leahy considered the possibility of a war between the Anglo-American powers and the Soviet Union. Wrote Leahy,

> The outstanding fact to be noted is the recent phenomenal development of the heretofore latent Russian military and economic strength. . . . In contrast, as regards Britain several devel-

opments have combined to lessen her relative military and economic strength and gravely to impair, if not preclude, her ability to offer effective military opposition to Russia on the continent except possibly in defensive operations in the Atlantic coastal areas. In a conflict between these two powers the disparity in the military strengths that they could dispose upon the continent would, under present conditions, be far too great to be overcome by our intervention on the side of Britain. Having due regard to the military factors involved—resources, manpower, geography and particularly our ability to project our strength across the ocean and exert it decisively upon the continent—we might be able to successfully defend Britain, but we could not, under existing conditions, defeat Russia.[55]

Army leaders were no more eager to take on the Soviet Union. Memos by Generals Schuyler and Crane in the spring of 1945 explicitly rejected the notion that military force might be employed to achieve full implementation of the Yalta accords. Instead, the generals favored "diplomatic pressure," though exactly what they meant by this was not entirely clear.[56]

Could the Soviets have been opposed in Eastern and Central Europe without a war? In particular, could they have been compelled by Anglo-American military threats to retreat without a fight from territories already under their control? The answer may never be known, but given the intensity of Soviet insecurity and the immense importance attached by Soviet leaders to the establishment of a buffer zone of friendly states, it seems unlikely. There is no reason to regard Stalin's statement at Yalta—"The Polish question is a matter of life and death for the Soviet Union"—as other than a genuine reflection of his attitude.[57] Senator Burton Wheeler of Montana, a harsh critic of the Yalta accords, expressed the belief that if the United States had told the Soviet Union that it could not assume control of Poland, Latvia, Estonia, Lithuania, Rumania, and Bulgaria, then "Russia would not have had the nerve to do it."[58] But his was a minority view. Most American policymakers did not believe the Soviets would withdraw peacefully. Averell Harriman, one of the advocates of a firmer policy, later admitted that "There was no way we could have prevented any of these events in Eastern Europe without going to war with the Russians."[59]

In sum, while American (and British) officials were becoming increasingly suspicious of Soviet intentions in Eastern and Central Europe, they felt unable, for a combination of diplomatic, political, and military reasons, to adopt a strong policy of resistance. Such a policy necessarily envisaged the prospect of armed conflict with the Soviet Union, a course of action virtually no one in Washington or London was seriously prepared to contemplate.[60] In April 1945, Harriman told the American delegation to the United Nations Conference that "while we cannot go to war with the Soviet Union, we must do everything to maintain our position as strongly as possible in Eastern Europe."[61] The assumption that war with the Soviets was unthinkable remained essentially unchallenged.

THE END OF APPEASEMENT

Measured against its most immediate objectives, Anglo–American policy toward the Soviet Union appears to have been largely successful. Moscow did not conclude a separate peace with Berlin. At Yalta, Stalin committed his country to entering the war against Japan within two or three months after the conclusion of the war in Europe; it did so in August 1945. The Soviet Union became a charter member of the United Nations. Above all, war between the Soviet Union and the Western Powers was averted.

Unfortunately, membership in the United Nations did not produce the moderation of Soviet attitudes and behavior predicted by American policymakers. Far from relaxing its grip on the countries of Eastern and Central Europe, Moscow moved to tighten it. Communist control of the Polish government was cemented. Progress toward German unification stalled, with the Soviets maintaining their hold on the eastern portion of the country. Perhaps more importantly, Stalin sought to expand Soviet influence elsewhere, particularly in southern Europe and Asia Minor. As a result, the British and American governments began to rethink more seriously the wisdom of their conciliatory approach. The strategy was abandoned, as one author has written, "only slowly and in a disorganized manner."[62] Indeed, at the Potsdam Conference in July and August of 1945, the new leaders of the Western Powers, Harry Truman and Britain's Clement Attlee, did little to oppose the consolidation of Soviet hegemony in Eastern Europe.[63]

Nevertheless, after 1945 a policy of what came to be called "containment" gradually evolved.[64] Intellectual underpinnings for this strategy were provided, in part, by Churchill's "Iron Curtain" speech at Westminster College in Fulton, Missouri, during the summer of 1946, and subsequently by the publication in the July 1947 issue of *Foreign Affairs* of George Kennan's famous "X-article." The proclamation of the Truman Doctrine, which offered aid to Greece and Turkey, the implementation of the Marshall Plan for the economic reconstruction of Europe, and the formation of the North Atlantic Treaty Organization (NATO) were critical steps in its development. Also important was the establishment of the Federal Republic of Germany as an additional bulwark against westward expansion by the Soviets.

In June 1950, following the North Korean invasion of South Korea, which Americans widely believed could have occurred only with the prior approval of the Soviet government, the Truman Administration adopted NSC-68 as a statement of policy. This document accused the Soviet Union of being "animated by a new fanatic faith" and called upon the United States, together with it allies, "to support a firm policy intended to check and to roll back the Kremlin's drive for world domination."[65] A strategy of containment was now firmly in place.

Soviet Motives

A debate over the fundamental character of Soviet policy has divided historians of American foreign relations since the late 1940s. At the risk of oversimplification, three basic positions can be identified. Revisionist scholars of the Wisconsin School have argued that Soviet expansionism was driven mainly by insecurity. Soviet aims were limited and legitimate, and Anglo-American policy failed because it was insufficiently accommodating, not because it was excessively conciliatory. Orthodox historians have maintained precisely the opposite: that the Soviets' behavior was rooted in their communist ideology, which they hoped to spread throughout Europe and, if possible, the world. A middle ground has been occupied by those scholars who contend that Soviet expansionism was greedy in nature, but that this greed was not ideological in origin. Rather, they suggest, Moscow's territorial ambitions stemmed from the wish to extend the borders of the traditional Russian empire.[66]

Although archival evidence that might resolve the issue once and for all is still lacking, the truth about Soviet motives is almost certainly a combination of these positions. On the one hand, there is no question that the Soviets, and particularly Stalin, felt profoundly insecure. Russia had, after all, been invaded from the west three times in the previous century and a half: by Napoleon, by the forces of Wilhelmine Germany, and by Hitler's war machine. In addition, the Western powers had intervened in the Russian Civil War in an effort to overthrow the newly established Bolshevik regime. Beyond this history, there was Soviet communist ideology, which postulated the irreconcilability of socialism and capitalism and the inevitability of conflict between them. Finally, there was Stalin's own personality, which, as the purges of the 1930s suggest, bordered on paranoid. In short, Soviet insecurity during the early and mid-1940s was grossly overdetermined. Alan Bullock has written that in this period "Stalin's primary aim can be summed up as security after the traumatic experience of the war—the security of Russian territory and the security of the Stalinist system against any renewed threat from external enemies."[67] Given the circumstances, this was surely understandable.

On the other hand, the Soviets were also interested in territorial expansion for nonsecurity reasons. Whether these were principally ideological (the spread of communism) or national-imperial (the spread of *Russian* influence) is difficult to determine; because Russia, as the center of the Soviet Union, was the leader of the world communist movement, the two objectives were generally compatible, and it is not evident that Soviet leaders saw any distinction between them.

In any event, it is difficult to escape the conclusion that Soviet expansionism was driven by *both* severe insecurity and a healthy appetite for territorial aggrandizement. As William Taubman notes, Stalin's foreign policy was "simultaneously offensive and defensive. . . . His country was devastated, but that did not prevent him from contemplating the downfall, if only on the installment plan, of others."[68]

WHY APPEASEMENT FAILED—AND SUCCEEDED

Although the conciliatory policy pursued by Britain and the United States failed to produce a significant moderation of Soviet attitudes and behavior, it did gain the Western Powers' immediate objectives: Moscow's agreement to participate in the war against Japan and Soviet membership in the United Nations. Acquiescence to Soviet demands also succeeded in averting an armed struggle with the Soviet Union over Eastern and Central Europe. While a "cold war" of almost half a century ensued, avoidance of a major conflict between East and West must be regarded as an accomplishment of considerable significance.

Anglo-American appeasement failed to moderate Soviet behavior because the policy did not effectively address either of the major motives for Soviet expansion. Since Roosevelt and his advisers did not perceive the Soviets to be seeking territory for ideological and/or imperial reasons, they did not offer concessions designed to satisfy this desire. But even had they diagnosed the sources of Moscow's expansionist behavior more accurately, it is unlikely that they would have been more accommodating. Indeed, those who believed Soviet actions to be driven by communist ideology argued strenuously for a less conciliatory approach. Whether such a strategy would have been any more successful is a question to which we shall return shortly.

The central aim of Anglo-American policy, as Roosevelt conceived it, was "the reassurance of Stalin."[69] Unfortunately, this project proved far more difficult than he had imagined. As noted previously, the U.S. president hoped to cultivate a friendly, trusting relationship between himself and the Soviet leader. Stalin, however, was completely immune to FDR's legendary charm. He was not interested in friendship, but in doing what was best for himself and his country. Probably Stalin could not even "conceive of such a close, personal relationship" of the kind Roosevelt desired. "He had his friends of one day executed the next day." According to Eubank, "Stalin did not perceive politics as being based on close personal relationships. He only understood raw power sufficient to frighten his fellow citizens."[70]

Moreover, for a mixture of historical and ideological reasons, Soviet leaders viewed the United States and Britain as implacably hostile and dangerous. It followed from this that efforts at conciliation by the Western powers were not genuine, but acts of trickery and deception. In a now-famous passage, the Yugoslav Communist Milovan Djilas quotes Stalin as saying,

> Perhaps you think that just because we are the allies of the English that we have forgotten who they are and who Churchill is. They find nothing sweeter than to trick their allies. During the First World War they constantly tricked the Russians and the French. And Churchill? Churchill is the kind who, if you don't watch him, will slip a kopeck out of your pocket. Yes, a kopeck out of your pocket! By God, a kopeck out of your pocket! And Roosevelt? Roosevelt is not like that. He dips in his hand only for bigger coins.[71]

Whether or not Stalin really said this, it appears to have been an accurate reflection of his beliefs, beliefs that were not altered by Anglo-American concessions. It is ironic, given Western fears of a separate peace between Germany and the Soviet Union, that in April 1945 Stalin accused Britain and the United States of already having reached an agreement with Hitler whereby, in exchange for lenient peace terms, Germany would cease military resistance in the west, allowing Anglo-American forces to move rapidly to the east.[72] In fact, while Roosevelt and his advisers hoped that a conciliatory policy would transform Soviet perceptions of the West, the opposite actually occurred. British and American concessions were misinterpreted so as to correspond to the Soviets' pre-existing worldview.[73] Given the intensity of Soviet mistrust of Britain and the United States, this is hardly surprising. As Adam Ulam has written, "[I]t was impossible for the Soviets to abandon their suspicions about the intentions of the Western Powers. . . . Suspicion was built into the Soviet system; it was inherent in the character of its ruler."[74]

Ulam's conclusion, and that of others such as William Taubman, is that appeasement failed to reassure Stalin and the Soviets because they were incapable of being reassured. While this was almost certainly the case, it is important to note that certain aspects of Anglo-American policy worked to undermine the potentially reassuring impact of British and American concessions.

One problem, alluded to earlier, was the propensity of the United States in particular to make promises it was unable to keep. A case in point was the pledge in June of 1942 to open a second front in Europe before the end of the year. This pledge proved impossible to fulfill, and as diplomat Charles Bohlen later wrote, "the effect of making estimates which were not realistic was to deepen Soviet suspicion that the policy of the Western Allies was to bleed Russia white."[75]

A second and more serious problem was that, with respect to the question of Soviet control of Eastern Europe in the postwar period, the United States and Britain pursued a "two-track" strategy.[76] On the one hand, because they were unwilling to threaten or use military force against the Soviets, the Anglo-American powers accepted Soviet domination of the region. On the other hand, this acceptance came only grudgingly and was accompanied by considerable condemnation and hostility, particularly as it became apparent that Moscow was establishing an exclusive sphere of influence in violation of the agreements at Yalta. While by this stage relations between the Soviet Union and the Western Powers were almost certainly beyond salvaging, there can be little doubt that the "second track" of Anglo-American policy worked to dilute whatever reassuring effect the two countries' concessions might otherwise have had.

Given his suspicions of the Western Powers and their intentions, it is not surprising that Stalin failed to see the United Nations as offering any real guarantee of Soviet security. The U.N. was, after all, going to be dominated by the Western Powers and their friends. Moreover, a veto in the Security Council by either the United States or Britain (or France or China) would be sufficient to prevent the U.N. from taking effective action to protect Soviet interests. Rather than placing their trust in a new, untested international organization, Soviet leaders turned to more traditional methods to defend their country. In June 1946, Maxim Litvinov, the estranged former foreign minister, told CBS correspondent Richard Hottelet that the Soviet leadership was operating on "the outmoded concept of security in terms of territory—the more you've got the safer you are." Asked by Hottelet whether Western acquiescence to certain of Moscow's demands would "lead to good will and easing of the present tension," Litvinov replied that "It would lead to the West's being faced, after a more or less short time, with the next series of demands."[77]

In the final analysis, Anglo-American geopolitical concessions fell far short of what Moscow felt it needed for its security and what it desired for reasons of ideology and empire. The full scope of Soviet objectives is difficult to determine, but it is clear that they went well beyond the establishment of a buffer zone in Eastern and Central Europe. At the very least, in the near term, Moscow's aims included the expansion of Soviet influence in Western Europe, the Near East, and Asia. Over the longer term, Soviet leaders envisioned "even greater gains when the next Western economic crisis struck."[78]

Although Anglo-American concessions did not come close to satisfying Moscow's maximum aims, they did meet Soviet leaders' minimum objectives. These consisted of restoring the Soviet Union's pre-1941 borders, preventing close cooperation among neighboring countries to the west, and guaranteeing the survival of existing communist establishments outside the Soviet Union.[79] During the war, the defeat and disarmament of Germany were also regarded as essential.[80]

Satisfaction of these minimum objectives, while not producing any significant alteration in Soviet attitudes or behavior, succeeded in averting a potential conflict between the Soviet Union and the Western Powers. For reasons of security, these aims were considered essential by Soviet leaders, who might have been prepared to engage Britain and the United States in battle had they been opposed.

WAS AN ALTERNATIVE POLICY POSSIBLE?

Anglo-American appeasement achieved the Western Powers' most immediate and least ambitious goals: prevention of a separate peace, Soviet entry into the Pacific war, Soviet participation in the United Nations, and avoidance of armed conflict between the Soviets and the West. It failed to produce moderation in Soviet behavior, including a tolerance of independent, democratic regimes in Eastern and Central Europe.

Would an alternative strategy have fared any better? Two possibilities existed. The first was a strong deterrent/compellent approach, which the Western Powers might have adopted as early as 1941, perhaps in conjunction with the issuing of Lend-Lease aid. The second was a mixed strategy that would have combined concessions with threats in some unspecified fashion.

As noted previously, the hardline approach was considered and rejected by American and British policymakers for a variety of reasons. Early in the war, it was feared that adoption of such a policy might lead Soviet leaders to sue for peace. Subsequently, it was feared that such a policy would cause the Soviet Union to decline to enter the war against Japan and to refuse membership in the United Nations. By late in the war, it seemed obvious that the price of such an approach would be armed conflict with the Soviet Union, a prospect few were prepared to contemplate.

Whether these concerns were valid can, of course, be debated. There were, as mentioned earlier, several reasons to think that Stalin would not be inclined to negotiate a separate peace with Germany. The Soviets might have entered the war against Japan on the basis of their own self-interest in the acquisition of Far Eastern territory, regardless of the nature of Anglo-American policy. Stalin had told Cordell Hull in October 1943 that Russia would eventually join the war in the Pacific, a pledge from which he never retreated, though he did subsequently attach certain conditions.[81] Perhaps the Soviets would even have been willing to join the United Nations, absent a conciliatory policy by the Western Powers, on the assumption that action contrary to Soviet interests could better be prevented from within the organization than from without.

While a plausible case can be made for them, these outcomes were at best uncertain and at worst unlikely. A deterrent/compellent policy would have put at risk all of the immediate aims for which Western policymakers labored. This was a danger that they were not prepared to face, and it is difficult, in retrospect, to quarrel with their decision. Moreover, such a policy would not have addressed the Soviets' profound sense of insecurity; indeed, it would almost surely have exacerbated it. For this reason, it is doubtful that a strategy of resistance would have produced any long-term moderation in Soviet behavior. If anything, the likely effect would have been the opposite.

The second option—a mixed strategy—was not given serious consideration by Western policymakers as a coherent strategy. It was adopted to a limited extent, de facto, as Roosevelt and Churchill sought to resist Soviet demands in Eastern and Central Europe. However, they were unwilling or unable to back their resistance with any kind of credible threats.

Given the dual character of Soviet motives, a mixed strategy probably made more sense than a purely conciliatory approach or an undiluted hardline policy. Nevertheless, it is hard to see how adoption of such a strategy would have done much to advance Western interests. In fact, policymakers in Washington and London were trapped in a dilemma that became more apparent when, following Roosevelt's death, new president Harry Truman gradually moved American policy in a more confrontational direction. Concessions—aimed principally at addressing Soviet insecurity—not only did nothing to reassure the Soviets as to Western intentions, but had the effect of encouraging Soviet aggressiveness by helping to foster the belief that the Western Allies were weak and could not effectively oppose Soviet territorial expansion. Firmness—directed toward the greed-driven component of Moscow's policy—promoted Soviet belligerence by making the Russians feel increasingly insecure. In the words of one historian, American policymakers "were damned if they did and damned if they didn't: conciliation struck Stalin as trickery or näiveté, and toughness only confirmed the Soviets' image of America as an unreconstructed enemy."[82] Under these circumstances, no policy—not even a mixed strategy of concessions and threats—offered much hope of ultimate success.

CONCLUSION

Anglo-American efforts to appease the Soviet Union in the years between 1941 and 1945 were partly successful. The most ambitious aim was not achieved: a moderation of the expansionist tendency of Soviet policy through participation in a postwar collective security organization. More immediate, less far-reaching objectives were, however, realized. The collective security organization—the United Nations—was established, with the Soviet Union as a charter member. A separate peace between Moscow and Berlin was averted; the Soviets entered the Pacific War against Japan. Most crucially, armed conflict between the Western Powers and the Soviet Union was prevented. Half a century later, the Soviet Union no longer exists and its empire has disintegrated. The Baltic states, Poland, eastern Germany, and other territories seized by Moscow are independent of Russian control and have democratically-elected governments. While roughly fifty years of Soviet domination produced great hardships, and its legacies will undoubtedly linger for some time, the unfulfilled objectives of Anglo-American policymakers in the mid-1940s have now been realized. In view of this, avoidance of war with the Soviet Union appears an even more valuable accomplishment.

There were those in the late 1940s and early 1950s who suggested that by allowing the Soviet Union to incorporate into the Soviet empire the Baltic states, Poland, and eastern Germany, the policy of appeasement might work to undermine the vitality of Soviet communism. In 1945, George Kennan wrote that the Soviet government now had the responsibility "to hold the conquered provinces in submission." There was "little doubt that many of the peoples concerned will be impatient and resentful of Russian rule." For this reason, "the great question of Russia's new world position" was whether the Soviet Union would "make of its conquests a source of strength rather than weakness."[83] Five years later, Joseph Kennedy offered a prediction that now seems remarkable for its prescience: "It may be that Europe for a decade or a generation or more will turn Communistic. But in doing so, it may break of itself as a unified force. Communism still has to prove itself to its peoples as a government that will achieve for them a better way of living. The more people that it will have to govern, the more necessary it becomes for those who govern to justify themselves to those being governed. The more peoples that are under its yoke, the greater are the possibilities of revolt."[84]

Over time, the Soviet empire became a considerable burden for Moscow. In order to keep captive populations quiescent, Soviet leaders were forced to subsidize the economies of their East European satellites, to the detriment of their own. By some estimates, oil and raw material subsidies to Eastern Europe totaled $22 billion in 1980 alone.[85] Moreover, the stationing and equipping of military forces in Eastern Europe for the purposes of internal and external security contributed to Soviet defense spending that may have reached 30 percent of Soviet GNP.[86]

On this basis, it could be argued that by allowing Soviet territorial expansion the policy of appeasement contributed to the collapse of the Soviet Union and the ending of the Cold War on terms favorable to the United States.[87] While there is merit to this claim, it must be acknowledged that the costs of empire were further and significantly increased by the strategy of containment, which not only prevented the Soviet Union from making certain additional territorial acquisitions—as in Korea—but rendered the maintenance of Soviet control over its existing possessions more difficult and more expensive.[88]

Indeed, in hindsight, Western policymakers appear to have adopted the right policies at the right times in their relations with the Soviet Union. Between 1941 and 1945, Great Britain and the United States made concessions that sacrificed no vital interests of their own but satisfied most of the Soviet Union's minimum objectives. In particular, Moscow was permitted to establish a buffer zone in Eastern and Central Europe. While this did not provide the Soviets with a real sense of security, it was enough to forestall the perceived need for immediate military action, as well as to secure other Western goals.

After 1945, the Soviet Union sought to attain some of its more ambitious maximum goals, which did threaten British and American vital interests. In response, the United States, with British support, abandoned appeasement and adopted a strategy of containment. This approach was also largely successful. The Soviets did not regard their maximum aims as being essential in the short term and so felt little urgency regarding their achievement.[89] As Kennan predicted in his "X-article," Soviet leaders proved unwilling to push their program of expansion to the point of a direct military confrontation.[90] Hence, while relations between the superpowers were tense, crises periodically occurred, and proxy wars were fought, the spread of Soviet influence was for the most part contained without a major conflict.

5

AMERICAN APPEASEMENT OF IRAQ, 1989–1990

Right now, George Bush is trying to soothe Hussein's paranoia
and temper his megalomania. It's not likely to work.
                                Morton Kondracke, "Saddamnation"

There was some reason to believe that perhaps improved relations
with the West would modify the behavior. . . . I think if everybody
had the benefit of total hindsight, why you'd go back and say, hey,
this didn't make much sense.
                                George Bush, *Public Papers*

During the late 1980s, the administration of President George Bush sought
to improve relations between the United States and the government of
Iraq with the aim of procuring certain modifications in Iraqi behavior.
With respect to domestic policy, American officials hoped that Iraq might
more fully respect the human rights of its citizens, especially the Kurds,
against whom poison gas had recently been used. With respect to foreign
policy, they hoped that Iraq would become less threatening to its neighbors in the Persian Gulf region. This meant not only that it would refrain
from overt acts of aggression, but that its chemical and nuclear weapons
programs might be curtailed. As Alexander George has noted, the American strategy was not simply to conciliate Iraq by satisfying the country's
needs and demands.[1] More ambitiously, it was to socialize and reform
Iraqi leader Saddam Hussein—in the words of one presidential adviser,
"to make this guy a reasonably responsible member of the international
community."[2] Ultimately, the policy failed. Iraqi behavior remained fun-

damentally unchanged, and on 2 August 1990, Iraqi forces invaded and rapidly overran Kuwait.[3]

THE TILT TOWARD IRAQ UNDER REAGAN

In 1980, war broke out between Iran and Iraq. The Reagan administration, anxious to preserve access to Persian Gulf oil for the United States and other oil-dependent countries, determined that it was in the U.S. interest that neither side win decisively and that some balance of power in the region be maintained. The following year, concern over the prospect of a rapid Iraqi victory led American officials to allow the government of Israel to ship several billion dollars' worth of arms to Iran. By 1982, however, the military situation was reversed, and American intelligence reported that Iraq was on the verge of collapse, causing American officials to fear that Iran, with its Islamic fundamentalist regime, might achieve a dominant position in the region.[4] As a result, U.S. policy shifted to support of Baghdad, a stance that was maintained to the end of the Reagan presidency.[5]

America's tilt toward Iraq began in February 1982, when the Reagan administration removed the country from its list of states sponsoring international terrorism. Although the Iraqi government had expelled Abu Nidal, best known as the man behind the *Achille Lauro* hijacking, there was little reason to believe its support of terrorist activities had diminished, let alone ceased. Noel Koch, head of the Pentagon's counterterrorism program, and Robert Sayre, the coordinator of counterterrorism in the State Department, both opposed the action, but were overruled because of the administration's desire to assist Iraq.[6] Removal from the list made Baghdad eligible for export credits financed by the U.S. government. In 1983, Iraq received more than $400 million in loan guarantees from the Agriculture Department's Commodity Credit Corporation (CCC). These guarantees, designed to promote exports of American agricultural products, enabled the Iraqi regime to purchase wheat, rice, and other foodstuffs with which to feed its population. Over time, additional CCC credits were extended to Iraq; through 1988 they totaled approximately $2.8 billion.[7]

The Reagan administration also saw to it that Iraq received credits from the Export-Import Bank. Eximbank officials were at first reluctant to extend loan guarantees to Baghdad, fearing it was too risky. Indeed, it was not clear that granting such credits would be permissible under the terms of the bank's charter, which required "reasonable assurances of re-payment." Nevertheless, in June 1984, after personal entreaties to Will-iam Draper, chair of the Eximbank, from Vice President George Bush, an old college friend, the Eximbank approved $484 million in loan guaran-tees for the construction of an oil pipeline in Iraq. Although Iraq was suspended from participation in Eximbank programs in 1986 for repay-ment failures, intense lobbying by Bush subsequently convinced the chair-man (now John Bohn) to issue another $200 million in revolving loan guarantees.[8]

The American government furnished additional economic assis-tance to the Iraqi regime in other ways. Prior to 1981, the United States imported no petroleum from Iraq. By 1988, however, it was buying 126 million barrels, a figure that in 1990 had increased to 187 million barrels, making the United States the world's foremost consumer of Iraqi oil.[9] In March of 1987, the Reagan administration agreed to allow Kuwaiti oil tankers to sail under the American flag and began assigning the ships naval escorts to protect them from attack by Iran.[10] With its oil revenues secure, the Kuwaiti government could continue to help finance Iraq's war effort.

In November 1984, the United States restored full diplomatic rela-tions with Baghdad. Shortly thereafter, American officials began provid-ing intelligence information to the Iraqi regime. Satellite imagery, Iranian communications intercepted by the United States, and assessments by the Central Intelligence Agency (CIA) were shared with Iraq in an effort to reveal weaknesses in Iran's military position. These practices continued throughout the rest of the Iran-Iraq war.[11]

Perhaps the most important, and certainly in the final analysis the most controversial, aspect of the Reagan administration's tilt toward Iraq was its effort to enhance Iraq's military capabilities. Between 1985 and 1990, the Reagan and Bush administrations allowed Iraq to purchase $1.5 billion in advanced technology items from American suppliers. In all, the U.S. government approved 771 separate sales. So-called "dual use" items (those having both civilian and military applications) constituted a sub-stantial portion of these exports. Two hundred seventy-three licenses for the transfer of dual use products valued at $782 million were issued by the Department of Commerce. In many cases, approval came over the objections of other government agencies, especially the Pentagon.[12] Ac-cording to Stephen Bryen, the Defense Department's undersecretary for trade security policy from 1985 to 1988, "It was routine for our recom-mendations to be ignored."[13] Indeed, as time went by, "It became very difficult for us to stop anything."[14] Among the American goods sold to Iraq during the 1980s were "advanced computers, radio equipment, graphics terminals that could be used to design rockets and analyze their flights, machine tools, computer mapping systems, and imaging devices for reading satellite pictures."[15] Also on the list: helicopters (allegedly for civilian transportation and crop dusting), high-speed oscilloscopes useful in processing data from nuclear tests, a powder press "suitable for the compaction of nuclear fuels," and technology for the production of ethylene, a key ingredient in thiodiglycol, the chemical precursor for mustard gas. By some estimates, as much as 40 percent of the equipment at Saad 16, a military-industrial installation for aircraft construction, missile design, and nuclear weapons research, was made in America.[16] A number of the Scud missile launchers targeted by the United States during the Gulf War were produced by an American truck manufacturing firm, Terex Corporation, at its plant in Motherwell, Scotland.[17]

Although the United States did not sell weapons directly to the Iraqi regime, its friends and allies served as conduits. According to U.S. intelligence sources, American arms were shipped regularly to Jordan, Egypt, and Kuwait "with advance White House knowledge and approval of their transshipment to Iraq." U.S. weaponry also reached Iraq through black marketeers. Included among the American arms to end up in Iraqi hands were HAWK anti-aircraft missiles, Huey helicopters equipped with TOW anti-tank missiles, and MK-84 bombs.[18] Finally, the United States government encouraged its allies to sell their own arms to the Iraqi regime. Britain, for example, sold billions of dollars' worth of tanks, missile parts, and artillery to Iraq. France sold Mirage fighters, Exocet missiles, and its 155-mm howitzer, "the most expensive, powerful, and sophisticated in the world." West Germany furnished supplies to six Iraqi plants producing nerve and mustard gas. According to an intelligence official, "The billions upon billions of dollars of shipments from Europe would not have been possible without the approval and acquiescence of the Reagan administration."[19] It should be noted that while all this was going on, the U.S. government was also engaged in "Operation Staunch," an effort to halt arms transfers to Iran.

U.S. APPEASEMENT UNDER BUSH, 1989–1990

The principal purpose of the Reagan administration's policy was not to influence the domestic or international behavior of Iraq, but to furnish support for that country in its struggle with Iran. However, this policy had the effect (perhaps partly intended) of establishing political contacts and economic connections between Iraq and the United States, as well as creating a brief history of limited cooperation. By the late 1980s, then, some foundation for further strengthening U.S.-Iraqi ties appeared to have been laid. When the Iran-Iraq war ended in August of 1988, policymakers in Washington continued to pursue close relations with Baghdad. According to Bruce Jentleson, "The prevailing view . . . was that while the war-induced need for an alliance of convenience had subsided, new and expanded bases for a U.S.-Iraqi relationship were developing."[20]

In its final months, the Reagan administration embarked upon what could be regarded as a nascent appeasement strategy. U.S. officials and many analysts outside of government believed Saddam Hussein had gradually become less extreme, so that a conciliatory approach now had the potential to reduce tensions with Iraq. Although a member of the State Department's policy planning staff, Zalmay Khalilzad, produced a memorandum arguing that Iraq represented the main threat to peace in the Persian Gulf region and the United States should therefore act to contain Iraqi expansion, his recommendation for a confrontational strategy was rejected out of hand. When the Senate unanimously passed the Prevention of Genocide Act of 1988, which would have imposed stringent sanctions on Iraq in retaliation for its gassing of Kurdish civilians, the administration and its allies in the business community lobbied House committee members so vigorously and so successfully that the sanctions bill never reached the floor for a vote. Toward the end of Reagan's presidency, the U.S. government actually increased the rate at which licenses for the export of dual-use technologies to Iraq were approved.[21]

George Bush succeeded Ronald Reagan as president of the United States in January 1989. As Jentleson writes, "The Bush administration took up where the Reagan administration left off."[22] In the spring and summer of 1989, U.S. officials conducted a "strategic review" of America's Persian Gulf policy.[23] This review culminated in the issuing of National Security Decision Directive 26 (NSD-26), signed by President Bush in October. The document recognized that certain aspects of Iraqi behavior were troubling and that the country might pose a threat to stability in the Persian Gulf region. Iraq's possession and recent use of chemical weapons against the Kurds, its active nuclear program, and its interference in the internal affairs of other states in the area received particular mention, as did its less-than-stellar record on human rights. Nevertheless, NSD-26 regarded good relations with Iraq as crucial to America's long-term interests and was optimistic about the possibility of manipulating Iraq's behavior in positive directions.[24] Toward this end, a conciliatory approach was advocated: "The U.S. Government should propose economic and political incentives for Iraq to moderate its behavior and to increase our influence with Iraq."[25] The carrots would be accompanied by sticks, for NSD-26 also stated that "Iraq should be told that the United States would impose economic and political sanctions and urge its allies to do so if Baghdad resumed its use of chemical weapons, used biological weapons, or tried to develop a nuclear weapon in violation of international accords."[26] As the policy was initially conceived, Deputy Secretary of State Lawrence Eagleburger's later description of it as "a mix of incentives and disincentives" was not entirely inaccurate.[27]

As implemented, however, the policy consisted mainly of inducements. In November 1989, a month after an unpleasant meeting between Secretary of State James Baker and Iraqi Foreign Minister Tariq Aziz, at which Aziz accused the United States of seeking to undermine the Iraqi regime, the Bush administration approved a new $1 billion in CCC loan guarantees to Iraq, to be made in two installments of $500 million each.[28] The approval came over the objections of the Treasury Department and the Office of Management and Budget (OMB), and despite growing suspicion that previous CCC loan monies had been diverted from commodity programs into weapons procurement through the illegal activities of the Atlanta branch of the Banca Nazionale del Lavoro (BNL).[29] On 17 January 1990, Bush issued an executive order permitting the Export-Import Bank to furnish additional credits for trade with Iraq. Overriding members of Congress who sought to end the program, Bush declared that cutting off Eximbank guarantees was "not in the national interest of the United States."[30]

The conciliatory gestures made by the Bush administration did not produce the desired results. Indeed, there followed what Assistant Secretary of State John Kelly called "the spring of bad behavior," as Iraq and its leader, Saddam Hussein, became increasingly belligerent.[31] On 24 February, Saddam Hussein told a meeting of the Arab Cooperation Council (ACC) in Amman, Jordan, that the decline of the Soviet Union placed the United States in an unchallenged position in international affairs. As a result, he warned, America might be tempted to commit "follies against the interests and national security of the Arabs." If the Arab people were not careful, "the Arab Gulf region will be governed by the U.S. will."[32]

The next month witnessed further events that cast doubt upon the willingness of Iraq to moderate its behavior. On 9 March, the government of Iraq placed Farzad Bazoft, an Iranian-born journalist for the *London Observer*, on trial. Bazoft, who had been arrested some months before while investigating an explosion at an Iraqi weapons facility, was charged with being an Israeli spy. Ignoring pleas for leniency from Great Britain and elsewhere, the Iraqi court convicted Bazoft and sentenced him to death. Less than a week later, he was hanged. Also in March, Iraqi agents were apprehended in Britain, seeking to smuggle electronic triggers for detonating nuclear weapons back to Iraq. Finally, American intelligence detected the construction of six missile launchers at a base in western Iraq, a location from which Scud missiles would be capable of reaching Israeli territory.[33]

On 1 April, Saddam Hussein delivered a speech to members of the Iraqi Armed Forces General Command in which he admitted that Iraq now possessed binary chemical weapons and warned that if Israel launched an attack against Iraqi industry, "by God, we will make fire eat up half of Israel."[34] The Bush administration, which termed the remarks "deplorable and irresponsible," was by now becoming increasingly concerned about Iraq's intentions, and on 16 April an interagency Deputies Committee met at the White House to review American policy.[35] The group agreed that no further commodity loan guarantees to Iraq should be issued. In May, the Bush administration suspended the second $500 million tranche of CCC credits that had been authorized the preceding November.

Although suspension of the loan guarantees moved U.S. policy in a less conciliatory direction, American policymakers wanted to "narrow" rather than to "shut" the window of opportunity for cooperation with Iraq, and attempts to cultivate improved relations with the Baghdad regime continued well into the summer of 1990.[36] The flow of dual use and other advanced technologies remained unabated, despite the recommendation of Dennis Kloske, undersecretary for export administration in the Department of Commerce, that an embargo on such items be enacted. Kloske later told a subcommittee of the House Foreign Affairs Committee that "the State Department adamantly opposed my position, choosing instead to advocate the maintenance of diplomatic relations with Iraq," a stance that was upheld by an interagencies Deputies Committee to which the matter was referred.[37] In the fifteen days before the invasion of Kuwait, the Bush administration approved licenses for the export of $4.8

million in advanced technology to Iraq. Included in this figure were $2.5 million of computers slated for the secretly renamed Ministry of Industry and Military Industrialization (formerly the Ministry of Industry and Minerals), headed by Saddam Hussein's son-in-law, Hussein Kamel Hasan, as well as more than $1 million of computers, flight simulators, and other items headed to Saad 16.[38] A mere two days prior to Iraq's attack on Kuwait, a Pennsylvania company was granted a Commerce Department license to export forges and computer hardware useful in the production of 16-inch gun barrels.[39] The day before the invasion, approval was given for the sale of $695,000 of sophisticated data transmission equipment.[40] When Iraqi troops crossed the border into Kuwait, sixty-one licenses for the export of goods valued at $107 million were still pending at the Department of Commerce.[41]

All efforts by the Congress to impose economic and other sanctions on Iraq were resisted strenuously by the Bush administration, which worried that such action would only antagonize Saddam Hussein and eliminate whatever chance remained of enticing him in a positive direction. Arguing against a sanctions bill, an administration supporter, Senator Richard Luger of Indiana, told his colleagues, "Passage of this legislation would badly undercut any possibility we have of influencing Iraqi behavior in areas from the peace process to human rights, terrorism to proliferation."[42] Some agencies within the administration continued working even to reverse the suspension of credit to Iraq. On the eve of the Iraqi invasion of Kuwait, April Glaspie, the American ambassador in Baghdad, assured the Iraqi government that the State Department was still seeking to thaw the frozen commodity loan guarantees.

In the end, the efforts to appease Saddam Hussein and the Iraqi regime failed. On 17 July, the Iraqi leader made a speech in which he attacked the United States, saying that "the imperialists . . . have chosen to wage an economic guerrilla war with the help of those agents of imperialism, the leaders of the Gulf states. Their policy of keeping oil prices at a low level is a poisoned dagger planted in Iraq's back."[43] Ominously, he warned that "if words fail to afford us protection, then we will have no choice but to resort to effective action to put things right and ensure the restitution of our rights."[44] On 20 July, Iraq began to mobilize its military forces; within a few days, more than 100,000 Iraqi troops had massed near the border with Kuwait.

The U.S. government repeatedly pressed Baghdad for a clear statement of its intentions, and stressed that America would defend its interests in the Gulf region. However, most observers in Washington, as well as those in the Arab world, felt that Iraq's mobilization was essentially a bluff, designed to intimidate Kuwait into making territorial and economic concessions, but not presaging an actual invasion.[45] Even the CIA, which concluded by 25 July that Saddam Hussein would likely initiate military action against Kuwait, did not believe he would seek to occupy the entire country.[46]

In part because of this belief, and because they did not want to provoke Saddam Hussein into action he might not otherwise take, American policymakers made only the most lukewarm efforts to deter the Iraqi leader. On the one hand, U.S. officials repeatedly emphasized America's determination to protect its interests in the region and warned that "there is no place for coercion and intimidation in a civilized world."[47] At the same time, however, the American government pointedly refused to commit itself to military intervention in the event of an Iraqi attack. State Department spokeswoman Margaret Tutwiler noted at a briefing on 24 July that "we do not have any defense treaties with Kuwait and there are no special defense or security commitments to Kuwait."[48] Assistant Secretary of State John Kelly told a House committee a week later, "We have no defense treaty relationship with any Gulf country," although he stressed that "we support the security and independence of friendly states in the region." Responding to a question, Kelly declined to state what American policy would be regarding the use of force should Iraq decide to invade Kuwait.[49] Finally, on 25 July, in a much-criticized interview with Saddam Hussein, Ambassador Glaspie told the Iraqi leader that the United States had "no opinion on the Arab-Arab conflicts, like your border disagreement with Kuwait." While she apparently warned Hussein that the United States would defend its interests in the Persian Gulf, her remarks were widely interpreted as giving a "green light" to Iraqi aggression.[50]

It is impossible to say what impact U.S. efforts to appease Iraq would have had on a more robust deterrent strategy had such a strategy been attempted. One can argue, as does Bruce Jentleson, that the continual offering of inducements without requiring reciprocation "could not but undermine American credibility."[51] There is, however, little evidence regarding Iraqi perceptions to support such a conclusion and no way of knowing whether the effect would have been fatal. The Iraqis may have viewed the United States as "a paper tiger,"[52] but Saddam Hussein's remarks expressing doubts about the willingness of the United States to fight contain no references to American concessions, emphasizing instead other actions, including the rapid withdrawal from Lebanon following the bombing of the Marine barracks in 1983.[53] In any event, the feeble attempts at deterrence failed. On 2 August 1990, Iraqi forces crossed the border into Kuwait.

IRAQI MOTIVES AND OBJECTIVES

In the months following the invasion of Kuwait, Saddam Hussein was pilloried, depicted as a greedy, aggressive dictator seeking to establish Iraq's hegemony in the Persian Gulf region. Said President George Bush, "We're dealing with Hitler revisited, a totalitarianism and a brutality that is naked and unprecedented in modern times."[54]

There is no doubt that the Iraqi president was (and presumably remains) a highly ambitious ruler. A man who compared himself to Nebuchadnezzar, the ancient king of Babylon, as well as the late Egyptian leader Gamal Abdel Nasser, he encouraged the development of a cult of personality.[55] The Baath Party, of which he was leader, espoused an ideology committed to "the ultimate goal of Arab unity," which was to be achieved "through armed struggle."[56] Saddam Hussein was determined to accomplish Arab unity under Iraq's—and his—leadership. As he declared in a 1979 speech, "The glory of the Arabs stems from the glory of Iraq. Throughout history, whenever Iraq became mighty and flourished, so did the Arab nation. That is why we are striving to make Iraq mighty, formidable, able, and developed, and why we shall spare nothing to improve the welfare and to brighten the glory of Iraq."[57] Those who have studied Hussein's career believe that his objective, from the time he became president, "was to make Iraq the dominant power in the Persian Gulf and in the Arab world."[58] One has described Iraq under his rule as "a despotism lusting for regional supremacy."[59]

How much territorial acquisition this ambition implied is hard to tell, but the tiny emirate of Kuwait was an obvious early target. In addition to having vast reserves of oil (about which more later), Iraqis considered it to be part of Iraq. Iraq's claim to Kuwait was based on the fact that the emirate had been part of the former Ottoman province of Basra and on the belief that Iraq, as the legal successor to the Ottoman Empire, had inherited that territory. The separation of Kuwait from the remainder of Basra by Great Britain in 1922 and the 1961 agreement between that country and Kuwait, by which the latter became independent, were thus regarded by Iraqis as illegitimate actions that could, if necessary, be reversed by force when the time was ripe. Six days after the 1961 pact was concluded, Gen. Abdel Karim Qassen, the president of Iraq, expressed a position held by subsequent Iraqi leaders, including Saddam Hussein: "We shall extend Iraq's borders to the south of Kuwait. Iraq and nobody else concludes agreements about Kuwait, so we regard this agreement between Kuwait and Britain as illegal from the date of its operation. No individual, whether in Kuwait or outside, has the right to dominate the people of Kuwait, for they are the people of Iraq."[60]

Although the enhancement of his personal power and the achievement of regional dominance by his country were strong motivators for Saddam Hussein, they do not fully explain why he decided to attack Kuwait in the summer of 1990. Given the status of its chemical and nuclear weapons programs, Iraq would have been in a much stronger military position a few years down the road. This was particularly true if it contemplated opposition from the United States, itself a major nuclear power. As Janice Gross Stein points out, a rational leader motivated by greed and the opportunity to commit an act of aggression would presumably have waited.[61]

The evidence suggests that Saddam Hussein's decision to attack Kuwait in August 1990 was in fact prompted more by considerations of need than of opportunity. As a radical dictator, Hussein's rule lacked legitimacy based on political institutions and depended instead upon his ability to "deliver the goods." For this reason, during the 1970s, he employed Iraq's new-found oil wealth to finance "massive development and social welfare programs aimed at broadening his own support base" in Iraq. Among his domestic reforms were "rapid improvements in housing, education, and medical services," as well as "legislation on social security, minimum wages, and pension rights."[62]

The war with Iran had proved disastrous from the standpoint of Hussein's domestic policy. By 1986, "economic development [had] been arrested and reversed; social cohesion [had] begun to show signs of strain; and ... the people's morale [had] sunk deeper into despair."[63] At the war's end, the decade-long struggle had cost the country nearly half a trillion dollars, and the economy was in shambles. Experts put the cost of reconstruction at as much as $230 billion. Unfortunately, Iraq's oil revenues, about $13 billion per year, were not enough to allow the country to tread water, let alone rebuild. With imports totaling approximately $17 billion, debt payments another $5 billion, and transfers by foreign workers $1 billion, Iraq was running a balance of payments deficit of roughly $10 billion per year. Of the $80 billion owed to foreign creditors, more than a third was short-term debt that had to be repaid to Europe, Japan, and the United States in hard currency.[64] Under these conditions, the prospects for economic reconstruction looked dismal indeed.

Iraq's only major source of hard currency, which would enable it to repay its loans—and perhaps finance the development of an economic infrastructure—was, of course, the sale of petroleum abroad. But oil prices had declined from around thirty dollars a barrel in the mid-1970s to less than half of that amount. In the first six months of 1990, the price of oil fell precipitously, from $20.50 to $13.00 per barrel.[65] Saddam Hussein told the Arab League in May that each time the price of oil dropped by a dollar a barrel, Iraq lost $1 billion a year.[66] Later that summer, his foreign minister, Tariq Aziz, estimated that falling oil prices had cost Iraq's treasury nearly $90 billion in the preceding decade.[67]

The situation, from the Iraqi perspective, was thus becoming increasingly desperate. A potentially restive population, whose expectations had been raised by the reforms of the 1970s and the "promised fruits of the 'historic victory'" over Iran, could be placated only if there were "an immediate economic breakthrough."[68] But this seemed virtually impossible, given Iraq's mountainous foreign debt, its stagnant economy, and the fact that the country lacked the means of obtaining funds sufficient to address these problems. As a consequence, the government of Saddam Hussein came to see itself as being in a virtual state of siege. In May 1990, Hussein reminded the other Arab states that "war is fought with soldiers and much harm is done by explosions, killings, and coup attempts—but it is also done by economic means." He accused them of waging "a kind of war against Iraq" and warned that Iraq had "reached a point where we can no longer withstand pressure."[69]

Kuwait was the most serious offender in Iraqi eyes. Its overproduction of petroleum in violation of OPEC quotas had been particularly excessive. Moreover, Kuwait had been pumping oil from the disputed Rumailah field, some of which lay beneath Iraqi soil, and which the government of Iraq claimed as its own. By Iraqi estimates, Kuwait had extracted as much as $2.4 billion worth of oil from this field between 1980 and 1990. In July 1990, Foreign Minister Aziz told the Arab League that "The government of Kuwait has, indeed, committed a double aggression against Iraq: first by seizing part of its land and its oilfield and then by despoiling its national wealth. Such an act can be compared to an act of military aggression. Then deliberately trying to strangle the Iraqi economy at a time when Iraq is already subject to ruthless Imperialist-Zionist threats is also an act of aggression as serious as military aggression."[70]

By the summer of 1990, Iraqi leaders were convinced that Kuwait was involved in "a conspiracy to destroy Iraq. . . . a conspiracy to bring about the economic collapse of Iraq, followed by its political collapse and a change of regime." They also believed, however, that "Kuwait was too small to do this without backing from a superpower."[71] That superpower was, of course, the United States.

The notion that Iraq was menaced by a U.S.-led conspiracy was a recurrent theme in Saddam Hussein's speeches. On 24 February 1990, he noted that with the disintegration of the Soviet Union, the United States had "emerged in a superior position in international politics." Until a new balance of forces was formed, "the U.S. [would] continue to depart from the restrictions that govern the rest of the world." If the Arab states were not careful, "the Arab Gulf region [would] be governed by the U.S. will," and oil production and prices would "be fixed in line with a special perspective benefitting [*sic*] U.S. interests and ignoring the interests of others."[72] At a meeting of the Arab League on 28 May, the Iraqi leader again railed against the United States and its ally, Israel, stating:

> The United States has demonstrated that it is primarily responsible for the aggressive and expansionist policies of the Zionist entity against the Palestinian Arab people and the Arab nation. . . . It would not have been possible for the Zionist entity to engage in aggression and expansion at the Arabs' expense if it did not possess the force and political cover provided by the United States—the main source of the Zionist entity's aggressive military force, and the main source of its financial resources. . . . Arab security and interests are on the receiving end of these American policies. . . . This is not a policy of friendship. It is a harmful policy that threatens the security and vital interests of the Arab nation.[73]

While such remarks may have been calculated in part to appeal to the anti-American attitudes of his audience, one expert testified before Congress in the winter of 1990 that "The conspiracy theories [Saddam Hussein] spins are not merely for popular consumption in the Arab world, but genuinely reflect his paranoid mindset. He is convinced that the United States, Israel, and Iran have been in league for the purpose of eliminating him."[74]

After the invasion of Kuwait, Foreign Minister Aziz stated that Iraq's economic difficulties were "a major factor" in the government's decision to attack. Said Aziz, "We were desperate, and could not pay our bills for food imports. It was a starvation war. When do you use military power to preserve yourself?"[75] While it is hard to know how much of his claim was a justification designed to put the best possible light on Iraq's aggression, it is generally consistent with other evidence.[76]

In sum, the aggressive behavior of Iraq and its president, Saddam Hussein, was motivated by both greed and need. As a long-term objective, Hussein wanted to expand his power and influence throughout the Persian Gulf region and to make himself undisputed leader of the Arab world. In the short term, he felt himself and his country to be under virtual attack from other Arab countries and from an imperialist-Zionist conspiracy led by the United States. April Glaspie later speculated that Saddam Hussein went ahead with the invasion of Kuwait, despite warnings that America might intervene, because he believed the United States would eventually "force a fight on him."[77] A subsequent statement by Tariq Aziz seems to confirm her view: "The Americans had decided long before August 2nd to crush Iraq, and there was nothing [our] government could do to stop them."[78] The invasion of Kuwait thus served a dual purpose. As Jerrold Post concluded, Saddam Hussein's aggression was "instrumental in pursuing his goals, but it [was] at the same time defensive aggression."[79]

WHY APPEASEMENT FAILED

American appeasement of Saddam Hussein failed at two levels. It failed at the long-run goal of producing a more harmonious relationship between Iraq and the United States and a mellowing of Iraq's domestic and international behavior. More immediately, it also failed to prevent Iraq's invasion and conquest of Kuwait.

As the preceding analysis suggests, there were three motives behind Iraq's aggressive behavior that an appeasement policy might have addressed: (1) Saddam Hussein's desire for the expansion of his personal power and the eventual achievement of regional hegemony by Iraq, (2) his fears of domestic challenge to his rule, rooted mainly in Iraq's economic problems, and (3) his related concern over the external threat to Iraq he believed was posed by a U.S.-led imperialist-Zionist conspiracy. While each of these was important, the second was probably foremost in Saddam

Hussein's mind at the time of the invasion of Kuwait. Whatever the relative significance of these motives, American policy did not address any of them in a satisfactory manner.

Since the United States was not eager to see Iraq become a regional hegemon, it is not surprising that the American government did not offer concessions designed to help Saddam Hussein achieve this goal. Unintentionally and quite ironically, the sophisticated technology and weaponry provided by the United States and its allies did enhance Iraq's capacity to pursue regional supremacy by force. In this way, they probably made conciliation all the more difficult by reducing Baghdad's incentive to settle for lesser concessions.

Exactly what—if anything—Iraq would have settled for is hard to determine. Although Iraqis had long regarded Kuwait as part of their national territory, Saddam Hussein's most immediate and primary motive for invading Kuwait appears to have been Iraq's deteriorating economic situation and the perception that Kuwait was in large measure responsible for it. At the Arab League summit in late May, the Iraqi leader accused Kuwait of conducting economic warfare against Iraq and demanded billions of dollars in reparations, as well as territorial concessions.[80] In a July letter to the secretary-general of the Arab League, the foreign minister, Tariq Aziz, demanded that oil prices be raised to more than $25 per barrel (roughly double the existing price), that Kuwait stop pumping from the Rumailah field and pay for what it had already extracted, that Arab states accept a moratorium on the repayment of loans made to Iraq, and that "an Arab plan similar to the Marshall Plan" be devised to assist Iraq in its postwar recovery.[81]

The Kuwaiti government eventually gave a little ground. At the end of June, the emirate offered Iraq $500 million in assistance over three years. This fell far short, however, of the $10 billion to $27 billion demanded by Baghdad on different occasions. On 10 July, the Kuwaiti government agreed to halt temporarily the overproduction of oil and to abide by its OPEC quota, reserving the right to reconsider in several months.[82] Beyond this, it simply would not go. A letter to the secretary-general of the Arab League in late July rejected Iraq's accusations against the emirate and stated that "The sons of Kuwait, in good as well as bad times, are people of principle and integrity. By no means will they yield to threat and extortion."[83]

The United States, though offering its own incentives to Iraq, refused to pressure Kuwaiti leaders into doing the same. When, in late June,

the American ambassador proposed encouraging the Kuwaiti government to be more responsive to Iraqi demands, he was directed by the
State Department "to reiterate the American commitment to defend
Kuwait."[84] In the final analysis, neither Kuwait nor the United States
made any concessions that substantially addressed Iraq's economic difficulties. In the context of the country's $80 billion foreign debt, its dete-
riorating infrastructure, and its declining oil revenues, the commodity
loan guarantees furnished by the United States appear a mere drop in the
bucket, hardly enough to affect Iraqi policy. It is true that the economic
problems confronted by the Iraqi regime were largely of Saddam Hussein's
own making. His war with Iran and the resultant expenditures on arms,
which absorbed nearly 40 percent of Iraq's GNP, had depleted his country's
treasury. April Glaspie was almost surely right when she testified that the
United States "couldn't and shouldn't have prevented him from going
bankrupt."[85] Still, given the meagerness of American concessions in relation to the economic catastrophe facing Iraq, it is small wonder that they
had so little effect.

If American concessions did not alleviate Saddam Hussein's perceived need to take aggressive action for economic reasons, neither did
they provide him with much reassurance regarding the external threat
posed by the alleged Zionist-imperialist conspiracy. It is doubtful there
was much prospect for reassuring the Iraqi leader, given the intensity of
his fears. As April Glaspie noted in testimony before Congress, "It is very
hard to persuade somebody of anything if they think you are irredeemably hostile."[86]

Two problems negated any reassuring effect that might have been
produced by American gestures toward Iraq. The first was the relative
insignificance of the concessions that were offered. Given the immense
difficulties facing Iraq, America's offering of only the most modest economic assistance could easily be interpreted as indifference or even hostility. The second, and perhaps more important, was the conflicting signals
that were emanating from Washington. At the same time that the Bush
administration was seeking to convince Saddam Hussein of America's
benign intentions, organs of the U.S. government, including some within
the executive branch itself, were giving the Iraqi leader a quite different
impression.

As noted previously, relations between the Bush administration and
the Iraqi government got off to a rocky start when in October 1989
Foreign Minister Aziz told Secretary of State Baker that Iraq had not seen

"enough improvement" in relations with the United States since the end of its war with Iran. He complained of a "propaganda campaign against Iraq in the U.S.—particularly by the Congress," citing "congressional moves to legislate economic and political sanctions." He was disturbed by reports that "some American agencies" were trying to destabilize Iraq. He accused the United States of sowing suspicion of Iraqi intentions among Iraq's neighbors in the Persian Gulf.[87] Don Oberdorfer has suggested that the Iraqi government may have gained knowledge of U.S. military briefings to friendly Arab states which "identified Iraq as a potential threat in the region."[88] Aziz said later that Baghdad had also received information that the CIA was advocating the overthrow of the Iraqi regime in conversations with Iraqi dissidents both at home and abroad.[89]

In any event, developments in the spring of 1990 did nothing to dispel Iraq's suspicions. On 15 February, the Voice of America (VOA) broadcast an appeal to public opinion to mobilize against dictators around the world. Iraq was specifically mentioned and Saddam Hussein condemned as a tyrant. The editorial claimed to be "reflecting the views of the U.S. government."[90] Not surprisingly, the Iraqi government interpreted the broadcast as an effort by the United States to "incite revolution" in Iraq.[91] The American ambassador quickly disavowed the editorial, telling Baghdad, "It is absolutely not United States policy to question the legitimacy of the government of Iraq nor interfere in any way with the domestic concerns of the Iraqi people and government."[92] A few weeks later, a group of five U.S. senators led by Minority Leader Robert Dole met with Saddam Hussein. In an effort to alleviate the Iraqi leader's fears, this delegation expressed sympathy for his concerns, informed him (erroneously) that the author of the VOA editorial had been removed from his position, and tried to convince him that only the U.S. media, not the government, was hostile to Iraq.[93] But the damage had been done.

Other events had a similar effect. Less than a week after the VOA broadcast, the Department of State issued its annual human rights report. The document devoted twelve pages to detailing human rights abuses in Iraq and identified Saddam Hussein as "the worst violator of human rights."[94] Appalled, the Foreign Affairs Committee of the House of Representatives proposed a resolution condemning Iraq. Only after considerable lobbying was the Bush administration able to block its passage.

The State Department's human rights report, the VOA broadcast, and the efforts by Congress to impose economic sanctions diluted whatever reassuring effect American concessions might have had on Iraq. In his 25 July meeting with April Glaspie, Saddam Hussein recited a long list of grievances against the United States, accusing "some circles" in the U.S. government, "including the CIA and the State Department," though not President Bush and Secretary of State Baker, of favoring policies inimical to Iraqi interests.[95] Glaspie later told a House committee that in spite of U.S. efforts to cultivate his friendship, "[Hussein] remained as convinced as he had been for the previous 20 years the United States was irredeemably hostile."[96]

Securing a modification, via concessions, of Iraq's foreign and international behavior would have been difficult—and perhaps impossible—even had American policy been well conceived and executed. Saddam Hussein's ambitions, while not Hitlerian in scope, were extensive. His economic needs were enormous. His insecurities were sufficiently great that it may not be an exaggeration to call him paranoid. Whether the U.S. government could have offered anything that would have satisfied his ambitions or relieved his fears seems doubtful. Regardless, in retrospect it is clear that American concessions fell far short of what might have been required.

THE FAILURE TO ADJUST POLICY

The policy of appeasement pursued by the Bush administration was not, in the beginning, an unreasonable one. It was by no means clear that Saddam Hussein was incorrigible. As the assistant secretary of state for Near Eastern Affairs, John Kelly, told Congress in June of 1990, during the late 1980s the Iraqi government had taken a number of steps suggesting a desire for better relations with the United States and the willingness to adopt more moderate policies both domestically and internationally. It had, for example, expelled the terrorist organization of Abu Nidal, cooperated with the Arab League in seeking a settlement of the Lebanese civil war, participated in the Paris Review Conference of the 1925 Geneva Chemical Weapons Protocol, adopted a more supportive stance on Arab-Israeli peace talks, and was even discussing a new constitution that would provide a greater measure of human rights for Iraqi citizens.[97] Some analysts outside the government were equally impressed. One regional expert predicted that the end of the war with Iran would "bring more democracy" to Iraq, accepting the claim of Iraqi officials that Saddam Hussein "'is much concerned about democracy. . . . He thinks that it is healthy.'"[98] Given the evidence, it was quite possible to discount the

Eximbank's April 1989 warning that Iraq might soon go to war with Syria, Saudi Arabia, or Kuwait "over simmering territorial claims."[99]

The tragedy of U.S. policy toward Iraq, as of British policy toward Germany in the 1930s, was not that appeasement was attempted but that it was pursued, essentially unaltered, long after it was clear that it was unlikely to succeed. There were, in principle, two adjustments policymakers in Washington could have made. The first would have been to offer more substantial concessions, hoping that these would succeed where previously modest offerings had not. Given the meagerness of America's economic assistance to Iraq, this approach made a certain amount of sense, but it was never considered, presumably because domestic political opposition would have made it virtually impossible to pursue.

The second alternative was to abandon appeasement and to adopt a more confrontational approach. This strategy was, in fact, advocated by some within the Bush administration. In January 1990, two junior members of the State Department's policy planning staff sought to revive Zalmay Khalilzad's earlier recommendations in a paper entitled, "Containing Iraq."[100] In April, during the "spring of bad behavior," the head of the policy planning office, Dennis Ross, and the assistant secretary of state for Near Eastern Affairs, John Kelly, approached Secretary of State Baker and recommended that limited sanctions be imposed on Iraq. Baker allegedly agreed. However, the interagency Deputies Committee, to which the matter was referred, determined only that commodity loan credits should not be renewed.[101] That same month, an undersecretary in the Department of Commerce, Dennis Kloske, recommended that export controls on dual use technologies be tightened. He repeated the suggestion in June. On both occasions, he was rebuffed by his superiors.[102] For later revealing to Congress his disagreement with administration policy, Kloske was relieved of his position; as noted earlier, sales of advanced technology continued right up to the invasion of Kuwait.

Despite the increasingly bellicose signals from Iraq, the continuing pressure from Congress for the imposition of sanctions, the pleas from the Israeli government that the United States shift to a more confrontational policy, and the advice of some members of its own administration, the White House clung to its conciliatory approach.[103] As John Kelly told a House subcommittee in April 1990, it remained U.S. policy "to attempt to develop gradually a mutually beneficial relationship with Iraq in order to strengthen positive trends in Iraq's foreign and domestic policies."[104] Whether such trends could be identified was, however, open to question.

Congressman Tom Lantos (D-Calif.) responded to Kelly with a scathing critique of the administration's position:

> With all due respect, Mr. Secretary, I detect an Alice in Wonderland quality about your testimony . . . You talk about Iraq using poison gas against its own people, diplomats engaged in murder plots in the United States, and the government smuggling nuclear triggers from here and from the U.K. and other places. . . . Then you express the hope, which boggles the mind, that somehow this will change and Iraq under Saddam Hussein will turn in the direction of being a responsible and civilized and peace loving and constructive member of the international community. At what point will the Administration recognize that this is not a nice guy?[105]

Kelly admitted to the Senate Foreign Relations Committee in mid-June that Iraq's behavior had not improved.[106] Nevertheless, he and his superiors in the administration continued to oppose the imposition of sanctions.

The failure of the U.S. government to respond to clear signals that its strategy was not working suggests, as one former Reagan Defense Department official remarked, that "the Bush administration sort of put Iraq policy on autopilot after the end of the Iran-Iraq War."[107] Why was this so? Why did the administration pursue its conciliatory policy well after it should have been obvious—and was obvious to many—that Iraq's behavior was not becoming more moderate, but rather more belligerent and threatening? One explanation is what Bruce Jentleson has called the "full-plate" defense: that the U.S. government was so consumed by other events in the world that it failed to devote sufficient attention to the problem of Iraq.[108] It is true that 1989 and 1990 were very busy years for makers of American foreign policy. The Cold War was ending. The Soviet Empire and even the Soviet Union itself were disintegrating. German reunification was in progress. It is also true that in the State Department, the same man, Dennis Ross, head of the policy planning staff, bore primary responsibility for Soviet, Middle Eastern, and Persian Gulf policy. According to Morton Kondracke, Ross later admitted "that one reason State did not pay attention to the rising menace of Saddam Hussein in early 1990 was his and [Secretary of State James] Baker's preoccupation with German reunification and Soviet affairs."[109]

Ross's admission notwithstanding, it would be inaccurate to say that Iraq was ignored by U.S. policymakers. On the contrary, administration officials devoted considerable time and energy to conciliating Saddam Hussein. That their attention did not lead to a reversal of this policy was, at the most fundamental level, a consequence of the fact that Saddam Hussein's receptivity to appeasement was "treated as a premise, not a hypothesis."[110] Arguments to the contrary were never seriously considered, but were rejected out of hand. Lawrence Eagleburger later claimed that U.S. policy was designed "to probe, test, and encourage the Iraqis while being wary of their intentions."[111] His statement, however, attributes to American strategy a provisional character it simply did not possess. As evidence mounted that Saddam Hussein could not be conciliated, it was disregarded because a mindset prevailed within the administration that held he could be.[112]

At least in part, this mindset had its origins in the American obsession with Iran, whose Islamic fundamentalist regime had held U.S. citizens hostage in 1979–80. An enemy of Iran must be a friend of the United States.[113] A hardline policy toward Iraq would give aid and comfort to a more dangerous adversary. Such logic persisted even after the end of the Iran-Iraq war.[114] It is also possible that U.S. officials continued to believe Saddam Hussein could be appeased because to admit otherwise would have meant having to abandon a strategy they had followed for nearly a decade, to admit that their policy was misguided and was not producing the expected results.

A more important reason for the persistence of "the mindset" was the fact that there appeared no viable alternative to conciliation. Administration officials did not believe economic sanctions would be an effective lever against Baghdad. Since other countries were unlikely to cooperate in a trade embargo, Iraq would simply buy its goods elsewhere. Nothing would be gained, and a valuable export market would be lost. At the time of the invasion of Kuwait, for example, nearly a quarter of American rice exports went to Iraq. John Kelly told the Senate Foreign Relations Committee in June 1990 that there was "virtually zero expectation that any other nations would join us in the imposition of sanctions against Iraq, and therefore it would be the American farmer and the American exporter who would in effect be punished."[115]

The most extreme version of a confrontational strategy, a deterrent approach backed by threats of military force, encountered similar objections. There was no enthusiasm in the United States for sending large numbers of troops to the Persian Gulf region. America's European allies were generally unconcerned about Iraq, so their support could not be anticipated. And America's friends in the Middle East were convinced that Iraq would not invade Kuwait; indeed, they warned the United States against doing anything that Saddam Hussein might construe as a provocation. Under these circumstances, it is not easy to see how the Bush administration could have confronted Saddam Hussein with a deterrent threat that he would have taken seriously. As Don Oberdorfer has written, "Before the invasion, it would not have been credible to Saddam— or, for that matter, to officials of the administration in Washington—for the United States to warn that it might send 500,000 troops and spearhead an unprecedented international effort to reverse the aggression."[116]

A final reason for the administration's refusal to abandon appeasement and move to a more confrontational strategy was that U.S. officials believed Saddam Hussein's aggressive behavior was motivated more by fear and insecurity than the desire for territorial aggrandizement and regional supremacy. Adopting sanctions and issuing threats against Iraq might, they worried, worsen the situation and provoke the very behaviors the administration was seeking to prevent. As John Kelly wrote in February 1990, urging the release of an additional $500 million in CCC credits, refusal to approve the loan guarantees "will feed Saddam's paranoia and accelerate his swing against us."[117] Kelly's concern may have been justified, for there is some evidence that the suspension of commodity credits in April was interpreted by the Iraqi government as a hostile act. According to Tariq Aziz, the freeze was imposed at a point when Iraq's need for imported foodstuffs was particularly acute. Its timing helped convince him that "the Americans had stopped listening to us and had made up their minds to hit us."[118]

CONCLUSION

America's conciliatory policy toward Iraq in 1989–1990 had short- and long-term objectives. The long-run goal was to produce a moderation of Iraq's domestic and, especially, international behavior by creating a friendlier U.S.-Iraqi relationship. This objective necessarily subsumed within it the short-run goal of preventing an overt act of Iraqi aggression, such as the invasion of Kuwait.

As a long-term strategy, appeasement was probably doomed to failure because, in a very real sense, Saddam Hussein was virtually unappeasable.

His aim of supremacy in the Persian Gulf region and the Arab world could not be met—or even approached—by concessions that it was in the power (or the interests) of the United States to make. His exceedingly suspicious, even paranoid personality also made fundamentally altering "his strategic image of the United States as an unrelenting enemy determined to destroy his regime through economic warfare and covert action" highly problematic.[119]

In the short term, it is arguable (though not, of course, provable) that an invasion of Kuwait could have been prevented by the offering of appropriate concessions. Saddam Hussein's decision to attack in August 1990 appears to have been driven mainly by Iraq's deteriorating economic condition, which many Iraqis believed was the result of a U.S.-inspired conspiracy to destroy their country. Given this, efforts by the United States, together with Kuwait and other Arab states, to relieve Iraq's economic distress might have had some chance of success.[120] Unfortunately, the concessions offered by the United States, and especially by Kuwait, did not come close to providing such relief. Nor did they affect Iraq's belief in a U.S.-led conspiracy. In the context of American criticisms of Iraq's human rights practices, the Voice of America broadcast, and congressional efforts to enact sanctions against Iraq, the modest concessions had little or no reassuring effect.

Because Iraq was motivated by greed and opportunity, as well as by need, it might, in hindsight, have been wise for the United States to have combined increased concessions with a more robust deterrent position.[121] Although the issuance of threats would probably have undermined the reassuring impact of larger concessions, this effect could have been minimized by signaling clearly that the threats would be carried out only in the event of Iraqi aggression. Ameliorating the economic imperative for seizing Kuwait, together with eliminating the opportunity to attack with impunity, could have prevented the invasion, if one assumes—as seems reasonable given the evidence—that Iraq's fear of the United States and of a U.S.-led conspiracy would not have been a sufficient cause. In any event, the complexity of these calculations, and uncertainly about their validity, illustrates the inherent difficulties of pursuing a mixed strategy with an adversary possessing a combination of motives.

It can still be wondered, of course, whether a strong deterrent strategy could have produced a modification of Iraqi policy and prevented the invasion of Kuwait. Given the lack of support for such an approach in the United States, among the European allies, and among America's friends in the Middle East, establishing a credible deterrent would certainly have been difficult. One-time assistant secretary of state Richard Murphy has said, "It is conceivable that a very blunt, harsh threat—you take one step toward Kuwait, and we'll clobber you"—might have deterred Iraq.[122] But the enormous pressures produced by Iraq's economic problems suggest otherwise. Indeed, Iraq's foreign minister, Tariq Aziz, stated in June 1991 that Iraqi leaders decided to proceed with the invasion of Kuwait despite the fact that "We expected an American military retaliation from the very beginning."[123] U.S. officials made a mistake in adhering to an appeasement policy long after there was virtually no prospect of its success. It is not clear, however, that an alternative strategy would have produced a more favorable outcome.[124]

The failed appeasement of Iraq illustrates clearly the unwisdom of making concessions that significantly increase a greed-driven adversary's ability to engage in acts of aggression. The transfers of sophisticated technology and weaponry by the United States addressed (unintentionally) Iraq's desire for regional supremacy, but did so by enhancing Baghdad's capacity to seek this objective by force. While need rather than opportunity appears to have been the crucial motive for Iraqi leaders in their decision to attack Kuwait, to the extent that opportunity mattered, American concessions helped to provide it. Offering Iraq the means to commit aggression was, not surprisingly, an ineffective way of preventing it.

6

AMERICAN APPEASEMENT OF NORTH KOREA, 1988–1994

The administration's inducement strategy is the only one that the American public and the international community will support economically, militarily and politically at this time. In some ways, then, it is the only available strategy. But upon examination, it appears more effective than the alternatives even if the world would support them.

> George Perkovich, "The Korea Precedent"

If this is appeasement, Neville Chamberlain would have been a hero.

> Jessica Mathews, "A Good Deal with North Korea"

During the late 1980s and early 1990s, the United States government, under the leadership of Presidents Bush and Clinton, pursued a policy with respect to North Korea that bore considerable resemblance to the Bush administration's approach toward Iraq. The immediate and most critical objective of U.S. strategy was the abandonment by Pyongyang of its accelerating nuclear weapons program, which American defense officials declared "must be stopped in advance without fail."[1] Its ultimate aim was more ambitious: to transform what Clinton "labeled a 'rogue state' into a responsible member of the global community."[2] In hearings before a subcommittee of the Senate Committee on Foreign Relations, special ambassador Robert Gallucci testified that the U.S. government wanted "to bring North Korea into the family of nations." If it succeeded, not only would the nuclear issue be resolved, but North Korean behavior might improve in other areas, including conventional arms control and human rights.[3] American policymakers hoped, he later said, to see "a rapprochement between North and South" and, eventually, "the reduction of tensions on the Korean peninsula."[4]

On 21 October 1994, after a series of difficult and protracted negotiations, the United States and North Korea signed an "Agreed Framework" to resolve the nuclear impasse.[5] In the four-page accord and the accompanying two-page secret codicil, the United States promised to arrange the construction of two proliferation-resistant light-water nuclear reactors in North Korea, at a cost of approximately $4 billion. Washington also agreed to see that Pyongyang received 3.65 million barrels of heavy oil per year. Perhaps most importantly, the United States pledged to end its efforts to isolate North Korea politically and economically, and to work toward the normalization of economic and diplomatic relations, beginning with the opening of liaison offices in the two capitals within six months.

In exchange, the government of North Korea promised to freeze immediately its nuclear program. It agreed to refrain from refueling its existing 5 megawatt research reactor and to halt construction of two much larger reactors. Furthermore, it pledged to cease operations at its plutonium processing plant and seal it. These facilities would be monitored by the International Atomic Energy Agency (IAEA), which would have the right to conduct "special inspections." After a period of approximately five years, the IAEA would also be allowed to visit two suspected nuclear waste sites to which investigators had previously been denied access. Approximately 8,000 spent fuel rods currently in a storage pond would be transferred out of the country. Pyongyang agreed, within a period of approximately ten years, to dismantle all three of its existing nuclear reactors as well as its plutonium plant. In addition, the North Korean government pledged to conduct talks with its South Korean counterpart aimed at improving the two countries' mutual relations.

It is, at this writing, too early to know the final outcome of this case. Thus far, however, the agreement has held. North Korea has frozen its nuclear program, and progress has been made toward implementation of various elements of the accord. The policy castigated by former defense secretary Caspar Weinberger as "the Appeasement of North Korea" has been a success and one of the more apparent foreign policy triumphs of the Clinton administration.[6]

U.S. Concern over North Korea's Nuclear Program

North Korea's desire for a nuclear capability originated during the Korean War, apparently as a response to discussion, in the United States, of the possibility of using American nuclear weapons in the fight against North Korean and Chinese forces. By the mid-1960s, the North Korean government had, with the assistance of China and the Soviet Union, established a nuclear research center at Yongbyon, about sixty miles north of Pyongyang. This complex contained, among other things, a small (2–4 megawatt) reactor supplied by the Soviet Union.[7]

In 1980, North Korea began construction of a much larger (20–30 megawatt) reactor at Yongbyon. Based on the British "Calder Hall" design of 1950s vintage, this graphite-moderated reactor was completed in 1986. While North Korean officials maintained that the new facility was intended solely for peaceful purposes, it was capable of producing in its spent fuel substantial amounts of the plutonium needed for nuclear weapons. Moreover, its size was "unusually large for a civilian research program," and it lacked the electric lines and transformers typically associated with the production of electrical power.[8] For these reasons, the discovery of the reactor by American intelligence in the early 1980s provoked considerable concern in Washington. At the behest of the Reagan administration, the Soviet Union pressured North Korea to accede to the Nuclear Nonproliferation Treaty (NPT), which it did in December 1985. Pyongyang refused, however, to sign an agreement placing the Yongbyon facility under IAEA safeguards.

During the 1980s, North Korea began building two additional reactors: a 50–200 megawatt facility at Yongbyon and a 600–800 megawatt facility near Taechon. Together the reactors would, upon completion, be capable of producing 180 to 235 kilograms of plutonium per year—enough for between forty and fifty nuclear devices.[9] The discovery of these facilities, along with the detection of a suspected plutonium reprocessing plant under construction at Yongbyon in late 1988 and early 1989, fostered concern in Washington, as well as in Tokyo and Seoul, that North Korea was close to acquiring nuclear weapons.[10] The revelation during the Persian Gulf War that Iraq's nuclear program had been much more advanced than previously suspected served to heighten this fear. In November 1991, the Bush administration, which had been quietly negotiating with Pyongyang for three years in an effort to achieve better relations, "declared that a nuclear-armed North Korea would be 'the most serious threat to peace and stability' in Asia."[11]

American policymakers were loath to see a North Korean nuclear capability for a number of reasons.[12] There was, first, the possibility that Pyongyang, with its reputation for behavior that was irrational and contrary to international moral and legal norms, might actually use the weapons, perhaps for terrorist purposes. In 1983 an explosive device planted by North Korean agents in Rangoon, Burma, had narrowly missed killing the entire South Korean cabinet. Four years later, a North Korean bomb had destroyed a South Korean jetliner en route from Bahrain to Bangkok, Thailand, causing the deaths of 115 persons. A second concern was that if North Korea acquired nuclear arms, the capacity of America's nuclear umbrella to deter a conventional attack against South Korea would be undermined. The North's oft-repeated aim of unifying the Korean peninsula, by force if necessary, might be acted upon. Even if these dismal scenarios did not come to pass, South Korea and Japan, confronted with North Korean nuclear weapons, might move to develop their own arsenals, leading to a costly and potentially destabilizing regional arms race.[13] Finally, there was the danger that North Korea might export nuclear technology to other "rogue" regimes, thus weakening the prospects for controlling proliferation worldwide.

BUSH ADMINISTRATION POLICY

Efforts by the Bush administration "to slowly coax North Korea into a broader engagement with the outside world and compel Pyongyang to be a reasonable and responsible international actor" began in October 1988.[14] The U.S. government announced "four unilateral actions: to open diplomatic contacts, to encourage non-governmental DPRK visits to the U.S., to facilitate American citizens' travel to the DPRK and to allow exported goods to North Korea that meet basic human needs." A series of low-level diplomatic meetings took place in Beijing between U.S. and North Korean representatives during 1989 and the first half of 1990. During the talks, American officials told their North Korean counterparts that the Bush administration would be looking for certain "positive actions" by Pyongyang in response to the U.S. initiatives. These included "real progress in the North-South dialogue; inclusion and implementa-

tion of an IAEA safeguards agreement; credible assurances opposing terrorism; confidence-building measures; and a regular process of returning
Korean war remains." DeSaix Anderson, deputy assistant secretary of state,
told a congressional subcommittee that these were "not preconditions,
and the DPRK does not need to do all of them first. If the DPRK takes
steps to improve relations, we can take further steps."[15]

During the next two years, the North Korean regime did in fact
take some "positive actions." In May 1990, Pyongyang returned the first
set of remains of Americans missing in action from the Korean War. In
September, meetings between the prime ministers of North and South
Korea began in Seoul. On the agenda: "the North's proposals on politi-
cal-military issues and the South's ideas on an array of personnel exchanges and economic agreements."[16] That same month, the North Korean
government expressed an interest in establishing diplomatic relations with
its long-time enemy, Japan.[17] In 1991, Pyongyang renounced international terrorism and declared its readiness to take part in efforts to control
it.[18] Finally, the North Korean regime announced its willingness to enter
the United Nations along with South Korea, in effect recognizing the
legitimacy of the South Korean state.[19]

North Korea's nuclear program, however, remained a fly in the oint-
ment, as Pyongyang continued to refuse to sign an IAEA safeguards agreement. Before it would place its nuclear activities under international
supervision, a North Korean government official said, two conditions
would have to be met. First, the United States must either permit North
Korean inspection of American nuclear weapons in South Korea or remove them from the country. Second, the United States must furnish
"legal assurances" to North Korea that American nuclear arms would not
be used against it.[20]

The Bush administration moved toward compliance with these demands. In September 1991, President Bush announced plans to end the
deployment of ground- and sea-launched tactical nuclear weapons on
foreign soil, including those in South Korea. The following month, the
administration declared its intent to remove air-based tactical nuclear
weapons from the Korean peninsula as well.[21] In December, South Korean President Roh Tae Woo announced that there were no longer any
nuclear weapons in South Korea.[22] While maintaining a "neither-con-
firm-nor-deny" policy with respect to the issue, Bush said he "would not
argue" with Roh's statement, thus admitting the point. In January, the
president said, "to any who doubted that (President Roh's) declaration,

South Korea, with the full support of the United States, has offered to open to inspection all of its civilian and military installations, including U.S. facilities."[23]

At the same time the U.S. government was attempting to gain North Korean acceptance of IAEA safeguards, it was, with the cooperation of its South Korean ally, seeking to secure Pyongyang's cooperation in a separate, bilateral inspections regime. In December 1991, the United States and South Korea announced that they would permit North Korea to inspect any military installation in South Korea if North Korea would allow them the same right of access to its facilities.[24] Later that month, Pyongyang and Seoul issued a Joint Declaration on a Non-Nuclear Korean Peninsula, in which each undertook not to "test, produce, receive, possess, deploy, or use nuclear weapons," nor to "possess facilities for nuclear reprocessing or uranium enrichment." The agreement specified mutual inspections as a means of verification, but did not contain any details. Rather, it left the procedures for monitoring compliance to be determined by a still-to-be-established Joint Nuclear Control Commission (JNCC).[25]

Additional inducements followed. With Washington's approval, the South Korean government offered to suspend the annual Team Spirit joint military exercises conducted by the two countries if North Korea would accede to an IAEA safeguards agreement and join a bilateral inspection regime. On 7 January 1992, Seoul announced cancellation of Team Spirit for that year.[26] The Bush administration also authorized Arnold Kanter, undersecretary of state for political affairs, to meet in New York with Kim Yong Sun, the secretary for international affairs of the Korean Workers Party, to discuss "the potential for improvements in relations between the United States and North Korea." It was the highest-level meeting between representatives of the two countries in almost forty years.[27]

The conciliatory approach seemed to work. In his conversations with Kanter, Kim said that Pyongyang was prepared to place its nuclear program under IAEA supervision and to establish a bilateral inspection regime with South Korea.[28] On 30 January, North Korea signed the IAEA safeguards agreement.[29] In early May, North Korean representatives submitted their required declaration of nuclear facilities to the IAEA.[30] Hans Blix, director general of the IAEA, subsequently traveled to North Korea, touring its facilities at Yongbyon, as a prelude to the first official inspections. While there, Blix became concerned that Pyongyang might be hiding additional nuclear installations, so he requested that IAEA "officials" be allowed to "visit" sites not on the list submitted by North Korea. The North Koreans agreed.[31]

Unfortunately, things soon began to unravel. During the summer and fall of 1992, IAEA inspectors conducted six on-site investigations of North Korean nuclear installations. From evidence it gathered the IAEA concluded that, contrary to Pyongyang's assertions, North Korea had engaged in the reprocessing of spent fuel on multiple occasions and that it possessed more plutonium than it had admitted.[32] Sensitive to its perceived failings in the case of Iraq, the IAEA adopted a stern approach, accusing Pyongyang of not disclosing all its nuclear facilities.[33] Requests to visit two suspected nuclear waste sites at Yongbyon were rejected by the North Korean government.[34] Meanwhile, despite some initial progress, JNCC talks aimed at the formation of a bilateral inspection regime proved unfruitful, as relations between North and South Korea soured, a result of Seoul's discovery of a North Korean spy ring and the announcement that the U.S. and South Korean governments had agreed, "in principle," to conduct Team Spirit exercises in 1993.[35]

CLINTON ADMINISTRATION EFFORTS
TO COERCE NORTH KOREA

Policymakers in the new Clinton administration thus confronted a rapidly deteriorating situation. On 25 January 1993, the South Korean government, citing the North's intransigence on the matter of inspections, announced that Team Spirit '93 would be held in March.[36] In late February, the IAEA Board of Governors met to discuss the inspections issue. Among the evidence it considered was a series of aerial reconnaissance photos of the Yongbyon nuclear complex provided by the United States.[37] The Board passed a resolution calling upon North Korea to implement fully IAEA safeguards "without delay." It set a deadline of one month for the North Korean government to allow "special inspections" at two suspected nuclear sites, warning that if Pyongyang did not comply, "further measures" would be taken.[38] The North Korean government rejected the demand, claiming that it infringed upon North Korean sovereignty.[39]

Team Spirit exercises began on 9 March. Three days later, the government of North Korea declared its intention to withdraw from the NPT, effective 12 June. Through its ambassador in China, the regime warned that it would take "a strong defensive countermeasure" if Western countries imposed economic sanctions in response.[40] Despite this, the Clinton administration began discussions with its allies on a policy to deny North Korea "oil, gas, other raw materials and even food." Secretary of State Warren Christopher told a congressional subcommittee that the U.N. Security Council would soon be considering the issue.[41] At the same time, as the date for the pullout neared, American officials expressed a willingness to make some concessions, including North Korean inspections of U.S. military bases in South Korea and additional assurances that Washington did not plan to use nuclear weapons against North Korea.[42] Although negotiations produced no resolution, on 11 June, the North Korean government announced that it would "suspend" its withdrawal from the NPT and would continue to allow IAEA inspectors to monitor some of its nuclear installations.[43]

The North Korean announcement did not resolve the issue of "special inspections" at the two suspected nuclear waste sites. In July, American officials stated their intention to seek the imposition of stiff economic sanctions, under the auspices of the U.N. Security Council, unless Pyongyang retreated.[44] The sanctions, however, never materialized, in part because of doubts regarding their efficacy. U.S. officials recognized that North Korea, which had long followed a philosophy of "juche," or self-reliance, was relatively immune to economic pressure. As one analyst asked, "How do you isolate the world's most isolated country?"[45] Moreover, sanctions would not have any immediate effect, and North Korea's acquisition of nuclear weapons might well be imminent. Former Reagan administration official Richard Perle testified to Congress that "economic sanctions, to be truly painful, have to remain in place for a long time." He concluded that "the hope that Kim Il Sung would renounce his nuclear program and dismantle it to a degree that would satisfy us in response to economic sanctions is wildly improbable."[46] Kathleen Bailey of the Center for Security and Technology at the Lawrence Livermore National Laboratory was equally pessimistic, warning that U.S. policymakers would have to deter the North Koreans from using their nuclear capability because "we cannot deter them from developing it."[47]

There were, in addition, more serious problems. The support of China, North Korea's one remaining ally and its principal economic partner, was essential to a program of sanctions. Beijing was opposed, however, presumably because it viewed North Korea's nuclear program as an internal matter not subject to interference by the international community.[48] Moreover, America's main allies on the issue, South Korea and

Japan, were also reluctant to participate. An estimated 150,000 Koreans sympathetic to Pyongyang resided in Japan. Every year, this group sent $600 million or more in hard currency back to North Korea. If sanctions, including a prohibition on the transmission of such funds, were imposed, Japanese officials feared retaliation in the form of riots and acts of terrorism.[49] The government in Seoul was more concerned about the prospect of a military attack on South Korea if Pyongyang felt boxed into a corner.[50] Kim Jung Woo, adviser to the National Unification Board, warned that "if the pressure for the North Koreans becomes intolerable, there will be a type of Waco, Tex., situation—an effort at joint suicide with South Korea. This is why we have no choice but to try to appease the North Koreans."[51]

The Clinton administration took such fears seriously. Visiting South Korea, U.S. Secretary of Defense Les Aspin expressed his concern that "the wrong kind of pressure" could cause North Korea to "lash out."[52] A senior U.S. military official noted that "There is a very fine line between coercing North Korea to do what you want them to do, and provoking a tremendous disaster."[53] William Perry, Aspin's successor, stated that if sanctions were required, the United States would "have to take seriously the risk of war."[54] He later told a congressional panel that the Pentagon had been prepared, in the event sanctions were imposed, to send 10,000 additional troops to South Korea and had "detailed plans for a full-scale U.S. deployment."[55] For these reasons, while the United States never abandoned the option, and on several occasions coupled inducements with threats of sanctions, a policy of economic pressure came to appear increasingly problematic.

An alternative strategy, one more decisively rejected by U.S. officials, was a preventive surgical strike on North Korea's nuclear facilities. In January 1995, Perry told the Senate Foreign Relations Committee that the Clinton administration had discussed "going in and taking out the nuclear reactor," but that "I did not recommend that course of action to the President."[56] Although the secretary of defense maintained that the United States possessed the capacity to carry out such an attack, the administration feared that "North Korea's 1.1 million-member army might quickly respond by leveling Seoul."[57] Unlike Perry, civilian military analysts were generally unconvinced that a surgical strike was feasible, citing a lack of accurate intelligence (which would make targeting difficult) and the possibility that North Korea had "dug in" some of its facilities, rendering them invulnerable to conventional weapons. Said one, military strikes against North Korean nuclear installations are "a non-option."[58] The air force and U.S. intelligence agencies concurred with this assessment, concluding that "a military strike against the nuclear complex at Yongbyon . . . had a relatively low chance of success because so much of the complex is hidden in hillsides or underground."[59] Said one official, "Even if we wiped out everything we saw, we would never know if we got it all."[60]

THE SHIFT FROM STICKS TO CARROTS

Sensitive to the domestic political dangers of appearing "soft" in the realm of foreign affairs, the Clinton administration probably felt "more secure 'warning' Pyongyang than . . . 'offering' Pyongyang any inducements."[61] Nevertheless, the difficulties associated with coercive, punitive strategies eventually encouraged the administration to change course, adopting a conciliatory approach described by one official as "Walk softly and carry a big carrot."[62] In late November 1993, Washington and Seoul agreed to try to resolve the nuclear impasse with Pyongyang by means of a so-called "package deal," in which the United States would "offer a series of small concessions and larger promises of future aid to North Korea—and steps toward diplomatic recognition—in return for immediate, limited inspections of its nuclear sites."[63] On 23 November, in New York, the offer was extended to North Korean officials, accompanied by a warning that the United States and South Korea would seek the imposition of sanctions through the U.N. Security Council if no agreement were reached. A week later, the North Korean government issued a statement condemning the United States and saying that "pressure will produce a very dangerous consequence." More hopefully, North Korea left open the possibility of a negotiated settlement, saying that if Washington accepted Pyongyang's own "package solution, all problems related to the nuclear issue, including the compliance with the safeguards agreement, will be solved, and it will not take much time." While North Korea's desiderata were not specified, U.S. officials understood them to include "everything from full diplomatic recognition to financial aid and commercial nuclear reactors."[64]

Between December 1993 and October 1994, U.S. and North Korean negotiators sought to arrive at a "package deal" that was acceptable to both sides. Progress was slow and less than steady. In early December, the United States proposed a settlement virtually identical to that of the previous month: "to cancel [Team Spirit exercises] and to begin talks over economic aid and diplomatic recognition if North Korea allows full inspection of its nuclear plants and begins an active, continuous dialogue with South Korea." The warning about possible economic sanctions was repeated; indeed the offer was described as the "last one" that would be made before the case was taken to the Security Council. North Korean officials issued a belligerent response, declaring that if a negotiated settlement were not reached "it would be the United States that would regret this" and that relations between the two Koreas were "an internal affair of our nation" and none of Washington's business.[65]

Within two weeks, North Korean diplomats told American officials they were prepared to allow IAEA inspectors access to their seven officially declared nuclear sites.[66] U.S. optimism was short-lived, however, for in late January the IAEA announced that North Korea had rejected the necessary inspection procedures.[67] Fearing the eventual outbreak of war, Washington declared its intent to send Patriot missiles to South Korea to protect airfields and port facilities.[68] The Pentagon also announced a new military strategy in the event of a North Korean invasion of the South. The plan called for a rapid counteroffensive designed to seize Pyongyang and overthrow the government of Kim Il Sung.[69] North Korea responded predictably, accusing the United States of "the insidious intention to unleash a new war in Korea" and warning that in the event of such a conflict North Korea would prevail.[70]

After a tense week, the North Korean government again announced its willingness to allow IAEA inspectors access to its seven officially declared nuclear installations.[71] The inspections began on 1 March, but soon hit a roadblock: North Korean officials refused to allow inspectors to conduct tests crucial to determining how much plutonium had been produced. Without this knowledge, it was impossible to know whether North Korea was still actively engaged in the pursuit of nuclear weapons.[72] The Clinton administration now began to fear that a diplomatic settlement could not be reached. One official told the press, "This time the North went too far. There are no more carrots." The U.S. government canceled scheduled talks with North Korean representatives and accelerated planning for Team Spirit exercises with South Korea.[73] It also decided finally to ask the U.N. Security Council to impose economic sanctions against North Korea, despite the fact that it remained unclear whether the Council would be willing to take such action.[74]

On 20 March, the North Korean government stated that it would no longer permit inspections of its nuclear facilities and warned that it would carry out its threat to withdraw from the NPT if the United States and South Korea went ahead with Team Spirit. It accused Washington of committing "a perfidious act," which, it said, "may bring the Korean nation back to the phase of confrontation and war."[75] The Clinton administration continued its military buildup in South Korea as it sought to obtain support in the Security Council for a sanctions resolution.[76] But China was still opposed. The best the U.S. government could get was a statement, weaker than a resolution, calling on North Korea to allow inspections. The threat of sanctions, should Pyongyang refuse to comply, was made only "obliquely."[77]

On 15 May, North Korea announced that it had begun extracting fuel from its largest reactor, possibly as a prelude to its reprocessing into weapons-grade plutonium.[78] After IAEA inspectors reported that the North Koreans had destroyed evidence of the possible diversion of fissionable material into weapons production, the U.S. government issued a strong call for the imposition of economic sanctions against Pyongyang.[79] American intelligence detected preparations for possible action on the part of the North Korean military. On 7 June, the North Korean government warned that "sanctions mean outright war."[80] While suggesting that such threats should not necessarily be taken at face value, special ambassador Robert Gallucci informed a congressional subcommittee on 9 June that the administration was "certainly not ignoring what may be the defense implications of a sanctions resolution."[81]

Into the crisis stepped former U.S. president Jimmy Carter, who traveled to Pyongyang as a private citizen and held a series of direct meetings with North Korean leader Kim Il Sung, beginning on 16 June. Openly critical of his government's efforts to impose sanctions, Carter announced that North Korean officials had told him they were willing to allow international inspections of their nuclear facilities and to freeze their nuclear program. Convinced of Pyongyang's commitment to peace, he returned to Washington declaring that the crisis was over.[82]

The Clinton administration, embarrassed by this spectacle and fearful that a well-intentioned but naive Carter had been hoodwinked by the North Koreans, sought to distance itself from his initiative. It did not, however, want to miss an opportunity to resolve the crisis. On 22 June, therefore, the U.S. government sent a letter to Pyongyang offering to suspend the American campaign for economic sanctions and to begin high-level talks on the inspections issue.[83] The following day, with North

Korea's reply in hand, President Clinton announced that Pyongyang was willing to freeze its nuclear program temporarily and to open talks in Geneva in July. He said that the push for sanctions would be halted upon the beginning of negotiations. Perhaps most importantly, he signaled that the United States would no longer insist that North Korea divulge information concerning its past nuclear activities.[84]

On 8 July, shortly before talks were scheduled to open, Kim Il Sung died. Following a postponement, the talks began on 5 August. Eight days later, U.S. and North Korean negotiators announced they had reached an agreement. North Korea was prepared, it said, to open its nuclear facilities to international inspection and to seal its plutonium reprocessing plant. In exchange, the United States promised to assist North Korea in the acquisition of light-water nuclear reactors and to provide for the country's energy needs until the reactors were in operation. The United States also pledged to reduce barriers to trade and investment, and to exchange diplomatic representatives, ultimately working toward the "full normalization" of relations.[85] On 15 August, South Korea formally offered to provide the nuclear reactors to North Korea.[86]

The apparent resolution of the dispute nearly foundered, during the ensuing months, on two issues: North Korea's refusal to allow inspections at its two suspected nuclear waste sites and its unwillingness to accept nuclear reactors from South Korea.[87] In late September, the United States announced a brief suspension of talks, citing lack of progress. Robert Gallucci, the chief U.S. negotiator, denied the existence of a "deadlock," but it appeared the two countries had reached an impasse.[88]

Discussions soon resumed, however, and on 18 October, U.S. and North Korean negotiators announced they had reached a breakthrough.[89] On 21 October, the two governments signed the Agreed Framework, details of which have been outlined above. Critics of the accord argued that the price was too high, and that it rewarded Pyongyang for doing nothing more than fulfilling its obligations under the NPT. Some were skeptical about North Korea's willingness to uphold its part of the bargain, citing its past behavior and the conclusion of the Defense Intelligence Agency (DIA) that "the North Koreans will continue its [sic] nuclear weapon program despite any agreement it signs to the contrary."[90] Many feared other potential proliferators would see the pact as an invitation to blackmail the United States into making similar concessions.[91] James Baker, secretary of state in the Bush administration, condemned the agreement as consisting of "all carrot and no stick."[92] Like former defense secretary Weinberger, Senator John McCain labeled the accord an act of "appeasement."[93]

The Clinton administration countered by pointing out that most of the cost of the pact would be underwritten not by the United States but by South Korea and Japan. America's financial obligation, Gallucci told a Senate subcommittee, would only be "in the tens of millions of dollars."[94] Supporters of the agreement rejected the idea that it set a bad precedent and would encourage other potential proliferators to follow the North Korean example. Some argued that no other member of the NPT possessed the kind of bargaining position enjoyed by North Korea, which had the capacity to produce rapidly a substantial nuclear arsenal, which displayed a callous disregard for international legal niceties, and which was controlled by a totalitarian regime able to engage in potentially dangerous policies unconstrained by popular objections.[95] Others noted that in signing the Agreed Framework, North Korea had actually given up a great deal, including the legal right it possessed, under the NPT, to manufacture plutonium.[96] Gallucci testified, "We do not believe there are states out there . . . that will look at this and get any comfort from it."[97] The danger that Pyongyang might later renege on its commitments could not, the special ambassador admitted, be ruled out. But he insisted that if it did so, the United States could move swiftly to impose economic sanctions, including the denial of enriched uranium needed as fuel for the light-water reactors. Even if the agreement collapsed, a temporary freeze on North Korea's nuclear program would be to America's advantage.[98]

In a press conference, President Clinton celebrated the Agreed Framework as helping to "achieve a longstanding and vital American objective—an end to the threat of nuclear proliferation on the Korean Peninsula." The accord was, he said, "good for the United States, good for our allies, and good for the safety of the entire world. It's a crucial step toward drawing North Korea into the global community."[99]

NORTH KOREAN MOTIVES

The Clinton administration believed—or at least hoped—that it was possible to present the North Koreans "with an option in terms of economics and political reentry into the international community that they would find appealing enough" to abandon their nuclear activities.[100] Whether the North Korean government would be willing to bargain away its nuclear program depended, of course, on the reasons for its existence and on whether Pyongyang's objectives could be addressed by American concessions.[101]

Because of a lack of information, it was—and remains—difficult to discern the motives behind North Korea's nuclear program. There was, not surprisingly, considerable disagreement among American observers on this point. The most malign interpretation was that Pyongyang sought to acquire nuclear weapons for purposes of aggression. The North Korean government had proclaimed repeatedly the goal of reunifying the Korean peninsula, by force if necessary. Some analysts feared that North Korea's nuclear capability was intended to neutralize the deterrent effect of the American nuclear umbrella, paving the way for a conventional attack on the South.[102] A few went even further. In a particularly extreme statement, former Reagan administration official Richard Perle declared that Pyongyang possessed "imperial ambitions that go beyond the Korean peninsula to include pretensions to third world leadership." North Korea was, he said, "the most dangerous state in the world today."[103]

At the other end of the spectrum were those observers who believed that North Korea's nuclear program was motivated by a profound sense of strategic insecurity. North Korean nuclear weapons, they argued, were intended to protect North Korea from an attack by the United States. They might also serve as a hedge against South Korea's eventual acquisition of its own nuclear arsenal. Fears of an American or an American-South Korean attack presumably owed their origins to the Korean War, which had never officially ended. Annual Team Spirit exercises, "a rehearsal for war on the peninsula," undoubtedly contributed to North Korean apprehension, as did "repeated suggestions" from American and South Korean analysts and officials that the Yongbyon facility be destroyed in a surgical air strike.[104]

At the same time U.S. and South Korean intentions were creating unease in Pyongyang, the ability of North Korea to defend itself was becoming increasing doubtful. The country's major nuclear ally, the Soviet Union, had vanished, replaced by a non-communist Russia less sympathetic to Pyongyang. In September 1991, Moscow established diplomatic relations with South Korea. The following year, on a visit to Seoul, Russian president Boris Yeltsin announced his intention to cut off military aid to North Korea. He also said that Russia, contrary to the terms of the 1961 Soviet-North Korean mutual defense treaty, might not intervene on behalf of North Korea in the event of war. Nor would Russia provide further nuclear assistance to Pyongyang unless the regime agreed to sub-scribe to IAEA safeguards. North Korea's other nuclear ally, China, also moved to distance itself, establishing diplomatic relations with Seoul, ex-panding commercial ties with the South, and announcing in 1992 that Pyongyang would henceforth be required to pay for Chinese oil with hard currency. At the same time, the balance of conventional forces on the Korean peninsula, long favorable to the North, was shifting, perhaps decisively, in favor of the South. In sum, the North Korean regime con-fronted, from its perspective, a rapidly deteriorating international envi-ronment. Given the situation, Pyongyang probably viewed its nuclear program as "a vital strategic asset."[105]

A third school of thought held that North Korea's drive to acquire nuclear weapons was a natural outgrowth of the philosophy of "juche," inspired by Kim Il Sung, which stressed "self-reliance and independence from foreign influence." According to this perspective, nuclear weapons were intended to provide North Korea with a sense of accomplishment as well as with status in the international community. They would also presumably enhance support for the regime among the North Korean people.[106]

Finally, there were observers who believed that North Korea's nuclear program was a bargaining chip, a lever by which to force the United States and other countries to make political and especially economic con-cessions. Peter Hayes, for example, argued in December 1993 that "North Korea wants to normalize its relations with the United States, and thereby with the rest of the world. The nuclear issue is a perfect battering ram to pound on the American door until the United States agrees to drop its political and legal barriers to trade, investment, and aid."[107]

It is true that by the early 1990s, the North Korean economy was in shambles. Between 1989 and 1993, the country's gross national product declined every year. South Korean analysts estimate that North Korea's GNP fell by roughly 15 percent during the first three years of this period. Part of the negative growth was attributable to Russia's decision, in 1990, to stop providing North Korea with oil at below-market prices. Two years later, the Chinese government demanded payment in hard currency for petroleum purchased by Pyongyang. The result was that North Korea was able to afford only about a third of the oil required for its economy, leading to a fall in industrial production of as much as 40 percent.[108]

Food was also becoming increasingly scarce.[109] The 1990 harvest was 30 percent below that of the previous year, partly because of a shortage of fuel needed to operate agricultural machinery. To make up the shortfall, North Korea was forced to import large quantities of rice from Thailand. There were rumors of food riots in remote areas near the Chinese border. Diplomats in Pyongyang reported the existence of "widespread malnutrition," noting that many people were not receiving their full allotment—a meager four and a half pounds—of red meat and chicken each month, while others were getting meat only once or twice a year. In 1992, the North Korean government took the extraordinary step of urging the North Korean people to begin eating only two meals a day.[110]

Foreign observers detected little unrest among the North Korean population. Nevertheless, it seems clear that economic problems, with their "potentially destabilizing political consequences," were a major concern in Pyongyang.[111] William Taylor and Michael Mazarr wrote in 1992 that "North Korea is obsessed with economic development."[112] That same year, the North Korean deputy prime minister stated with respect to Pyongyang's efforts to attract foreign capital and technology: "It is for our own survival."[113]

It is probable that Pyongyang's nuclear ambitions reflected a combination of these motives.[114] It is also likely that the importance of each varied from person to person and group to group within the North Korean power structure. One American analyst claimed that there was "an increasingly sharp policy conflict within the ruling Workers Party, especially over the issue of whether the North should continue to pursue a nuclear weapons program." On one side were an "old guard" of unreconstructed cold warriors, "centered in the armed forces and a military-industrial complex that includes the nuclear establishment." This group, intensely distrustful of American and South Korean motives, feared that Washington and Seoul would try to exploit North Korea's growing strategic vulnerability in order to pursue Korean reunification according to the German model—i.e. absorption of the North by the South. Members believed a nuclear capability to be essential to the ultimate survival of the North Korean regime and were unwilling to give it up under virtually any conditions.[115]

Arrayed against the "hard-liners" were the "moderates" or "pragmatists." They, too, feared for the survival of the North Korean regime, but saw the primary threat as internal rather than external, and as rooted in North Korea's deteriorating economic situation. In the eyes of the moderates, Pyongyang's nuclear program—and high levels of defense spending more generally—represented a diversion of human and financial resources from productive to nonproductive uses that the North Korean economy could ill afford. More importantly, it precluded a much-needed expansion of trade with an infusion of capital and technology from the United States and other countries. The moderates were, therefore, willing to abandon the North's nuclear program in return for "external economic help."[116]

ANATOMY OF SUCCESS

Because we have so little information about the internal workings of the North Korean government, it is difficult to say conclusively why North Korea agreed to renounce its nuclear ambitions. The most plausible explanation, however, is that U.S. concessions addressed the most important objectives of North Korean leaders and, perhaps, helped pragmatists overcome the opposition of hard-liners.[117] High-level negotiations with the United States, which resulted in promises of the normalization of political and economic relations, provided the North Korean regime with a heightened sense of status in the international arena. The Bush administration's removal of nuclear weapons from the Korean peninsula and the Clinton administration's decision to work toward normalized relations with North Korea undoubtedly helped to ease Pyongyang's strategic insecurity. The agreement to furnish light-water nuclear reactors and heating oil, and to expand commercial and financial interactions, presumably created a somewhat more benign image of American intentions among North Korean leaders. Hyperbolic, but illustrative nonetheless, were the remarks of North Korea's deputy foreign minister, Kang Sok Ju, who hailed the conclusion of the Agreed Framework as an event of "great historical significance because it has removed the abnormal and horrendous distrust that has marked relations between our countries for too long."[118]

Most importantly, the promise of increased trade and investment gave North Korean leaders hope that their economy might become revitalized. In comments to members of the press following the conclusion of the Agreed Framework, American officials said they believed Pyongyang was finally willing to abandon its nuclear program "because it desperately needs to forge new political ties that could lead to foreign investment and revive its shattered economy." According to one U.S. diplomat, the North Koreans wanted "to begin to attend to . . . economic questions and regime stability and pulling themselves out of the slump they have been in for the past four years. The nuclear issue was the impediment, and it had to be solved."[119]

In pursuing their inducement policy, U.S. officials exhibited an exceptional degree of patience. Six years passed between the Bush administration's initiatives of October 1988 and the signing of the Agreed Framework. During much of this period, prospects for success were altogether uncertain. Apparent progress was frequently followed by disappointment. Some called for the Clinton administration to abandon the effort. In February 1994, for example, nonproliferation expert Kathleen Bailey told a congressional subcommittee that the United States had "negotiated with Pyongyang for months with no resultant change in North Korea's behavior. This policy amounts to appeasement and it has got to stop. North Korea has eaten all the carrots, now it is time for the stick."[120] Others agreed.

Despite the crescendo of criticism, U.S. officials persisted in seeking a negotiated settlement. In June 1994, Special Ambassador Gallucci admitted that "it may be there is nothing in terms of a negotiation that will bring the North Koreans around to satisfying us on the nuclear issue." Nevertheless, he argued, this was far from clear. Given the potential consequences of a resort to sanctions, the United States, he said, had an obligation to "explore the proposition at least that there is a possibility that the whole issue can be settled through a negotiation in which the North Koreans are brought into the international community."[121]

Looking back, the wisdom of Gallucci's point appears obvious, but it is essentially the same argument that was offered by British policymakers during the 1930s to justify their approach to Germany and by Bush administration officials in support of their policy toward Iraq. In those cases, of course, the continuation of a conciliatory strategy in the face of mounting evidence of its ineffectiveness proved disastrous. Was the Clinton administration merely lucky, or were the signals sent by North Korea really more favorable than those emanating from Berlin and Baghdad?

Although ambiguous, the evidence regarding North Korean intentions did seem to indicate that a negotiated settlement was possible. As William Taylor told a congressional subcommittee, there occurred in the early 1990s "important . . . changes in the behavior of the DPRK." Pyongyang agreed to participate in united Korean sports teams, signed a "barter deal" to send coal and cement to South Korea in exchange for rice, invited foreign scholars and retired officials to visit, accepted simultaneous entry with South Korea into the United Nations, engaged in high-level meetings with South Korean diplomats, concluded an "agreement of reconciliation, nonaggression, cooperation and exchange" with the ROK, and promised to sign an IAEA safeguards agreement. These and other actions suggested an unprecedented flexibility on the part of Pyongyang and a real desire for improved relations with its adversaries.[122]

Critics of appeasement could and did point to less promising aspects of North Korean behavior. Taken as a whole, however, Pyongyang's policy was at worst inconsistent, even erratic, but not implacably hostile. Bellicose statements were often issued in conjunction with those expressing hopes for a peaceful resolution of the dispute. Aggressive actions—or threats of them—were frequently followed by retreat. While it was not unreasonable to conclude, as some did, that inducements were likely to fail, it was also not unreasonable to conclude that they stood a decent chance of success, assuming that the proper package could be created. The evidence confronting British statesmen during the 1930s and American policymakers concerned with Iraq during the 1980s was much less ambiguous.

While strict reciprocity on the part of North Korea was demanded by neither the Bush nor Clinton administration, U.S. policymakers, unsure of North Korea's intentions, were wary of conceding too much without evidence of Pyongyang's good faith. Virtually nothing of substance—certainly nothing that was irreversible—was given up prior to the conclusion of the Agreed Framework. Nuclear weapons could be redeployed in South Korea if necessary. High-level diplomatic contacts could always be severed; economic sanctions could always be imposed. Time was not a significant problem because time was on the side of the United States rather than North Korea. Pyongyang's nuclear arsenal, if indeed one existed, was tiny and, for the present, undeliverable. The conventional balance on the Korean peninsula was shifting against the North. Meanwhile, the country's economy was headed downhill at an alarming rate. Unless the regime cooperated, its future existence would be imperiled.[123]

The insistence by U.S. officials that North Korea respond positively to American inducements as a precondition for conceding anything of real value was reflected in the Agreed Framework itself. The accord was structured so that it was to be implemented in stages. Only if North Korea were in full compliance with the terms of the agreement would each successive step be taken. In congressional testimony, Gallucci defined four specific "checkpoints" for U.S. policymakers: the conclusion of the contract for the two light-water reactors, which would require that North Korea have maintained its freeze on nuclear activities and be cooperating with the IAEA's monitoring of it; the delivery of equipment for construction of the first reactor, which would be contingent upon Pyongyang's full compliance with IAEA safeguards; the completion of the first reactor, which would not occur until all the spent fuel had been removed from the country; and the completion of the second reactor, which would take place only after all North Korea's nuclear facilities had been dismantled.[124]

By this means, the Clinton administration eliminated much of the risk associated with concessions. If North Korea ultimately renounces the Agreed Framework and restarts its nuclear program, it will have gained very little—some heating oil and perhaps some proliferation-resistant nuclear technology. "In the meantime," as Gallucci noted, its "program will have been frozen." His conclusion, that "the agreement does not leave us or our allies disadvantaged at any point if the North Koreans walk away," seems well founded.[125]

THE ROLE OF THREATS

Although U.S. policy consisted mainly of inducements, the threat of coercive measures was not entirely absent. As noted previously, the Clinton administration raised the prospect of economic sanctions recurrently from March 1993 onward. The United States did not explicitly threaten military action against North Korea in the event Pyongyang refused to abandon its nuclear program. Still, the vehemence of U.S. declarations that a North Korean nuclear arsenal was unacceptable, the continued large-scale U.S. military presence in the region, and the holding of Team Spirit exercises probably conveyed, implicitly, such a threat to North Korean leaders. In some sense, then, the U.S. government employed a mixed influence strategy in its approach to North Korea. Did U.S. threats contribute to the successful outcome of the case, or did appeasement succeed despite rather than because of them?

The argument that coercive threats helped convince North Korea to renounce its nuclear ambitions rests largely on the assumption that Pyongyang had aggressive designs which had to be deterred. Many Americans, especially conservatives, believed this; hence the condemnation of the Agreed Framework from persons on the right of the political spectrum. Apart from North Korea's almost ritual proclamation of its intent to reunify the Korean peninsula, by force if necessary, there is, however, little evidence to support this interpretation.

Early in the crisis, the *New York Times* published an editorial, "Don't Demonize North Korea," which argued that "The North's nuclear ambitions feed on its growing sense of vulnerability and isolation."[126] The "hard-liners" in North Korea (like the cold warriors in the United States during the period of U.S.-Soviet rivalry) do appear to have been driven much more by insecurity than by the desire for territorial aggrandizement. Threats by the United States and its ally, South Korea, tended to exacerbate this insecurity and to strengthen the political position of the conservatives by buttressing their claims that America was irredeemably hostile. Similarly, they tended to undermine the position of the moderates by undercutting their contention that if North Korea would abandon its nuclear ambitions she would find a United States ready to offer political and economic largesse.

In 1992 and 1993, U.S. and South Korean actions intended to pressure North Korea into a more accommodating stance backfired, reversing apparent progress toward the resolution of the nuclear dispute. According to Selig Harrison, the battle between the North Korean moderates and hard-liners "came to a head" in December 1991, at a meeting of the Central Committee of the Korean Workers Party (KWP). Moderates won a "conditional victory," with hard-liners agreeing to "test" the United States by suspending North Korea's push to acquire nuclear weapons. The Bush administration responded by making what it considered a significant concession: authorizing Undersecretary of State Arnold Kanter to meet with Kim Yong Sun, international affairs secretary of the KWP. In addition, Team Spirit exercises were suspended.[127] As noted previously, the North then signed an IAEA safeguards agreement and allowed inspections to commence.

But no tangible political or economic commitments were made by the United States, and "at the very time the reform elements in North Korea needed more 'ammunition' to consolidate their victory over the hard-liners, Washington, Seoul and Tokyo continued to apply more pressure." In June, just as IAEA inspections were beginning, Gen. Robert Riscassi, the commander of U.S. forces in South Korea, announced the resumption of Team Spirit exercises, apparently without consulting the South Korean government. According to a South Korean diplomat, this "statement had an immediate and discernable effect on the North's posture, vindicating the hard-liners' arguments that a 'soft' line would not yield results." The next month, in an unprecedented move, IAEA director general Hans Blix testified before a congressional subcommittee, giving the impression that the IAEA, which had angered North Korea with its stance on inspections, was acting in the service of the United States.[128]

Despite these false steps, in the fall of 1992 JNCC negotiations aimed at establishing a bilateral inspection regime were making headway. At their September meeting, North and South Korean representatives had settled on an "organizational format" and had agreed to begin discussing treaty language at their next meeting, scheduled for the following month. On 8 October, however, the South Korean government announced an agreement "in principle" with the United States that Team Spirit exercises would be held in 1993, noting that the decision could be reversed if bilateral inspections were conducted before the year was over. The hope in Seoul and Washington was that this would give South Korea "added bargaining leverage in the JNCC talks, especially on challenge inspections." Instead, North Korea denounced the decision and threatened "to suspend the peace process." The JNCC negotiations foundered.[129]

Finally, in January 1993, the South Korean government stated that Team Spirit exercises would be conducted in March. The beginning of these exercises was the trigger for North Korea's dramatic announcement of its intent to withdraw from the NPT. This announcement was followed by the Clinton administration's efforts to put together an international coalition that would enact strict economic sanctions against Pyongyang, efforts that appear in retrospect to have done little but alienate the North Korean regime. It was not until the United States abandoned its coercive approach and its insistence on North Korea's acceptance of inspections as a precondition for further negotiations, and agreed to discuss political and economic concessions in the framework of a package arrangement, that the nuclear impasse was ultimately resolved.

The Clinton administration was, to its credit, sensitive to the possibility that attempts to exert pressure might be perceived by the North Koreans as offensively motivated, rather than defensively, and that they would reinforce Pyongyang's insecurity, making a settlement more difficult. In July 1993, announcing plans to seek economic sanctions, Clinton himself stated, "North Korea must understand our intentions. We are seeking to prevent aggression, not to initiate it. As long as North Korea abides by the United Nations charter and international non-proliferation commitments, it has nothing to fear from America."[130] Such assurances, however, appear to have had little if any beneficial effect.

Coercive threats were probably prudent for an American government unsure of North Korean motives. In the final analysis, they did not prove fatal to the success of U.S. policy. Nevertheless, it appears that a mixed strategy probably delayed achievement of U.S. objectives by enhancing Pyongyang's insecurity and undermining the position of North Korean moderates who were willing to renounce their nuclear ambitions in return for what they considered appropriate concessions.[131]

CONCLUSION

In many respects, American strategy toward North Korea between 1988 and 1994 appears a model of successful appeasement. U.S. policymakers ultimately offered concessions that addressed effectively the North Korean government's most important objectives. When initial efforts at conciliation failed, American officials continued to negotiate, on the basis of what they believed to be sufficient evidence that the policy might ultimately work. At the same time, they did not—prior to the conclusion of the Agreed Framework or in the Agreed Framework itself—make any concessions that significantly diminished their ability to change course and adopt an alternative strategy if that became necessary. Indeed, they attempted to build an international coalition in support of economic sanctions and strengthened their military position on the Korean peninsula. Because North Korea's nuclear program was motivated in part by Pyongyang's insecurity, these actions probably delayed a resolution of the nuclear impasse by exacerbating the regime's feelings of vulnerability and strengthening the position of conservative forces within the North Korean power structure. Nevertheless, they did not preclude a settlement, and, given uncertainty about North Korea's intentions, may in hindsight be defended as prudent.

Whether North Korea will observe the provisions of the Agreed Framework and permanently abandon its nuclear weapons program cannot now be known. Difficulties in fleshing out the details of the pact arose almost immediately. Chief among these was North Korea's refusal, for reasons of "national pride," to accept nuclear reactors manufactured in South Korea, a condition the United States considered essential.[132] Between December 1994 and June 1995, talks on this issue were initiated and broken off on several occasions, with Pyongyang threatening to refuel its 5 megawatt research reactor if the United States did not back down. This obstacle was finally overcome when the two countries issued a joint statement referring to the reactors as "the advanced version of U.S.-origin design and technology," a formulation that allowed the North

Korean government to save face.[133] Left unresolved by the statement, however, was Pyongyang's new "demands for up to $1 billion worth of electrical power lines and other installations ancillary to the reactors."[134]

Although the signing of a contract to supply nuclear reactors to North Korea was delayed by the dispute over their origin, in other respects implementation of the Agreed Framework proceeded more or less on schedule.[135] The first shipment of heating oil, 50,000 metric tons, arrived in North Korea in January 1995. In March, KEDO (the Korean Energy Development Organization), a multilateral consortium headed by the United States, South Korea, and Japan, was established to furnish the reactors.[136] Discussions between representatives of the American and North Korean governments began on "consular and technical issues involved in setting up liaison offices."[137] Perhaps most importantly, North Korea froze its nuclear program. IAEA inspectors were stationed at Yongbyon to monitor the freeze. In February 1995, U.S. analysts believed that the North Korean regime was "complying meticulously with its nuclear commitments under the deal."[138] The initial signs were, therefore, generally quite positive.

Unfortunately, more recent events have cast some doubt on Pyongyang's willingness to uphold its side of the bargain. In late 1998, North Korea launched a multi-stage ballistic missile that violated Japanese airspace. The North Korean government explained that the alleged "missile" was a rocket attempting (and failing) to place a satellite in orbit, an explanation subsequently supported by U.S. officials. Japan nevertheless suspended its financial contribution to KEDO in protest. Perhaps more crucially, U.S. intelligence sources detected increased activity at an underground site at Kumchangni, long suspected as a possible location for nuclear weapons development. Policymakers in Washington demanded access to the site. North Korea refused, contending that it was still adhering to the Agreed Framework. It then agreed to allow access, but only following the payment of a large sum of money by the United States. As of this writing, Pyongyang has dropped its demand for money and has agreed, in principle, to allow U.S. inspectors access to the underground facility. Whether inspections will be held remains to be seen, as does what, if anything, they might reveal.

Some in the United States, especially Republican members of Congress, view these recent developments as evidence that North Korea never had any intention of abiding by the Agreed Framework. Others, however, point out that violations of the agreement on the part of North Korea, while suspected, have not been proved. The United States, by contrast, has demonstrably failed to live up to its side of the bargain. In particular, movement toward normalization of economic and diplomatic relations with North Korea has been minimal, and the United States has been late in delivering shipments of heating oil. Those with a more benign view of North Korean intentions suggest that Pyongyang is frustrated and is trying to regain the attention of the United States, which—occupied by events in Bosnia, Kosovo, Iraq, and elsewhere—has put U.S.-North Korean relations on the back burner. These analysts suggest that the greatest menace to the Agreed Framework is not North Korean perfidy, but insufficient priority attached to the U.S.-North Korean relationship by U.S. policymakers, together with a Congress hostile to Pyongyang and determined to undermine the Clinton administration's strategy, which it regards as ineffective and dangerous.[139]

Assuming that the U.S. government remains committed to the Agreed Framework, perhaps the biggest obstacle to North Korean adherence is the presence in North Korea of a powerful faction, centered around the military, which is opposed to the pact. On two occasions, Kim Jong Il, Kim Il Sung's son and successor, had to intervene and override the objections of this group in order to keep relations with the United States from sliding back into their rancorous former state. The first of these was the negotiation and signing of the Agreed Framework itself. The second occurred in December 1994 following the shooting down by North Korea of an American helicopter that had wandered into North Korean airspace. Despite objections from the military, Kim ordered the release of the pilot, who had been captured in the incident. American analysts have concluded that Kim, who is officially head of North Korean forces, has the political strength at this point to resist pressures for a return to confrontation. They note, however, that the military's position in North Korean society appears to be growing increasingly important.[140] Should the political situation in North Korea change, so that "hard-liners" gain ascendancy, the future of the Agreed Framework could well be in jeopardy.

It is also possible that the broad political aims of the United States and those of North Korea might ultimately come into conflict. The U.S. government, as noted earlier, views the Agreed Framework as a stepping stone toward an eventual rapprochement between North and South Korea and the pacification of the Korean peninsula. Improved inter-Korean relations are to be, from Washington's perspective, an important by-product of the accord. Pyongyang, however, seems largely uninterested in improving relations with Seoul, perhaps fearing that this will lead to Korean unification by the absorption of the North into the South. The North Korean regime appears concerned mainly to improve its relations with the United States, in part as a means of detaching the United States from its South Korean ally.[141] Whether these objectives will prove compatible is open to question.

Finally, there is the danger that the inducements offered and provided by the United States may eventually produce domestic side-effects that are undesirable from the perspective of the North Korean government, which will then be tempted to renounce them. American analysts note that although Pyongyang desires expanded international trade and investment relations in order to promote economic growth, it seems determined to resist the opening up of North Korean society, economically and politically.[142] While China seems to have accomplished this delicate balancing act thus far, it is unclear whether such a position is sustainable over the long term. In a congressional hearing of February 1994, Representative Tom Lantos (D-Calif.) wondered,

> If the carrots that are feasible to be offered by the United States and other members of the democratic community are all of a nature that would open up North Korean society to Western penetration, and basically those are the only carrots we are capable of offering—trade, investment, cultural contacts, all of the things which presumably are anathema to a police state, rigidly dictatorial society—is it realistic to view these as carrots, and why would the current leadership wish to open itself to these carrots which are so profoundly subversive to their very existence?[143]

Civilian analysts worried similarly that North Korea might view American inducements as "poison carrots."[144] Pyongyang's signing of the Agreed Framework and the observance of its terms thus far suggests that the North Korean regime does not currently hold this perception. Still, U.S. officials have expressed hope that the accord will "open the isolated, xenophobic nation to outside ideas" and "move its economy toward capitalism."[145] If such changes occur, and if the North Korean government proves unwilling to countenance them, a return to confrontation is possible.

7

TOWARD A THEORY
OF APPEASEMENT

The efficacy of . . . any strategy of conflict management depends
very much upon the adversary's intentions, the degree and kinds of
constraints that affect its leaders, and the political context in which
that strategy is pursued. Appeasement of a Hitler only elicits more
demands. But the same policy applied to a state with limited aims
may resolve important outstanding differences.

                    Richard Ned Lebow, "Conclusions"

Perhaps the greatest task of the prudent and responsible statesman
is to be able to judge when appeasement will and will not lead to
peaceful resolution of disputes.

                    Robert Gilpin, *War and Change in World Politics*

The preceding chapters have examined historical cases of attempted appeasement. This conclusion elaborates the principal themes and findings
that emerge from these cases and offers some "lessons" that may be of
interest to scholars and potential use to policymakers.

MAJOR FACTORS AFFECTING APPEASEMENT OUTCOMES

Defining appeasement outcomes is more complicated than it might initially appear. As noted in the opening chapter, the effectiveness of an
appeasement policy can only be evaluated in relation to its goals. These
tend to vary from case to case. Moreover, in many situations, policymakers
are pursuing multiple objectives. Some of these may be achieved, while

others, more ambitious, may not. Dividing appeasement outcomes into two categories—"successes" and "failures"—thus oversimplifies an often complex reality. Indeed, many attempts at appeasement are both successful and unsuccessful, and should be regarded as "partial successes" and/or "partial failures." In what follows, therefore, the terms "success" and "failure" refer to the results of a policy with respect to a particular objective; they are not intended to exclude the possibility of a mixed outcome overall.

As a diplomatic strategy, appeasement is predicated on the supposition that by offering concessions to its adversary, a state can remove causes of disagreement and reduce tensions, procuring in the process some modification of its opponent's behavior. Three factors appear to be most crucial in determining whether such a policy succeeds or fails. The first is the nature of the adversary, particularly the adversary's motives and the extent of its needs and/or desires. The second is the character of the inducements offered by the appeasing state, especially as these are perceived by the adversary. The third factor is the presence or absence of exogenous incentives for the opponent to respond favorably to the appeaser's initiatives.

The Nature of the Adversary

Some states are more difficult to appease than others. Indeed, with certain adversaries it is impossible to reduce tensions in any real or lasting way.

Most states that engage—or threaten to engage—in hostile behavior (e.g., the use of force) do so for instrumental reasons. That is, they view such behavior as a means to an end. Although the ends of states vary widely, they possess two basic underlying motives: greed and security. "Greedy" states pursue objectives for reasons that are not security-related. Their aims typically include material interests like territory, resources, and commerce. They may also include less tangible interests like prestige and the recognition of status by others. "Insecure" states may seek some of the same goals (e.g., territory); however, they do so not out of avarice but in order to guarantee their future existence.

While most states that engage or threaten to engage in hostile behavior are greedy and/or insecure—in fact, many are both—not all see this behavior in purely instrumental terms. Some states view the use of force as an end in and of itself. Their objective is not satiation of an appetite or amelioration of their insecurity; it is war. These are states that may initiate what Lebow has referred to as "justification of hostility crises," crises that serve as little more than a pretext for military action. The classic example of such a state is Nazi Germany in 1938–1939. Hitler did not merely seek territory in Central and Eastern Europe. He was resolved that this territory be acquired by force.

States whose primary motive in threatening and using force is a desire for war may be labeled "war-seeking." War-seeking states, such as Nazi Germany, cannot be appeased because inducements, if accepted, only delay them from the accomplishment of their intended purpose. Thus, as noted in chapter 4, Hitler's frustration at the outcome of the Munich Conference strengthened his determination to go to war in the Polish Crisis.

By contrast, states whose hostile behavior is instrumental—that is, greedy and/or insecure states—can in principle be appeased. With respect to the former, concessions may perform the purpose of satiation— to paraphrase Churchill, of feeding the crocodile so that it stops being hungry. With respect to the latter, concessions may perform a reassurance function, convincing the adversary that the status quo is not as menacing as it apparently believes. Whether appeasement succeeds in any given case, then, depends to a considerable degree upon the extent and nature of the target state's ambitions. A useful distinction in this regard, although one that is admittedly too simple, is among states whose objectives are limited, those whose objectives are extensive, and those whose objectives are unlimited.

Greedy states whose aims are limited may be termed "revisionist." Such states seek modest alterations in the international status quo, but do not desire far-reaching changes in the rules of the international system or a radical change in the international distribution of spoils. Greedy states that have more extensive ambitions, but whose aims are not infinite, may be termed "expansionist." Finally, those greedy states that seek to change the rules by which the international system operates or that desire far-reaching changes in the international distribution of spoils that would give them the dominant position may be labeled "hegemonic."

Similar distinctions may be made among states whose principal motive is the need for enhanced security. Those states that require relatively modest tangible or intangible improvements in their position may be called simply "insecure." Others, for which more extensive concessions are needed, may be termed "frightened." Finally, there are some states for which only the most extreme concessions, such as the surrender

Table 2. Types of Adversaries		Basic Motivation	
		Security	**Greed**
	Low	Insecure	Revisionist
Needs/Demands	**Moderate**	Frightened	Expansionist
	High	Paranoid	Hegemonic

of an opponent's sovereignty or unilateral disarmament, could produce a sense of security. These states may be labeled "paranoid."

The types of greed-driven and security-driven states that an appeaser may confront are shown in Table 2.

Because their demands and needs are least extensive, revisionist and insecure states are the most susceptible to appeasement. Expansionist and frightened states are more difficult to appease, although the potential for appeasement still exists. States that have truly hegemonic ambitions or whose governments are truly paranoid are incapable of being fully appeased, although in the case of the former at least, some partial appeasement may be possible.

Adding war-seeking states to our list of states motivated by greed or insecurity produces a typology of adversaries, and their appeasability, as shown in Table 3.

It is, of course, critical to understand that an adversary may not fall neatly into a single category. Many, perhaps even most, hostile states are motivated by both security and non-security objectives. Thus, for example, a state may be at the same time expansionist *and* insecure. Such a state can in principle be appeased, since concessions may address both its security needs and its non-security ambitions. However, the task is likely to be complicated. In particular, if the appeaser seeks to couple concessions with deterrent threats in order to discourage the advancement of additional demands (a problem that arises mainly among states motivated by greed), it runs the risk of heightening, rather than ameliorating, the target state's feelings of insecurity.

Table 3. Appeasability of Adversary	
Nature of Adversary	**Potential for Appeasement**
Revisionist	High
Expansionist	Moderate to Low
Hegemonic	Very Low to None
Insecure	High
Frightened	Moderate to Low
Paranoid	Very Low to None
War-Seeking	None

Our analysis of the nature of the adversary and its impact on appeasement outcomes lends support to the following propositions:

Proposition 1: That an adversary is war-seeking (or its hostile behavior is otherwise non-instrumental) is a sufficient condition for appeasement failure.

Proposition 2: That an adversary's hostile behavior is instrumental is a necessary, though not a sufficient, condition for appeasement success.

Proposition 2A: The less extensive the needs/demands of an adversary whose hostile behavior is instrumental, the more likely appeasement is to succeed.

Inducements and the Adversary's Perception of Them

If an adversary's behavior is instrumental, then whether an appeasement policy succeeds depends partly on whether or not the inducements offered are seen as meeting its needs and/or demands. Cases examined in this study reveal that efforts at appeasement may fail to fulfill the needs/

demands of a target state for three basic reasons: the inducements are *misdirected,* they are *insufficient,* or they are *misperceived.*

Misdirected inducements are those that are not appropriate to, or do not really address, the aims of the target state. Attempting to provide reassurance or recognition of status when one's adversary seeks substantial territorial or other material interests is unlikely to produce a significant reduction in tensions. Similarly, making concessions on the means by which an adversary might attain its goals, rather than on the goals themselves, is likely to be unproductive, or even counterproductive.

Misdirected concessions posed problems for appeasement in several cases. For example, the British (and French) decision to allow Germany to rearm during the 1930s enhanced the military capabilities of Hitler's regime while doing little or nothing to address the Nazis' territorial ambitions. American and other Western contributions to the arming of Iraq during the 1980s were similarly misguided.

> Proposition 3: A necessary condition for appeasement success is that inducements must address the needs/demands of the adversary.

Insufficient concessions are those that do address the adversary's needs and/or demands, but fall too far short of meeting them. Insufficient concessions played a role in virtually every appeasement failure examined in this study, perhaps most notably in British efforts to conciliate Nazi Germany, Anglo-American attempts to improve relations with the Soviet Union, and U.S. efforts to secure the friendship and cooperation of Saddam Hussein's Iraq.[1]

It is important to recognize that successful appeasement does not necessarily require the full satisfaction of every need or demand advanced by a diplomatic opponent. It does, however, require satisfaction of those needs/demands which the adversary regards as crucial—i.e. its minimum needs/demands. Thus, for example, Anglo-American appeasement of the Soviet Union in the 1940s succeeded in a limited sense because the territorial concessions made by the Western Powers fulfilled those objectives over which Moscow was probably prepared to fight.

> Proposition 4: A necessary condition for appeasement success is that inducements must meet at least the minimum needs/demands of the target state.

The magnitude of the concessions that an appeasing state is willing and able to offer depends on a number of factors. Historically, states have felt constrained from offering inducements for a variety of reasons. Sometimes these have been strategic. In the 1930s, for example, the British government refused to concede Germany a free hand on the continent of Europe because doing so would have upset the balance of power and compromised British security. Sometimes the reasons have had more to do with domestic politics. In the years prior to Iraq's invasion of Kuwait, the Bush administration was reluctant to extend significant economic and other concessions to the government of Saddam Hussein partly because doing so would have been enormously unpopular with the Congress and the American public. Sometimes the reasons have been primarily diplomatic, and have involved relations with third parties. The U.S. government did not pressure the Kuwaiti government to make meaningful concessions to Iraq because to do so would have seemed improper and would almost certainly have resulted in a hail of criticism from Arab states and other members of the international community. Although the Clinton administration eventually managed to offer the government of North Korea inducements that Pyongyang found acceptable, its freedom of action was at times circumscribed by the attitude of the South Korean government, which feared an overly conciliatory approach.[2]

Proposition 4A: A necessary condition for appeasement success is that the appeasing state possess both the capacity and the willingness to offer sufficient inducements.

Misperceived (or unperceived) inducements are concessions that are incorrectly viewed by the adversary as being unimportant or as not being concessions at all.[3] How inducements are perceived depends both on how they are transmitted and how they are received. Problems with transmission seem to be greater the farther a government engaged in appeasement departs from the unitary actor model. When multiple actors are involved in policy formulation and implementation, mixed signals may be sent to an adversary, which has difficulty deciding what the true policy of the appeasing state is. This problem was particularly acute in U.S. efforts to conciliate the government of Saddam Hussein. In this case, anti-Iraq attitudes manifested by the Voice of America, Congress, and even the State Department diluted the intended reassuring impact of economic concessions. By contrast, U.S. policy toward North Korea was more centralized and ultimately more effective. Under the leadership of Special Ambassador Gallucci, the Clinton administration, for the most part, spoke with a single voice.

Problems with reception seem to occur most frequently where the adversary is insecure. Too often, concessions are viewed with considerable suspicion—as "tricks," for example—or are simply lost amid the "noise" of a generally hostile relationship. Misperceived concessions were a problem in a number of cases, particularly the U.S. effort to conciliate Iraq and Anglo-American attempts to appease the Soviet Union.

It would be too much to claim that an adversary must perceive inducements with absolute accuracy in order for appeasement to succeed. Nevertheless, it seems evident that, in general, the greater the accuracy with which concessions are perceived, the better the prospects for success.

Proposition 5: The greater the accuracy with which an adversary perceives inducements, the more likely appeasement is to succeed.

The Presence (or Absence) of Incentives for the Adversary to Respond Favorably

When an appeasement policy meets some but not all of the adversary's needs/demands, a crucial factor in determining the outcome is the presence or absence of exogenous incentives—reasons other than the inducements offered by the appeasing state—for the target state to accept the appeaser's efforts to reduce tensions. At the international level, such incentives may flow from a threatening geostrategic environment. The target state may have other adversaries besides the appeasing state. The appeasing state, either through active cooperation or a benevolent neutrality, may be of assistance to the dissatisfied state in confronting its opponents. On the other hand, continuing to press the appeasing state might push it into cooperation with these same adversaries, with consequences that could be detrimental, even disastrous.

At the level of bilateral relations, incentives to comply with the appeasing state's desire for reduced tensions may be rooted in commercial and financial interactions, or ideological and cultural connections. They may also derive from the perception that pushing further, or too strenuously, would be unlikely to result in additional gains, or that the risk involved would be too great, because of potential opposition by the appeasing state.

At the domestic level, incentives for moderation may be generated by changes in the balance of political power caused by concessions. Especially where there is a debate over the intentions of the appeasing state (friendly vs. hostile), appeasement may strengthen the hand of advocates of cooperation, while weakening the position of more aggressive persons and factions. In such cases, the leadership may be constrained from issuing further demands or pursuing an aggressive course by the force of domestic opposition. Of course, this can only occur in political systems where some form of pluralism exists.

Cases examined in this study illustrate these factors. The favorable response of the United States to British appeasement between 1895 and 1905 occurred in part because of strategic incentives for Anglo-American cooperation, as well as profitable economic ties and social and cultural links. North Korea's decision to accept the Agreed Framework was partly the result of an increasingly adverse geostrategic context—abandonment by the Soviet Union/Russia and the growing capabilities of South Korea—and of a deteriorating economic situation within the DPRK itself.

The existence of strong incentives—beyond the inducements offered by the appeasing state—for the target state to modify its behavior creates a situation that is "ripe" for appeasement. A considerable degree of "ripeness" was clearly present in the case of British appeasement of the United States around the turn of the century, and in the case of American efforts to persuade North Korea to abandon its nuclear weapons program. At the other end of the spectrum lies the case of Nazi Germany, which was virtually unconstrained in its policy. Surrounded by relatively weak neighbors, convinced that it could achieve economic self-sufficiency, and facing little domestic pressure, the German government possessed no significant reasons to acquiesce in the reduction of tensions desired by British policymakers.

> Proposition 6: The prospects for appeasement success are greatly enhanced by the existence of other incentives for the target state to modify its behavior and acquiesce in the reduction of tensions.

MATCHING APPEASEMENT STRATEGY TO TARGET

Whether an attempt at appeasement succeeds or fails appears to depend, to some extent, on devising and implementing a strategy appropriate to a particular adversary. In a broad sense, appeasement strategies differ along two basic dimensions: (1) the degree of reciprocity which they require and (2) the extent to which they couple inducements with threats. On the first dimension, appeasement may vary between unilateral concessions and strict reciprocity. On the second, it may vary between pure inducements and inducements mixed with significant threats, including threats of military action. The sort of appeasement strategy that is most appropriate, and most likely to be effective, depends on the nature of the target state, its motives, and the particular context in which the policy is being attempted.

> Proposition 7: The greater the greed of the target state, the more appropriate for the appeasing state to require reciprocity and use threats in combination with inducements.

> Proposition 8: The greater the insecurity of the target state, the more appropriate for the appeasing state to offer unilateral concessions and follow a pure inducement strategy.

The logic of these propositions is clear. Insistence on reciprocity and the use of threats in combination with inducements may signal a greedy state that there is no free lunch, thus discouraging the issuance of future demands. Insistence on reciprocity in particular can also provide a means by which the appeasing state can ascertain, relatively early in the process, whether or not the target state is willing to modify its behavior in desired ways. If the target is unwilling to reciprocate, policymakers in the appeasing state can recognize the likelihood of appeasement failure and change course accordingly.

On the other hand, if the target state is insecure, then insistence on reciprocity may heighten this insecurity, giving the target the sense that the appeasing state is fundamentally hostile, does not recognize its legitimate interests, and is concerned not with reducing tensions but with extracting concessions. This problem is even worse in the case of a mixed strategy, where threats can easily exacerbate the fears of an anxious state.

If one divides states into two categories along the dimensions of greed and insecurity—low greed/high greed and low insecurity/high insecurity—it is possible to construct a four-fold typology of potential targets of appeasement. Such states may be characterized by: (1) low greed and low insecurity, (2) low greed and high insecurity, (3) high greed and low insecurity, and (4) high greed and high insecurity. What do the propositions presented above suggest about the appropriate strategy with respect to each type of target?

It may not be necessary to appease a state characterized by low levels of both greed and insecurity since a state that is neither greedy nor insecure is unlikely to have significant differences with other members of the international community. Given this, it should not be surprising that none of the cases considered in this study appear to have involved target states that fall into this category. Nevertheless, the logic of the two propositions suggests that if differences exist and appeasement is attempted toward a low-greed, low-insecurity adversary, it is likely to be successful regardless of the precise strategy employed. Unilateral concessions and a pure inducement strategy carry no dangers, and should fulfill the needs/demands of the target state with relative ease. At the same time, while insistence on reciprocity and the use of threats are unnecessary, they are also not likely to be counterproductive in the sense of creating insecurity so profound as to result in failure of the policy.

Target states that are characterized by a low level of greed but a high level of insecurity are best approached with unilateral concessions unmixed with threats. In such cases, inducements can satisfy the needs/demands of the target without provoking additional demands, while insistence on reciprocity or the use of threats may cause insecurity sufficient to prevent successful appeasement. The turn-of-the-century United States appears to have been a target of this type.

High-greed, low-insecurity target states demand insistence on reciprocity and the mixing of inducements with threats, for reasons discussed earlier. Nazi Germany is the prototypical example of this kind of target. Unfortunately, during much of the period of attempted appeasement, the British government refrained from the use of threats. While it did insist on reciprocity, when Germany proved unwilling to reciprocate, British policymakers failed (or perhaps more accurately, refused) to recognize that this signaled the probable failure of their policy and thus failed to make the appropriate adjustments.

High-greed, high-insecurity target states are the most problematic from the standpoint of appeasement. Indeed, propositions 7 and 8 argue for contradictory approaches. The target's greed should be addressed with a mixed strategy of inducements and threats requiring reciprocation in response to any concessions, but this is likely to exacerbate an already considerable insecurity. At least three of the target states examined in this study fall into the high-greed, high-insecurity category: the Soviet Union

Table 4. Matching Appeasement Strategies to Target States			
		Greed	
		Low	**High**
Insecurity	**Low**	Appeasement probably not necessary (no cases)	Reciprocity; Mixed Strategy (Nazi Germany)
	High	Unilateral Concessions; Pure Inducements (United States)	No clear strategy; anything beyond limited appeasement problematic (Soviet Union, Iraq, North Korea)

during the 1940s, Iraq, and North Korea. As these cases illustrate, what one might label "mixed-motive adversaries" are difficult to appease. Inducements may create the false impression that further demands will be fulfilled, while insistence on reciprocity and the use of threats heighten insecurity and raise tensions. The North Korean case shows that it is possible to reduce tensions and modify behavior with respect to a very specific, limited issue. However, there is no evidence that appeasement of high-greed, high-insecurity states can result in a fundamental relaxation of tensions and an alteration of a basic pattern of hostility and fear.

The typology of target states, with the appropriate appeasement strategy for each, is presented in Table 4.

AVOIDING EXPLOITATION

Critics of appeasement argue that the policy makes a state vulnerable to exploitation. Efforts at reducing tensions are perceived by the target state as an invitation to issue further demands, demands that the appeasing state may be unable to deny without going to war.

The problem does not appear to be, as is sometimes supposed, that appeasement leads a recipient state to expand the scope of its objectives. If one considers the ambitions of Nazi Germany, for example, it is apparent that appeasement did not actually cause leaders to increase their aims, which were already quite extensive. Hitler's ambitions, as recorded in *Mein Kampf,* did not grow dramatically during the 1930s. In fact, there is evidence to suggest that refusing to make concessions when demands are minimal is far more likely to stimulate an expansion of objectives than is the granting of concessions. For example, Barbara Tuchman has argued persuasively that American colonists of the late eighteenth century might well have been pacified by relatively minor British concessions on questions of taxation and representation. It was only when the British government rejected modest demands on these issues that the colonists decided that full independence from Britain was required.[4]

The danger of appeasement, then, is not so much that concessions will lead a target state to expand its objectives, but that they will increase its willingness to pursue already existing objectives. To use the appetite metaphor, rather than actually making a state hungrier, appeasement (it is alleged) simply makes it more daring and aggressive in the quest for food. It becomes more aggressive because it perceives reduced risks attached to aggression, appeasement being evidence of weakness and/or lack of resolve on the part of its opponent.

Whether a target of appeasement interprets the policy as evidence of weakness or irresolution depends on a number of factors, some of which already have been discussed. It depends first upon the motives of the state in question. A state for which the use of force is essential—i.e., one that desires war, though perhaps not too large a war—may well interpret concessions as a sign of weakness and a "green light" to commit aggression. Similarly, a greedy state seeking territorial or other gains may perceive concessions as indicating an opportunity to make additional demands and receive additional spoils. On the other hand, an insecure state is more likely to interpret concessions as evidence of benign intentions and good will. If concessions are seen as signs of weakness, the effect on an insecure state should be beneficial, since a weaker adversary is presumably less threatening than a strong one.

Proposition 9: The more a target state is motivated by greed, the greater the probability that appeasement will be interpreted as a sign of weakness or irresolution.

Proposition 10: The more a target state is motivated by insecurity, the lower the probability that appeasement will be interpreted as a sign of weakness or irresolution.

Another factor in determining how concessions are perceived by a target state is the process by which they are made. In this regard, appeasing states possess several mechanisms by which they can seek to discourage perceptions of weakness on the part of the target. First, they can make concessions that are conditional rather than unconditional, which require reciprocation or at least some evidence of improved behavior prior to the making of additional concessions. Second, appeasing states can make concessions after they have already established some reputation for firmness in dealing with the dissatisfied state. Finally, appeasing states can attempt to influence their adversary's interpretation of concessions by presenting them as being motivated by factors other than weakness. As Jervis writes, an actor who decides to back down "can mitigate the effect on his image by influencing others' interpretations of his behavior and convincing them not to take his retreat as an index to his lack of resolve."[5]

> Proposition 11: Appeasement is less likely to be interpreted as evidence of weakness or irresolution if concessions are made contingent upon reciprocation.

> Proposition 12: Appeasement is less likely to be interpreted as evidence of weakness or irresolution if the appeasing state has already established a reputation for firmness and strength.

> Proposition 13: Appeasement is less likely to be interpreted as evidence of weakness or irresolution if the appeasing state can convey the sense that concessions are not being made simply because of pressure, but because the target state's demands/needs are recognized as legitimate or just.

Finally, the impact of appeasement on the credibility of an appeasing state's promise to uphold its commitments seems to depend more upon capabilities than reputation. It is not so much the act of making concessions itself that undermines subsequent attempts at deterrence. It is the weakness in military posture that may be produced by these concessions. In other words, the "material effect" of appeasement is generally more damaging than the "psychological effect."

> Proposition 14: Appeasement is most likely to be interpreted as evidence of weakness if it results in a deterioration in the capability of the appeasing state to defend its commitments.

Support for propositions 9–14 can be found in various of the cases. The greediest states—Nazi Germany, Soviet Russia, Iraq—were those most likely to interpret appeasement as a sign of weakness or irresolution, while the less greedy, more insecure targets—the United States, North Korea—tended not to see an opportunity to advance more far-reaching demands. Failure of the United States to insist on reciprocity contributed to Iraq's view of Washington as unlikely to respond vigorously to aggressive moves in the Persian Gulf region. British policymakers confronting the United States around the turn of the century benefited from Britain's strength, especially that of her navy. British leaders also presented their concessions as fulfilling legitimate American demands. On the other hand, the British government during the 1930s failed to communicate to Hitler the belief that some of his demands were justified, thus leaving the impression that Britain was retreating involuntarily under German pressure. A decade later, the Roosevelt administration in the United States mounted a vigorous rhetorical campaign attacking Soviet advances in Eastern and Central Europe at the same time it was acquiescing to them. It would have been surprising had Stalin not interpreted American policy as weak since the United States was so clearly retreating against its will.

Whether concessions are perceived as indicating an opportunity for advancing further demands or committing further acts of aggression also depends on certain other factors, including the potential costs associated with such activities at several different levels. Simply stated, appeasement is less likely to elicit further demands or to promote further aggression in cases where the recipient of concessions has strong reasons to remain on cordial terms with the appeasing state. While these incentives may not be sufficient to cause the target state to abandon its most important objectives, they may, once these objectives have been met, dissuade it from aggressively pursuing additional aims to which it is less committed.

LESSONS FOR POLICYMAKERS

One of the purposes of this study is to provide guidance for policymakers contemplating a policy of appeasement vis-à-vis a particular adversary. Beyond the propositions elaborated above, the cases suggest a few basic lessons. Most of these fall into the category of common sense, but given the failure to observe certain of them in previous situations, perhaps they bear repeating here.

1. *Know your adversary.* This is by far the most important lesson. Unless

one understands an opponent and his motives, one cannot know the prospects for successful appeasement or how to devise an appropriate strategy. Failure to understand adequately the target state and its leaders contributed significantly to failed appeasement in several cases, including British efforts to conciliate Nazi Germany and American attempts to improve relations with Saddam Hussein's Iraq.

2. *Reevaluate policy on a regular basis.* Because a target state's motives are typically complicated and obscure, policymakers often will not be able to know their adversary as fully as they would like. A policy of appeasement, like any other policy, should be adopted provisionally, and its effectiveness evaluated regularly.

3. *Devise tests.* Sometimes it is difficult to know whether or not an appeasement policy is succeeding. The target state may make "tactical" adjustments in behavior designed to elicit further concessions which are hard to distinguish from genuine, "strategic" changes. Mistaking the former for the latter contributed to the failure of U.S. policy toward Iraq, while an accurate assessment of North Korean policy shifts enabled U.S. officials to adopt and implement an appropriate strategy in that case. It is thus important that policymakers find ways to test the target's response to appeasement. Among the questions that should be asked in evaluating its response: (1) Is the target state fulfilling the obligations it has assumed under the terms of any agreement(s)? (2) Is the change in behavior by the target state something that would be difficult to reverse? (3) Do these shifts in behavior by the target state impose any costs on it? (4) Does the target state appear to have strong internal and/or external incentives to modify its behavior? If the answer to each of these questions is affirmative, there is a good chance that a change in the target's behavior is strategic rather than tactical; if negative, then the opposite is likely to be true.

4. *Modify or abandon appeasement if evidence of ineffectiveness is strong.* This rule should be obvious, but it is one that British policymakers failed to observe during the 1930s. U.S. officials charged with America's Iraq policy during the 1980s did not do markedly better. Shifting emphasis from appeasement to another strategy—e.g., deterrence—may be more easily said than done. In a democracy, it requires, as Iklé notes, "both an official consensus and effective public agreement on the point at which appeasement . . . must be abandoned and any further demands by the opponent rejected, backed up by the threat of war."[6] Nevertheless, as the United States' experience in the early Cold War and Britain's experience during the 1930s illustrate, this condition is not impossible to meet.

5. *Maintain capacity for alternative policy.* If policymakers are going to shift to an alternative policy, it is necessary that the capacity for such a policy exist. Iklé writes, "The most dangerous phase in following a policy of 'appeasement' arises when initial concessions fail to pacify the opponent. . . . The switch to a policy of deterrence may be attempted without the requisite military preparations, precisely because in a period of appeasement such preparations usually lack popular support and would seem inconsistent with a stance of conciliation. Hence, the opponent cannot be confronted by a military capability threatening him with losses severe enough to outweigh his expected gains from aggression."[7] This was precisely what happened during the 1930s. British leaders allowed Britain's relative military capabilities and its relationships with various potential allies to deteriorate to such an extent that when they abandoned appeasement and adopted a strategy of deterrence they were unable to confront Hitler with a threat sufficient to dissuade him from attacking Poland. Conversely, American policymakers in the 1940s, despite their desire to conciliate the Soviet Union, retained sufficient military strength that when they abandoned appeasement and adopted a strategy of containment (deterrence), this new strategy was effective in the sense that Soviet leaders refrained from challenging American commitments in a way that might have led to a third world war. With an insecure adversary, there is some danger that maintaining the capacity for effective deterrence will exacerbate insecurity and undermine efforts to reduce tensions. This is probably unavoidable.

6. *Centralize policy implementation and speak with one voice.* Because the target state's perceptions of an appeasement policy are crucial, it is important that policymakers send consistent signals. Mixed messages can weaken the impact of conciliation, leading the target to wonder whether the appeasing state is really serious about wishing to reduce tensions or will live up to its commitments. In particular, U.S. efforts to appease Iraq during the 1980s were significantly damaged by the often conflicting signals emanating from Washington.

7. *Be patient and flexible.* Appeasement is often a slow process. Sometimes a series of inducements may be necessary before the desired change in an adversary's behavior is achieved. Where insecurity is an obstacle to reducing tensions, trust is crucial, and trust seldom develops overnight.[8] Putting together a package of concessions and reciprocal commitments acceptable to both sides can be difficult and laborious. The target state's behavior may be inconsistent and hard to interpret. For British policymakers

confronting the United States at the turn of the century and U.S. policymakers concerned with North Korea during the early 1990s, patience and flexibility proved vital. It took the better part of a decade for London to efface American hostility and mistrust, while the Agreed Framework emerged only after very difficult and protracted negotiations.

8. *Be aware of the advantages (and disadvantages) of incrementalism.* Appeasement may be attempted either through a comprehensive settlement resolving all outstanding differences, or by a piecemeal process that deals with an issue at a time. A comprehensive settlement may appear attractive, but it is likely to be difficult to achieve, particularly when tensions are severe and differences fundamental, as in the case of Britain and Germany during the 1930s, and the United States and the Soviet Union in the following decade. Insistence on a comprehensive settlement also eliminates the possibility of a mixed outcome; either appeasement succeeds completely or it fails completely. By contrast, an incremental approach to appeasement allows for partial success, an important consideration. Had the United States insisted upon resolving simultaneously all outstanding differences with North Korea rather than focusing upon Pyongyang's nuclear program, it seems unlikely that anything of value would have been accomplished. The disadvantage of incremental appeasement is that the appeasing state may have difficulty judging the extent to which tensions are really being reduced and the target state's behavior modified. Resolution of certain issues may appear significant, but actually matter little in the context of the two states' relationship as a whole. Indeed, partial successes can be quite illusory, as the British experience after Munich clearly demonstrates.

9. *Avoid passive appeasement.* Passive appeasement, as distinct from active appeasement, involves standing by while an adversary seeks to satisfy its needs or demands. It can be seen most clearly in the British approach to Nazi Germany in 1935–1936, but there were also elements of it in U.S. policy toward the Soviet Union after Yalta. Passive appeasement has the disadvantages of active appeasement, but lacks its advantages. Because it requires no action by the appeasing state, it may not be apparent to the target that passive appeasement represents part of a policy of tension-reduction and reflects a genuine desire to remove causes of disagreement. The appeasing state receives no credit for its restraint, which is likely to be interpreted either as a lack of interest or a lack of resolve. If passive appeasement is contemplated, it should be identified as a policy, with both its objectives and its limits made clear.

10. *Recognize that socialization requires more than setting an example.* In several of the cases, policymakers believed that their adversary's aggressiveness reflected, at least in part, a lack of appreciation for generally accepted standards of international behavior. If the target state could be brought into the international community—introduced to polite society, as it were—political leaders might learn its norms and act more appropriately. British statesmen in particular seemed at times to think that if they behaved in a conciliatory fashion toward Germany, the German government would observe how proper diplomacy was conducted and seek to emulate them. This study provides no evidence for the effectiveness of such an approach. While it is clear that in their actions Hitler, Stalin, and Saddam Hussein, for example, departed dramatically from community standards, this was not because they did not understand them. Rather, they rejected them and—in Hitler's case especially—used others' adherence to them to their advantage because they believed that more could be obtained by acting "outside the law" than within its boundaries. Had "playing by the rules" resulted in significant gains in territory, wealth, or security, these dictators might have agreed to abide by international norms, eventually internalizing them. This implies that states' aggressive behavior originates primarily in leaders' perceived interests (whether based in greed, security, or some combination thereof) and only secondarily in inadequate or improper socialization. Unless perceived interests are addressed effectively—as, for example, in the case of British appeasement of the United States—socialization is unlikely to occur.[9]

11. *Do not rely on personal relationships with the adversary's leader or leaders.* In at least two of the cases examined in this study, practitioners of appeasement were convinced that the policy would succeed if they could establish a close working relationship, even friendship, with the leader of the target state. Neville Chamberlain believed that he (and he alone) could develop a businesslike relationship with Hitler, based on common sense and mutual trust. Once this was accomplished, the two of them could rationally and peacefully negotiate the future of Europe. Chamberlain was wrong. Similarly, Franklin Roosevelt believed that he had the unique capacity to arrive at mutual understanding with Josef Stalin, and that their friendly relationship would influence Soviet policy in a positive direction. Roosevelt, too, was mistaken. This study provides no evidence that close personal connections between leaders of an appeasing state and leaders of a target state can be created, or that if created they enhance the prospects for successful appeasement.[10]

APPEASEMENT AND DETERRENCE

Although deterrence theorists often seemed to claim, especially during the Cold War, an almost universal applicability for threat-based approaches, recent critics have argued persuasively that deterrence is appropriate only under a limited range of circumstances. According to Lebow and Stein, for example, successful deterrence requires that the adversary be motivated by opportunity or greed rather than need, that leaders have the political freedom to modify their policy, that they accurately perceive the political and military situation, that they be vulnerable to the threats the deterrer is capable of making, and that they have not already committed themselves to a particular course of action. Additionally, deterrence is more likely to succeed with adversaries that are risk-averse rather than risk-acceptant.[11]

No one, it seems safe to say, has ever argued for the universal applicability of appeasement. And indeed, the cases examined in this study suggest that, like deterrence, appeasement is appropriate only under certain circumstances. What are they? First, the adversary must not be unalterably committed to the behavior the appeasing state seeks to modify. The use of force, for example, if contemplated by the opponent, must be viewed as instrumental to the acquisition of a particular objective, not as essential in and of itself. Second, the adversary must be susceptible to inducements that it is within the political and material capacity of the appeaser to make. If the adversary is motivated by opportunity/greed, this implies that there are limits to its demands; if motivated by insecurity, it implies that leaders are not impervious to the reassuring effects of an appeasement policy. The latter condition is most likely to be met when the adversary's insecurity is primarily a function of the appeaser's recent actions, rather than political leaders' ideology, worldview, or paranoid mentality.[12] Finally, the adversary must accurately perceive the appeaser's policy. At the very least, efforts to address the adversary's concerns must be regarded as such.

Confronted by a hostile state whose behavior they wish to change, policymakers have two basic options: deterrence (or compellence) or appeasement. Logically, such situations are of four possible types: (1) those in which deterrence alone can succeed, (2) those in which appeasement alone can succeed, (3) those in which either deterrence or appeasement can succeed, and (4) those in which neither deterrence nor appeasement can succeed. The most basic determinant of the category into which a situation falls is the primary motive of the target state. What is causing the adversary's behavior? If it is insecurity, then deterrence alone is inappropriate, though it may be useful as a strategy to buy time during which alternative ways of dealing with the adversary can be developed. Appeasement is appropriate in the sense that it can in principle address the source of the problem; whether it in fact does so depends on the origins and the intensity of the insecurity.

If the adversary is greed-driven, then the situation is more complex. Indeed, it appears useful to think of greed as consisting of two distinct components: intensity and range. Intensity refers to the level of commitment to a state's aims, including both the degree to which the aims are regarded as essential and to the degree of time-pressure or urgency with which they need to be obtained. Range refers to the extensiveness of the state's objectives. Deterrence theorists have noted that deterrence is problematic when a state is highly committed to a goal and when it experiences a sense of urgency with respect to its attainment. In such cases, even the threat of serious punishment may not be sufficient to dissuade the state from taking action. By contrast, deterrence is much easier when the adversary is less committed to the achievement of its goal and feels itself under little or no time pressure. Cases examined in this study suggest that, unlike deterrence, appeasement can succeed in pacifying an adversary that is highly committed to its goal. It becomes problematic, however, when the opponent has ambitions that are very extensive.

If one classifies greedy states according to the intensity and the range of their ambitions, one can construct a 2x2 table, indicating the appropri-

Table 5. Greedy States: Appeasement or Deterrence?

		Range of Aims	
		Low	**High**
Commitment to Arms	**Low**	Either Appeasement or Deterrence (Argentina in Falklands Crisis?)	Deterrence (Soviet Union—maximum aims)
	High	Appeasement (United States, North Korea, Soviet Union—minimum aims)	Neither Appeasement nor Deterrence (Nazi Germany, Iraq?)

ateness of deterrence and appeasement strategies. Adversaries whose ambitions are low-intensity, low-range can be addressed by either appeasement or deterrence. Neither appeasement nor deterrence is likely to succeed with an opponent highly committed to the attainment of extensive aims. Deterrence is appropriate with an adversary having extensive ambitions, but not highly committed to their achievement, while appeasement is appropriate with an adversary having limited aims to which it is highly committed.

Placing a historical case into a particular category requires counterfactual argumentation, since one must speculate about what would have happened had a different strategy been attempted. In this sense, it cannot be proved conclusively that a given case belongs in a given category. Nevertheless, it seems appropriate to make some effort to identify cases representing each type of situation.

The low-commitment, high-range category, it could be argued, is represented by the Soviet Union during the Cold War. Deterrence (containment) did in fact succeed in thwarting the Kremlin's most ambitious aims. It is unlikely that appeasement would have done so. The United States and the West more generally were incapable of offering inducements that would satisfy Moscow's territorial objectives, which were truly global. Nor could they reassure insecure Soviet leaders who not only had paranoid personalities (Stalin), but whose ideology told them that capitalist states were unalterably hostile to socialism.

The high-commitment, low-range category is represented by the Anglo-American relationship at the turn of the century, and perhaps by the U.S.-North Korean dispute over North Korea's nuclear weapons program. In each case, appeasement was largely successful, and in each it seems doubtful that deterrence or compellence (in the case of North Korea) would have worked as well. Policymakers in Britain around the turn of the century were not capable of presenting the United States with a strong and credible threat, and Americans were strongly committed to their aims. Compellence by economic sanctions proved impossible in the case of North Korea; compellence by military threats was never seriously considered, probably because U.S. policymakers did not believe such threats would be effective.[13]

None of the cases examined in this study appears to fall into the low-commitment, low-range category. The 1983 Anglo-Argentine dispute over the Falkland Islands might, however, be considered an example of this type of situation. The problem in this case was that the British government attempted neither to appease the Argentine junta—by entering into negotiations regarding the sovereignty of the islands—nor to deter it by threatening a military response in the event Argentina seized the islands. Had either policy been adopted, it seems likely that war would have been averted.

The high-commitment, high-range category is represented by the situation in Europe in 1938–1939. Hitler could not be appeased. His territorial ambitions were too extensive, and he was determined to have a war regardless of what he was offered by Britain and France. Nor, as it turned out, could he be deterred. The Western Powers presented him with a credible threat (though not a strong one, in immediate military terms), yet he decided to proceed with his attack on Poland.

The challenge for policymakers, of course, is to ascertain the nature of the situation with which they are faced. It would be foolish to pretend that this is ever likely to be easy; as the cases demonstrate, an adversary's motives are frequently complex and obscure. One can make genuine efforts to comprehend one's opponent and still fail. Nevertheless, recognition that different situations call for different policies, knowledge of the conditions that define each type of situation, and identification of methods for diagnosing the nature of the situation in a given case should be helpful. If this study contributes to our understanding in these areas, it will have fulfilled its purpose.

NOTES

In citing works in the notes, short titles have generally been used. Certain works have been identified by the following abbreviations.

DBFP, 1919–1939 Great Britain. Foreign Office. *Documents on British Foreign Policy, 1919–1939*, 1st series, 27 vols.; series 1A, 7 vols.; 2nd series, 21 vols.; 3rdseries, 10 vols. London: HMSO, 1946–.

DGFP, 1918–1945 Germany. Auswärtiges Amt. *Documents on German Foreign Policy, 1918–1945*, from the archives of the German Foreign Ministry, series C (1933–1937), 6 vols.; series D (1937–1945), 13 vols. Washington: USGPO, 1949–1983.

FBIS-EAS U.S. Foreign Broadcast Information Service. *Daily Report: East Asia.*

FBIS-NES U.S. Foreign Broadcast Information Service. *Daily Report: Near East & South Asia.*

FRUS U. S. Department of State. *Foreign Relations of the United States: Diplomatic Papers.* Washington: USGPO, 1861–.

Malta and Yalta U. S. Department of State. *The Conferences at Malta and Yalta, 1945.* Washington: USGPO, 1955.

TMWC International Military Tribunal (Nuremberg). *Trial of the Major War Criminals Before the International Military Tribunal,* 42 vols. Nuremberg, 1947–49.

1. The Study of Appeasement

1. Santayana, *Reason in Common Sense,* 284.

2. Strausz-Hupé and Possony, *International Relations,* 246–47.

3. The best explication and analysis of the "deterrence model" is found in Jervis, *Perception and Misperception,* chap. 3.

4. On containment, see Gaddis, *Strategies of Containment.*

5. Norman Podhoretz, for example, has referred to the Soviet Union as "Hitler with nuclear weapons." See Podhoretz, "Future Danger," 35.

6. See May, *"Lessons" of the Past,* 33, 81–86, 112–14; and Rystad, *Prisoners of the Past?* Patrick Morgan, however, argues that the concern of American policymakers with reputation and credibility is not really grounded in the experience of the 1930s, but is a reflection of insecurities rooted in the American political culture and in doubts about their ability to actually use nuclear weapons. American statesmen, he suggests, have em-

ployed the Munich analogy to rationalize or justify policies they were already disposed to pursue. See Morgan, "Saving Face," 151.

7. From "American Relations with the Soviet Union," a "Top Secret" report of September 1946, reprinted in Krock, *Memoirs,* Appendix A, 477.

8. Televised address of 8 August 1990, excerpts printed in *The Times* (London), 9 August 1990.

9. George Bush, remarks to officers and troops at Hickam Air Force Base, Pearl Harbor, Hawaii, 28 October 1990, *Bush Papers,* 1483.

10. The relationship between appeasement and engagement is explored in more detail later in this chapter.

11. Plano and Olton, *International Relations Dictionary,* 250.

12. See Draper, "Appeasement and Detente," 36.

13. Jack F. Kemp, speech at the Heritage Foundation, quoted in Clifford D. May, "Kemp Assails White House on Arms Control Proposal," *New York Times,* 23 May 1987. Pat Robertson quoted in John Dillin, "But Right-Wing Sniping at Treaty and Economy Worries Are Clouds," *Christian Science Monitor,* 11 December 1987.

14. "Conservatives Fire Back at Reagan," *Los Angeles Times,* 4 December 1987.

15. Gilpin, *War and Change in World Politics,* 193.

16. George, *Bridging the Gap,* 61–62.

17. Jervis, *Perception and Misperception,* 101. Jervis, however, clearly does not regard all threatening states as "aggressors," since he argues that "conciliation does not always lead to further demands. Appeasement often works, even when there are major conflicts between the countries" (90).

18. In his history of the Second World War, Winston Churchill wrote that "The subjugation of Czechoslovakia robbed the Allies of the Czech Army of twenty-one regular divisions, fifteen or sixteen second-line divisions already mobilised, and also their mountain fortress line which, in the days of Munich, had required the deployment of thirty German divisions, or the main strength of the mobile and fully trained German Army. . . . Besides this the Skoda Works, the second most important arsenal in Central Europe . . . was made to change sides adversely." Churchill, *Gathering Storm,* 336–37.

19. Jervis, *Perception and Misperception,* 58.

20. I shall argue in chapter 3 that this critique of Munich is incorrect. Not only did Hitler find threats of Anglo-French intervention on behalf of Poland to be credible, he perceived Munich as a humiliating defeat at the hands of his foes, rather than a great diplomatic triumph signaling their irresolution.

21. There does exist one comparative historical analysis of multiple cases of appeasement. See Karsten, "Response to Threat Perception," 120–63. Karsten, however, focuses exclusively upon the origins of the strategy rather than its results.

22. Jervis, *Perception and Misperception,* 90.

23. See especially Orme, "Deterrence Failures: A Second Look." Orme's article was a response to Lebow, *Between Peace and War,* in which Lebow claimed many deterrence failures flowed not from mistakes in policy, but from errors in the fundamental assumptions made by deterrence theory regarding the sources of states' aggressive behavior. Lebow replied to Orme, reasserting his position in "Deterrence Failure Revisited."

24. Snyder and Diesing, *Conflict Among Nations,* 185–89.

25. Huth and Russett, "What Makes Deterrence Work?" 517.

26. Compared to the chances of deterrence success if the previous encounter ended in a stalemate. Huth, *Extended Deterrence and the Prevention of War,* 80–81; and Huth, "Ex-

tended Deterrence and the Outbreak of War," 438. It should be noted that in their 1984 article, Huth and Russett did not distinguish between past confrontations involving the same adversary and those involving a different one, while Huth, in his more recent study, made this distinction. Huth found that only those concessions made to the same adversary undermined deterrence; backing down in a prior confrontation with a different opponent did not seem to affect adversely the defender's reputation in the cases that he examined.

27. Huth notes that "the defender's record of weakness might also have contributed to the initial decision by the potential attacker to threaten the use of force and risk a wider confrontation. An analysis of the origins of the immediate deterrence cases indicates that such calculations probably played an important role in about eight cases. . . . The defender's past behavior was not a consistently critical factor in decisions by the potential attacker to challenge extended-general deterrence and to threaten the use of force" (*Extended Deterrence and the Prevention of War,* 216–17).

28. Mercer, *Reputation and International Politics,* 23.

29. Fearon, "Signaling versus the Balance of Power and Interests," 261–65. Fearon hypothesizes that a selection effect explains the lower rate of immediate-deterrence success in cases in which a previous crisis occurred compared to those in which a previous crisis did not occur. He argues that the occurrence of a crisis signals a defender's willingness to resist a challenger's demands, even if the defender eventually backs down. Any subsequent challenge that is issued, therefore, is issued in the face of heightened expectations that the defender will use force to preserve its interests. Since the challenger has already taken the defender's presumed willingness to uphold a commitment into account when issuing its challenge, it is unlikely to be deterred by threats which merely confirm this willingness. In such cases, once general deterrence has failed, immediate deterrence is also likely to fail.

30. Mercer, *Reputation and International Politics,* 227.

31. Ibid, 214. Mercer's statement implies that adversaries do *sometimes* (even if only rarely) acquire reputations for lacking resolve. For some such cases, see George, "The Role of Force in Diplomacy," 46–50; and Blechman and Wittes, "Defining Moment: The Threat and Use of Force in American Foreign Policy." One of the weaknesses of Mercer's analysis is that he does not attempt to develop contingent generalizations, identifying the conditions under which states do and do not acquire reputations for irresolution. In my concluding chapter, I make some effort to do precisely this.

32. David Baldwin argues that positive sanctions (rewards and promises) are more costly when they succeed, while negative sanctions (threats of punishment or retaliation) are more costly when they fail. See Baldwin, "Power of Positive Sanctions," 28.

33. The primary aim of America's containment policy was to protect Western Europe from communism. Presidents Truman and Johnson feared that if the United States failed to defend its interests in East and Southeast Asia, Soviet leaders would not find American threats to defend Western Europe credible and might, therefore, be encouraged to attack.

34. For one such analysis, see Melman, "Limits of Military Power."

35. The leading member of the "America in decline" school is Paul Kennedy, who advanced the thesis in *Rise and Fall of the Great Powers.* For a much-abridged statement of his position, see Kennedy, "The (Relative) Decline of America." Needless to say, Kennedy's conclusions have not been universally accepted. For a contrasting view, see Nye, *Bound to Lead;* and Nye, "Misleading Metaphor of Decline." As the title of Nye's article suggests, some of the debate between "declinists" and "non-declinists" may be semantic. The two

sides agree that the share of world power possessed by the United States in the early years after World War II was artificially high, that this share has been decreasing, and that the United States must modify both its domestic and international policies in adjusting to its changing position. They disagree mainly on the causes of the "decline" (bad policy vs. secular trends largely beyond the control of the United States) and on the nature of the appropriate responses.

36. This suggests that Baldwin's generalization that positive sanctions are more costly when they succeed while negative sanctions are more costly when they fail (note 32) may not be entirely correct.

37. Huth, *Extended Deterrence and the Prevention of War;* Huth, "Extended Deterrence and the Outbreak of War"; Lebow and Stein, "Deterrence: The Elusive Dependent Variable."

38. Huth, *Extended Deterrence and the Prevention of War;* Huth, "Extended Deterrence and the Outbreak of War"; Lebow and Stein, "Beyond Deterrence."

39. The literature on deterrence is voluminous. Pioneering theoretical works include Kaufmann, *Requirements of Deterrence;* Schelling, *Strategy of Conflict;* Snyder, *Deterrence and Defense;* and Schelling, *Arms and Influence.* Empirical works may be divided generally into comparative case studies and quantitative analyses. Among the former are George and Smoke, *Deterrence in American Foreign Policy;* and Mearsheimer, *Conventional Deterrence.* The latter include works of Huth and Russett cited elsewhere in this chapter. Critiques of deterrence theory are found in George and Smoke, *Deterrence in American Foreign Policy,* and numerous other works by George; Jervis, Lebow, and Stein, *Psychology and Deterrence;* Lebow and Stein, "Beyond Deterrence"; and Lebow and Stein, "Rational Deterrence Theory." A good survey and review of the early literature is Jervis, "Deterrence Theory Revisited." For a critical assessment of quantitative studies, see Levy, "When do Deterrent Threats Work?"

The literature on compellence or coercive diplomacy is much less extensive than the literature on deterrence. In addition to Schelling, *Arms and Influence,* see George and Simons (eds.), *Limits of Coercive Diplomacy;* George, *Forceful Persuasion;* and Peterson, "Deterrence and Compellence."

40. Baldwin, "Power of Positive Sanctions."

41. Leng and Wheeler, "Influence Strategies, Success, and War."

42. Exceptions include Rosecrance, "Reward, Punishment, and Interdependence," and Patchen, *Resolving Disputes Between Nations,* chap. 9, "The Use of Positive Incentives." See also Cortright (ed.), *Price of Peace.* The contributors to the Cortright volume do employ case studies in order to develop hypotheses regarding the conditions under which incentives will and will not lead to the prevention of conflict.

43. There are some exceptions. See, for example, Weinberg, *Foreign Policy of Hitler's Germany.* Studies treating the reasons Britain adopted a policy of appeasement include Wheeler-Bennett, *Munich: Prologue to Tragedy;* Rowse, *Appeasement: A Study in Political Decline;* Gilbert, *Roots of Appeasement;* Middlemas, *Strategy of Appeasement;* Eubank, *Munich;* Ovendale, *"Appeasement" and the English Speaking World;* Mommsen and Kettenacker (eds.), *Fascist Challenge and the Policy of Appeasement;* and William Rock, *Chamberlain & Roosevelt.* Essays on the historiography of appeasement in the 1930s include William Rock, "British Appeasement (1930's)"; Watt, "Historiography of Appeasement"; Kennedy, "Appeasement"; and Richardson, "New Perspectives on Appeasement."

44. Gilpin, *War and Change in World Politics,* 193–94; Jervis, *Perception and Misperception,* 90; Lebow, "Conclusions," 223; Laqueur, "Psychology of Appeasement," 46.

45. Craig and George, *Force and Statecraft,* 250.

46. Ibid.

47. Kennedy, "Tradition of Appeasement in British Foreign Policy."

48. Ibid., 16, 39.

49. The change in the semantics of appeasement is reflected in the *Oxford English Dictionary*. In the first edition of the *OED*, published in 1933, there is no indication whatsoever that the word was employed as a term of derogation. In the second edition, published in 1989, the editors note that the term "appeasement" is "often used disparagingly" in reference to Chamberlain's efforts at conciliation and to efforts at conciliation more generally. An excellent discussion of the transformation of "appeasement" from a term of honor and justice to one of opprobrium is William Rock, *British Appeasement in the 1930s*, chap. 1, "The Meaning of Appeasement."

50. *Webster's Third New International Dictionary*, 103; emphasis added.

51. Morgenthau, *In Defense of the National Interest*, 137; emphasis added.

52. Strausz-Hupé and Possony, *International Relations*, 246.

53. Paul Kennedy makes this argument, noting with respect to appeasement that "it has proved impracticable to banish the expression." See Kennedy, "Tradition of Appeasement in British Foreign Policy," 15.

54. As many students of international politics have noted, there is no logical reason why deterrence must or should rely exclusively on threats; rather, it can be part of a broader influence strategy that also employs promises or rewards. See, for example, Milburn, "What Constitutes Effective Deterrence?" and George and Smoke, *Deterrence in American Foreign Policy*, 604–10. In fact, some scholars have defined appeasement as a form of deterrence, albeit one relying upon positive, rather than negative, sanctions. See Mueller, *Retreat from Doomsday*, 249.

Despite this, most scholars have conceptualized deterrence as a threat-based influence strategy. Thus Paul Huth writes, "I define deterrence as a policy that seeks to persuade an adversary, through the threat of military retaliation, that the costs of using military force to resolve political conflict will outweigh the benefits. A policy of deterrence, then, seeks to prevent an adversary from using military force to achieve foreign policy objectives through the threat of a counterattack" (Huth, *Extended Deterrence and the Prevention of War*, 15). For a variety of similar definitions, see Morgan, *Deterrence: A Conceptual Analysis*, 18–24.

55. The distinction between immediate and general deterrence receives a thorough discussion in Morgan, *Deterrence: A Conceptual Analysis*, chap. 2. The distinction between deterrence and compellence was first articulated by Schelling in *Arms and Influence*, 69–91.

56. An anonymous reviewer of the manuscript for this book suggested that the French withdrawal at Fashoda and the Soviet decision to remove its nuclear missiles from Cuba were cases of "strategic surrender" rather than appeasement. As originally defined by Paul Kecskemeti, strategic surrender is a policy of conceding defeat in war in order to avoid incurring the losses associated with a final, futile military engagement. See Kecskemeti, *Strategic Surrender*. Neither French policy in the Fashoda Crisis nor Soviet policy in the Cuban Missile Crisis meets Kecskemeti's definition because neither constituted capitulation in war. The concept of strategic surrender might, of course, be broadened to cover crises in which one party backed down in order to avert a conflict it felt certain to lose. However, in such cases the aims of an appeasement strategy—reduction of tensions and some modification of behavior on the part of the adversary—are clearly present. For this reason, strategic surrender in a crisis seems most appropriately viewed as a subcategory of appeasement, not a different policy altogether.

57. Schroeder, "Munich and the British Tradition," 224.

58. See especially Lebow and Stein, "Beyond Deterrence." Reassurance theory bears considerable resemblance and owes a considerable debt to the so-called "spiral model" of international politics, which also identifies insecurity as the source of aggressive behavior and prescribes conciliatory policies as a remedy. Early spiral theorists came largely from the fields of psychology and sociology, and include, among others, Osgood, *Alternative to War or Surrender;* and Etzioni, *Hard Way to Peace.* An excellent elaboration and analysis of the spiral model can be found in Jervis, *Perception and Misperception,* chap. 3. See also Glaser, "Political Consequences of Military Strategy."

59. See also the chapter "Reforming Outlaw States and Rogue Leaders" in George, *Bridging the Gap.*

60. George and Smoke first elaborated this methodology, which they termed "focused comparison," in *Deterrence in American Foreign Policy,* 95–97. It was refined, and renamed, by George in subsequent works. For the clearest explication, see George, "Case Studies and Theory Development" (1979); and George, "Case Studies and Theory Development" (1982).

61. On the comparative method, see, among others, Lijphart, "Comparative Politics and the Comparative Method"; Lijphart, "Comparable-Cases Strategy in Comparative Research"; Przeworski and Teune, *Logic of Comparative Social Inquiry;* and Skocpol and Somers, "Uses of Comparative History in Macrosocial Inquiry." The single best treatment of the comparative method is found in George, "Case Studies and Theory Development" (1982).

62. George and Smoke, *Deterrence in American Foreign Policy,* 96, 513, 519, 632–40.

63. The best-developed critique is Achen and Snidal, "Rational Deterrence Theory and Comparative Case Studies." As the title of the essay suggests, Achen and Snidal's argument is developed specifically in connection with deterrence theory. However, they intend it to apply in other contexts as well.

64. Achen and Snidal, "Rational Deterrence Theory and Comparative Case Studies." Virtually all works on the comparative method, including those by advocates, discuss these weaknesses.

65. See especially the following responses to the essay by Achen and Snidal: George and Smoke, "Deterrence and Foreign Policy"; Jervis, "Rational Deterrence: Theory and Evidence"; and Lebow and Stein, "Rational Deterrence Theory: I Think, Therefore I Deter."

66. This argument is made persuasively by George and Smoke in *Deterrence in American Foreign Policy,* 97, 628–42.

67. Achen and Snidal, "Rational Deterrence Theory and Comparative Case Studies," 167.

68. See Bennett and George, *Case Studies and Theory Development,* for a detailed examination of the strengths and limitations of case studies in the development of theory.

69. As the reader will later note, in order to avoid a mechanistic, repetitive presentation, I refrain from listing formally the questions and their answers in the case studies. Nevertheless, both questions and answers are implicit in the text and should be readily apparent.

70. On Tit-for-Tat, see Axelrod, *Evolution of Cooperation.* On GRIT (Graduated Reciprocation In Tension-reduction), see Osgood, *Alternative to War or Surrender;* and Osgood's earlier essay, "Suggestions for Winning the Real War with Communism." On the Firm-but-Flexible strategy, see Huth, *Extended Deterrence and the Prevention of War,* esp. 51–53.

71. The strategy of generosity from strength is discussed in Orme, "Circuitous Route to Peace."

72. Jervis, *Logic of Images in International Relations,* 197–201.

73. Karsten, "Response to Threat Perception."

74. Singer, "Appeasement Option," 6. It should be noted, however, that the definition of appeasement employed by Singer was a restrictive one, requiring that the states involved possess "relatively symmetric capabilities" (2).

75. White House, *National Security Strategy of Engagement and Enlargement.*

76. See, for example, Schulz, "United States and Cuba."

77. White House, *National Security Strategy of Engagement and Enlargement.* The military component of engagement, including the maintenance of existing alliances and continued deployment of troops overseas, receives particular emphasis in Nye, "Case for Deep Engagement," which articulates U.S. strategy in East Asia. At the time he wrote this essay, Nye was assistant secretary of defense for International Security Affairs.

78. See, for example, Shambaugh, "Containment or Engagement of China?" Shambaugh's notes provide an excellent guide to some of the literature on engagement.

79. On engagement with South Africa, see Coker, *United States and South Africa,* and Ungar and Vale, "South Africa." On Bush administration policy toward China, see Skidmore and Gates, "After Tienanmen."

80. Shambaugh, "Containment or Engagement of China?" 184. According to Shambaugh, the various types of engagement are distinguished from one another mainly by "the degree of punitive measures advocated for . . . violation of U.S. laws and of international rules and norms."

81. Shambaugh, "Containment or Engagement of China?" 185.

2. British Appeasement of the United States, 1896–1903

1. Gilpin, *War and Change in World Politics,* 194; Jervis, *Perception and Misperception,* 90; Lebow, "Conclusions," 223; and Kennedy, "Tradition of Appeasement in British Foreign Policy," 23–24.

2. I have previously examined the Anglo-American reconciliation, though not in connection with appeasement, in Rock, *Why Peace Breaks Out,* chap. 2. Much of the material for this chapter is drawn from that earlier study. Among the major sources on Anglo-American relations of the late nineteenth and early twentieth centuries are Bradford Perkins, *Great Rapprochement;* A.E. Campbell, *Great Britain and the United States;* Charles S. Campbell, *Anglo-American Understanding;* Gelber, *Rise of Anglo-American Friendship;* and Bertram, *Birth of Anglo-American Friendship.*

3. The best account of nineteenth-century Anglo-American relations is found in Allen, *Great Britain and the United States.*

4. Richard Olney, quoted in Bailey, *Diplomatic History of the American People,* 436.

5. Olney to Bayard, 20 July 1895, *Congressional Record,* 54th Cong., 1st sess., 28: 191–96.

6. Salisbury to Pauncefote, 26 November 1895, *Congressional Record,* 54th Cong., 1st sess., 28: 196–99.

7. *Congressional Record,* 54th Cong., 1st sess., 28: 191.

8. The Jameson Raid, led by Dr. Leander Starr Jameson, was part of a plan designed by Cecil Rhodes to unify South Africa under British rule. The plan called for British settlers in the Transvaal to begin an uprising. Jameson and his force would then march on Johannesburg under the pretext of defending the settlers' lives and property. However, the uprising never materialized, and the raiders were intercepted by the Boers and forced to surrender before reaching their destination.

9. Grenville, *Lord Salisbury and Foreign Policy*, 68. See also Grenville and Young, *Politics, Strategy, and American Diplomacy*, 170.

10. *Parliamentary Debates*, 4th ser., 37 (1896): 109–10.

11. Good accounts of Anglo-American diplomacy concerning an isthmian canal are in A.E. Campbell, *Great Britain and the United States*, 48–88; and Charles S. Campbell, *Anglo-American Understanding*, 213–39.

12. Good accounts of the Alaskan boundary dispute, and its resolution, are in A.E. Campbell, *Great Britain and the United States*, 89–126; and Bradford Perkins, *Great Rapprochement*, 162–72.

13. Roosevelt to Hay, 10 July 1902, quoted in Bailey, *Diplomatic History of the American People*, 508.

14. Bailey, "Theodore Roosevelt and the Alaska Boundary Settlement," 123–26.

15. Roosevelt to Lee, 6 June 1905, Morrison (ed.), *Letters of Theodore Roosevelt*, 4: 1207.

16. A superb treatment of the role of Canada, and its vulnerability to invasion by the United States, in the history of Anglo-American diplomacy is Bourne, *Britain and the Balance of Power*. See also Brebner, *North Atlantic Triangle*.

17. Memorandum on the Defence of Canada, 12 December 1897, quoted in Grenville and Young, *Politics, Strategy, and American Diplomacy*, 173.

18. George Davis, *Navy Second to None*, 168–71; Marder, *Anatomy of British Sea Power*, 442n.

19. The best analysis of Britain's strategic predicament at the turn of the century is Monger, *End of Isolation*. See also Friedberg, *Weary Titan*.

20. Marder, *Anatomy of British Sea Power*, 257.

21. Ibid., 255.

22. Admiralty memorandum, "Defence of Canada," 24 February 1905, quoted in Bourne, *Britain and the Balance of Power*, 382, 385.

23. Mitchell, *European Historical Statistics*, 449–52; U.S. Bureau of the Census, *U.S. Statistical Abstract, 1906*, 418, 426, 429, 465–66; Great Britain, Parliament, *Parliamentary Papers*, 1903, vol. 68 (Accounts and Papers, vol. 33), "Food Supplies (Imported)," 9.

24. See, for example, Whelpley, "American Control of England's Food Supply," 804–5; Norman Angell, *Daily Mail* (London), quoted in *Literary Digest*, 14 September 1912, 411; G.S. Clarke, "England and America," 193; and Gleig, "British Food Supply in War," 161–62.

25. 6 April 1897, *Parliamentary Debates*, 4th ser., 48 (1897): 642–76.

26. War Office, "Memorandum on the standards of defence for the naval bases of Halifax, Bermuda, Jamaica, and St. Lucia," 17 September 1903, quoted in Bourne, *Britain and the Balance of Power*, 361–62.

27. The definitive treatment of Anglo-Saxonism is Anderson, *Race and Rapprochement*.

28. Quoted in Dugdale, *Arthur James Balfour*, 1: 226.

29. In fact, the final settlement was substantially in accordance with British claims.

30. "The Alaskan Award," *Spectator*, 24 October 1903, 638.

31. Grenville, *Lord Salisbury and Foreign Policy*, 385–86.

32. Ibid., 67.

33. Pauncefote to Salisbury, 20 January 1899, quoted in Grenville, *Lord Salisbury and Foreign Policy*, 377, emphasis added.

34. Memorandum of 13 December 1900, quoted in Grenville, *Lord Salisbury and Foreign Policy*, 383.

35. Roosevelt to Holmes, 25 July 1903, Morrison (ed.), *Letters of Theodore Roosevelt*, 3:

530. Roosevelt was convinced that this letter played a key role in Britain's decision to capitulate. See Roosevelt to Holmes, 20 October 1903, *Letters of Theodore Roosevelt*, 3: 634.

36. Nevins, *Henry White*, 197.

37. Bayard to Gresham, quoted in McElroy, *Grover Cleveland*, 2: 178.

38. Lodge to White, 18 December 1900, quoted in Nevins, *Henry White*, 155.

39. Hay to Choate, 15 January 1900, quoted in Thayer, *Life and Letters of John Hay*, 2: 223.

40. Lodge to White, 18 December 1900, quoted in Nevins, *Henry White*, 155.

41. George Davis, *Navy Second to None*, 168–71; Marder, *Anatomy of British Sea Power*, 442n.

42. See Monger, *End of Isolation*, 8–10.

43. Kennedy, *Rise and Fall of British Naval Mastery*, 209.

44. Selborne to Curzon, 19 April 1901, quoted in Monger, *End of Isolation*, 72n.

45. Bourne, *Britain and the Balance of Power*, 341, 369–70.

46. Lebow, *Between Peace and War*.

47. Glaser, "Political Consequences of Military Strategy."

48. Roosevelt to Taft, 21 August 1907, Morrison (ed.), *Letters of Theodore Roosevelt*, 5: 761.

49. Healy, *US Expansionism*, 52.

50. May, *American Imperialism*, 222–23.

51. Dunning, *British Empire and the United States*, 291.

52. Allen, *Great Britain and the United States*, 175.

53. Spring Rice to Villiers, 12 April 1895, Gwynn (ed.), *Letters and Friendships of Sir Cecil Spring Rice*, 1: 175. Mary Leiter was shortly to marry Lord Curzon, a prominent British noble and diplomat.

54. Olney to Bayard, 20 July 1895, *Congressional Record* (Senate), 17 December 1895, 54th Cong., 1st sess., 28: 195.

55. 20 December 1895, *Congressional Record* (Senate), 54th Cong., 1st sess., 28: 259. Stewart was only one of many in Congress and in the press who saw the Venezuelan question as a matter of "honor" and the "assertion of manhood."

56. For a history of the Monroe Doctrine, see Dexter Perkins, *Hands Off*; and Dexter Perkins, *Monroe Doctrine*.

57. Thomas Bayard, private memorandum, 10 January 1896; quoted in Nevins, *Grover Cleveland*, 644.

58. A good account of Scruggs's background and his influence is found in Grenville and Young, *Politics, Strategy, and American Diplomacy*, chap. 5, "The Diplomat as Propagandist: William Lindsay Scruggs, Agent for Venezuela."

59. Scruggs, *Venezuelan Question*, 32.

60. Grenville and Young, *Politics, Strategy, and American Diplomacy*, 163.

61. Wheeler and Grosvenor, "Our Duty in the Venezuelan Crisis," 630.

62. *Atlanta Constitution*, 13 October 1895, quoted in Tansill, *Foreign Policy of Thomas Bayard*, 711.

63. Lodge, "England, Venezuela, and the Monroe Doctrine," 657–58.

64. British leaders did not prefer a pure inducement strategy. They moved in the direction of this strategy only when it became obvious that a policy requiring reciprocity on the part of the United States was unlikely to succeed. The sensitivity of British policymakers to U.S. responses to their appeasement policy and their willingness to adjust it as necessary were crucial to the outcome in this case.

65. Bradford Perkins, *Great Rapprochement*, 7.

66. Ibid., 167.

67. "The Nicaragua Scandal," *Saturday Review*, 22 December 1900, 782–83.

68. Harvey, "United States and Great Britain," 536.

69. "The Alaskan Surrender," *Saturday Review,* 31 January 1903, 128.

70. *Philadelphia Press,* quoted in *Public Opinion* 20 (23 January 1896): 107.

71. *New York Tribune,* quoted in *Public Opinion* 21 (19 November 1896): 646.

72. Salisbury's address to the House of Lords, 17 July 1896, *Parliamentary Debates,* 4th ser., 43 (1896): 5.

73. On the shift in American attitudes toward Britain beginning in early 1896, see Stephen Rock, *Why Peace Breaks Out,* 26–28.

74. Pauncefote to Salisbury, 26 May 1898, quoted in Charles S. Campbell, *Anglo-American Understanding,* 49.

75. Reginald Tower, memo enclosed in Pauncefote to Salisbury, 27 May 1898, quoted in Charles S. Campbell, *Anglo-American Understanding,* 50.

76. Olney's speech, which he delivered on 2 March, subsequently appeared in print as Olney, "International Isolation of the United States."

77. Memo by de Kay, 1 February 1896, quoted in Vagts, *Deutschland und die Vereinigten Staaten,* 1: 619.

78. Herbert to Lansdowne, 29 December 1902, Great Britain, Foreign Office, *British Documents on the Origins of the War,* 2: 164.

79. Roosevelt to Lodge, 27 March 1901, Lodge (ed.), *Selections from the Correspondence of Roosevelt and Lodge,* 1: 485.

80. Adams, "Spanish War and the Equilibrium of the World," 645.

81. U.S. Bureau of the Census, *Historical Statistics of the United States,* 550–53; U.S. Bureau of the Census, *Statistical Abstract of the United States, 1906,* 418, 427–28.

82. Harvey, "United States and Great Britain," 533.

83. Bacon, "American International Indebtedness," 276.

84. LaFeber, "American Business Community and Cleveland's Venezuelan Message," 396–97. LaFeber argues that the crash was more the consequence of a long-term weakness in the dollar than of the Venezuelan crisis; furthermore, its economic impact was limited because domestic American capital quickly filled the vacuum created by British withdrawals.

85. *Economist,* 4 January 1896, 15.

86. Pauncefote to Salisbury, 24 December 1895, quoted in Mowat, *Life of Lord Pauncefote,* 186.

87. For a complete discussion of the role of Anglo-Saxon nationalism in the relations of Britain and the United States during this period see Anderson, *Race and Rapprochement.*

88. Gelber, *Rise of Anglo-American Friendship,* 102.

89. Quoted in Washburn, "Memoir of Henry Cabot Lodge," 342.

3. British Appeasement of Germany, 1936–1939

1. One of the great difficulties in assessing how Chamberlain felt about Hitler is that his views tended to fluctuate. Although he frequently expressed his distrust of the German chancellor, there were also times when he argued (and perhaps believed) that Hitler could be relied upon to keep his word.

2. On the report of the Defence Requirements Committee, see Gibbs, *Rearmament Policy,* 93–127.

3. "Memorandum by Sir R. Vansittart on the Future of Germany," 7 April 1934, *DBFP, 1919–1939,* 2nd ser., 6: 975–90.

4. "Memorandum by Sir R. Vansittart on the Present and Future Position in Europe," 28 August 1933, *DBFP, 1919–1939,* 2nd ser., 5: 552.

5. Entry of 28 July 1934, quoted in Feiling, *Life of Neville Chamberlain,* 253.

6. Quoted in William Rock, *British Appeasement in the 1930s,* 46.

7. It should be noted that public opinion was influenced considerably by the Chamberlain cabinet's manipulation of the press, which overemphasized German strength and understated British capabilities, thereby exaggerating the difficulties of confronting Germany. The press also tended to overstate the prospects for successful appeasement. See Cockett, *Twilight of Truth.*

8. On the attitude of Commonwealth leaders and the pressure for a conciliatory approach they exerted on British policy, see Ovendale, *"Appeasement" and the English Speaking World;* and Weinberg, *Foreign Policy of Hitler's Germany,* 14–16.

9. On the attitude of the United States and the British government's belief that the United States could not be relied upon to support Britain in opposing Hitler, see Reynolds, *Creation of the Anglo-American Alliance,* 10–36; William Rock, *Chamberlain and Roosevelt;* and Ovendale, *"Appeasement" and the English Speaking World.*

10. Schroeder, "Munich and the British Tradition," 242.

11. In conversation with Thomas Jones, 28 April 1934, quoted in Jones, *Diary with Letters,* 129.

12. Henderson to Halifax, 1 April 1938, *DBFP, 1919–1939,* 3rd ser., 1: 109. See also Henderson's dispatches of 20 April and 12 May 1938, *DBFP, 1919–1939,* 3rd ser., 1: 174, 286–87.

13. Wendt, "'Economic Appeasement'—A Crisis Strategy," 161.

14. Overy, *War and Economy in the Third Reich,* 208.

15. Wendt, *Economic Appeasement,* 75.

16. A good discussion of attempts to cultivate the moderates is MacDonald, "Economic Appeasement and the German 'Moderates,'" 105–35.

17. "Memorandum by N. Chamberlain on Anglo-German Relations," 2 April 1937, *DBFP, 1919–1939,* 2nd ser., 18: 555.

18. Lanyi, "Problem of Appeasement," 319.

19. Quoted in Weinberg, *Foreign Policy of Hitler's Germany,* 96–97.

20. A good account is in Weinberg, *Foreign Policy of Hitler's Germany,* 67–77, 95–141.

21. Eden to Leith-Ross, 19 January 1937, *DBFP, 1919–1939,* 2nd ser., 18: 120.

22. Leith-Ross's report of his conversation with Schacht is printed in *DBFP, 1919–1939,* 2nd ser., 18: 188–95.

23. Halifax to Phipps, 11 February 1937, *DBFP, 1919–1939,* 2nd ser., 18: 221–25.

24. Eden to Phipps, 27 April 1937, *DBFP, 1919–1939,* 2nd ser., 18: 678.

25. The German record of this conversation is in *DGFP, 1918–1945,* ser. D, 1: 55.

26. *DGFP, 1918–1945,* ser. D, 1: 61.

27. Ibid., 64.

28. Summary of cabinet discussion of 24 November 1937, *DBFP, 1919–1939,* 2nd ser., 19: 573.

29. Halifax's report on his visit to Germany, *DBFP, 1919–1939,* 2nd ser., 19: 548.

30. Memorandum enclosed in Ribbentrop to Henderson, 4 March 1938, *DGFP, 1918–1945,* ser. D, 1: 242.

31. For these instructions see Eden to Henderson, 12 February 1938, Eden to Henderson, 16 February 1938, and Halifax to Henderson, 27 February 1938, *DBFP, 1919–1939,* 2nd ser., 19: 890–92, 908, 976. In mid-February, Eden resigned as foreign secretary and was

replaced by Halifax. Eden, who preferred a tougher line toward Germany and Italy than did Chamberlain, had come to be regarded (along with the Foreign Office generally) by the prime minister as a chief obstacle to the success of his appeasement policy.

32. *DGFP, 1918–1945,* ser. D, 1: 243.

33. Ibid., 247.

34. Ibid., 243.

35. Henderson to Halifax, 5 March 1938, *DBFP, 1919–1939,* 2nd ser., 19: 994.

36. Henderson to Halifax, 4 March 1938, *DBFP, 1919–1939,* 2nd ser., 19: 987.

37. MacDonald, "Economic Appeasement and the German 'Moderates,'" 114–15.

38. German Foreign Ministry to German Embassies in Italy, Great Britain, France, and the United States, 22 November 1937, *DGFP, 1918–1945,* ser. D, 1: 69.

39. There is some evidence that Chamberlain remained inclined to continue a "piece-meal" appeasement strategy toward Germany even after the Nazis' seizure of Czechoslo-vakia. Sir John Simon recorded in his diary that Chamberlain was prepared to consider a "Polish Munich" on 2 September 1939. However, the cabinet was so adamantly opposed that the prime minister was precluded from pursuing such an agreement. William Rock, personal correspondence to author.

40. See Newton, *Profits of Peace,* for an excellent discussion of Anglo-German eco-nomic relations as well as economic conditions in Britain, Germany, and Europe more generally.

41. Eden recognized that increasing Germany's economic strength would increase its capacity to commit aggression, and for this reason he was careful to argue that Britain should make concessions only within the framework of a broader settlement that would include arms limitations and Germany's return to the League of Nations. Eden, *Facing the Dictators,* 362–63.

42. I do not mean to suggest that this was the only basis for German policy, or even necessarily the most important one. Clearly, Hitler's ambitions were also driven by other factors, including his racial theories and his own personal need for power.

43. Overy, *War and Economy in the Third Reich,* chap. 7.

44. Quoted in Carroll, *Design for Total War,* 96.

45. Ibid., 102. There has long been a debate between realist and liberal theorists of international politics regarding the effects of economic interdependence. Realists have seen it as a source of vulnerability and a cause of conflict, while liberals have seen it as a source of common interests and a cause of peace. Hitler's view, of course, supports the realist claim, but one recent analysis suggests that both realists and liberals are sometimes right (and wrong), depending on the circumstances. See Copeland, "Economic Interde-pendence and War."

46. Carroll, *Design for Total War,* 95–96.

47. Hitler, *Mein Kampf,* 3.

48. Ibid., 181.

49. Hillgruber, *Germany and the Two World Wars,* 50.

50. Quoted in Henderson to Halifax, 5 March 1938, *DBFP, 1919–1939,* 2nd ser., 19: 994.

51. Henderson, memorandum of 12 September 1937, *DBFP, 1919–1939,* 2nd ser., 19: 288. See also memo of 4 October enclosed in Henderson to Eden, 10 October 1937, *DBFP, 1919–1939,* 2nd ser., 19: 388.

52. Kennedy, "Mahan *versus* Mackinder," 34–85; and Stephen Rock, *Why Peace Breaks Out,* 71–73.

53. Hitler, *Hitler's Secret Book*, 74.

54. Frank, *Im Angesicht des Galgens*, 230.

55. Weinberg, *Foreign Policy of Hitler's Germany*, 1.

56. See below.

57. Murray, *Change in the European Balance of Power*, 4.

58. In fact, as Murray points out, Germany's war effort *was* significantly weakened by the imposition of a blockade by its enemies. See Murray, *Change in the European Balance of Power*, 326–34.

59. In 1936, Hitler authorized a Four-Year-Plan, which called for expanding the exploitation of domestic raw materials and increasing production of synthetic substitutes. As Carroll notes, the plan was not itself intended to achieve autarky, but to prepare the German economy for the wars of conquest that would make Germany self-sufficient. Carroll, *Design for Total War*, chap. 7.

60. Carroll, *Design for Total War*, 102.

61. Quoted in Carroll, *Design for Total War*, 104.

62. Ibid.

63. Weinberg, *Foreign Policy of Hitler's Germany*, 2.

64. *Parliamentary Debates* (Commons), 5th ser., 311: 735, and 317: 355–56.

65. William Rock, *Neville Chamberlain*, 215.

66. Ibid.

67. For a good discussion of Plan Z, see Fuchser, *Neville Chamberlain and the Pursuit of Appeasement*, 136–41.

68. Fuchser, *Neville Chamberlain and the Pursuit of Appeasement*, 144; Taylor, *Munich: Price of Peace*, 749, 822.

69. Fuchser, *Neville Chamberlain and the Pursuit of Appeasement*, 179.

70. Alexandroff and Rosecrance, "Deterrence in 1939," 406.

71. Another aspect of British policy during the 1930s which largely ruled out a deterrent strategy was the failure of British policymakers to strengthen relations with potential allies: France, the United States, and the Soviet Union. The chiefs of staff advised in 1937 that it was essential for Britain to "draw her friends closer to her" (William Rock, personal correspondence with author). But little was done in this regard. To be fair, how much could have been done is open to question, especially in view of France's desire not to provoke Germany, isolationist sentiment in the United States, and the extreme ideological gulf between Great Britain and the Soviet Union.

72. Huth, *Extended Deterrence and the Prevention of War*, 137.

73. Dirksen to German Foreign Ministry, London, 10 July 1939, *DGFP, 1918–1945*, 6: 892.

74. *DGFP, 1918–1945*, ser. D, 7: 141.

75. Ibid., 297.

76. Seligo, "Political Situation Report," transmitted to the chief of the Reich Chancellery, 7 July 1939, *DGFP, 1918–1945*, ser. D, 6: 876. Löwisch, memorandum of 24 August 1939, *DGFP, 1918–1945*, ser. D, 7: 301–2. See also Bräuer, the chargé d'affaires in France, to the Foreign Ministry, 25 August 1939, *DGFP, 1918–1945*, ser. D, 7: 303–4.

77. Weizsäcker, diary entry of 23 August 1939, *Weizsäcker-Papiere*, 159–60.

78. Weizsäcker, diary entry of 25 August 1939, *Weizsäcker-Papiere*, 160.

79. *TMWC*, 39: 107.

80. Dahlerus's paraphrase; memorandum of 24 July 1939, *DBFP, 1919–1939*, 3rd ser., 6: 748.

81. Hesse, *Hitler and the English,* 79. It is, of course, possible that Hess and especially Ribbentrop were saying one thing to Hesse and quite another to Hitler.

82. The attitude of the German generals is more difficult to determine. However, according to Wilhelm Keitel, chief of the Armed Forces High Command, by May 1939 German military leaders believed Britain and France would come to Poland's aid. See Keitel's testimony at Nuremberg in *TMWC,* 10: 514. The great lengths to which Hitler apparently felt forced to go in order to convince his generals that the Western Powers would not intervene (see below) supports Keitel's assertion.

83. An account of the 14 August address is contained in extracts from the notebook of Gen. Franz Halder, chief of the Army General Staff, *DGFP, 1918–1945,* ser. D, 7: 551–56. Three accounts of the 22 August address exist: an unsigned memorandum, *DGFP, 1918–1945,* ser. D, 7: 200–206, and *TMWC,* 26: 338–44; the notes of Hermann Böhm, *TMWC,* 41: 16–25; and Halder's notebook, *DGFP, 1918–1945,* ser. D, 7: 557–59.

84. Extract from Halder notebook, *DGFP, 1918–1945,* ser. D, 7: 555.

85. Report by Lochner of the Associated Press, contained in Ogilvie-Forbes to Kirkpatrick, 25 August 1939, *DBFP, 1919–1939,* 3rd ser., 7: 258.

86. The allusion here is, of course, to *Hamlet,* act 3, scene 2, wherein the queen utters her famous line: "The lady protests too much, methinks."

87. Aigner, *Ringen um England,* 64. Similarly, Josef Henke has argued that Hitler's statements can be read as "efforts to soothe an army leadership which regarded Hitler with suspicion." Henke, *England in Hitlers politischen Kalkül,* 288. Henke contends that Hitler firmly believed in the probability of Anglo-French intervention and that his remarks on 22 August were a "show of artificial confidence" (289).

88. Henke, *England in Hitlers politischen Kalkül,* 265–66.

89. Ibid., 274. Hesse had apparently been informed of Hitler's views by Ribbentrop (278, note 153).

90. Huth, for example, writes that by the afternoon of 25 August, "Hitler's calculation that Britain would back down in the end was shattered." By 1 September, Hitler had decided to attack Poland "even at the risk of war with Britain." Huth, *Extended Deterrence and the Prevention of War,* 135, 136.

91. Chamberlain to Hitler, 22 August 1939, *DBFP, 1919–1939,* 3rd ser., 7: 170–71.

92. Jodl, diary entry of 24 August 1939, quoted in Henke, *England in Hitlers politischen Kalkül,* 288.

93. Weizsäcker wrote in his diary on 23 August, "The Führer reckons that on August 24, with the news of our coup in Moscow, Chamberlain will be ousted and the idea of the guarantee abandoned." *Weizsäcker-Papiere,* 159.

94. Mussolini to Hitler, 25 August 1939, *DGFP, 1918–1945,* ser. D, 7; 285–86. The Italian dictator did offer to fight if Germany would furnish her with military supplies and raw materials he deemed necessary to combat Britain and France. The list, submitted on 26 August, was, however, too extensive for the Germans—perhaps as Mussolini intended. See *DGFP, 1918–1945,* ser. D, 7: 309–10.

95. Keitel, *Memoirs,* 89. See also Göring's testimony at Nuremberg in *TMWC,* 9: 596–97.

96. Operation White (*Fall Weiß*) was the German code for the invasion of Poland. There has been some question as to whether the decisive factor leading Hitler to postpone Operation White was the signing of the Anglo-Polish Treaty or Italy's refusal to stand with Germany. Jodl and Göring testified at Nuremberg that the crucial factor was the conclusion of the Anglo-Polish Treaty. See *TMWC,* 15: 422, and 9: 597. See also Hesse's

account of his 27 August meeting with Ribbentrop, Hess, and Göring in Hesse, *Hitler and the English,* 79. Logic suggests that the signing of the Anglo-Polish Treaty is necessary, if not sufficient, to explain Hitler's decision, since Italian assistance would presumably have mattered only if Britain (and France) were expected to enter the war on Poland's behalf. In any event, the two were clearly linked in Hitler's mind.

97. Hitler to Mussolini, 26 August 1939, *DGFP, 1918–1945,* ser. D, 7: 314. See also Hitler to Mussolini, 27 August 1939, *DGFP, 1918–1945,* ser. D, 7: 347.

98. Franz Halder, diary extract, 28 August 1939, *DGFP, 1918–1945,* ser. D, 7: 565.

99. Franz Halder, diary extract, 31 August 1939, *DGFP, 1918–1945,* ser. D, 7: 569. Additional confirmation that Hitler now believed the Anglo-French threat to intervene is provided by Dahlerus, who reported on 29 August that, according to Göring, "Hitler was fully alive to fact that Great Britain was not bluffing." Henderson to Halifax, 29 August 1939, *DBFP, 1919–1939,* 3rd ser., 7: 360.

100. The German text of this document is in *TMWC,* 34: 456–59. English translations are in Nuernberg Military Tribunals, *Trials of War Criminals,* 10: 704–5; and *DGFP, 1918–1945,* ser. D, 7: 477–79.

101. One of the accounts, the unsigned memorandum, does record Hitler as stating that "Our enemies are little worms. I saw them in Munich." *TMWC,* 26: 343. See also *DGFP, 1918–1945,* ser. D, 7: 204.

102. For a good discussion of this in the international relations literature, see Lebow, *Between Peace and War,* 102–12.

103. It might be argued that Hitler did not misperceive the Anglo-French commitment to Poland at all. For although the Western Powers formally declared war on Germany two days after the invasion of Poland, they made no effort to render substantial military assistance to that country. Had Germany not attacked France in May of 1940, Britain and France might never have become involved. See Mearsheimer, *Conventional Deterrence,* chap. 3.

104. Hofer, *War Premeditated,* 55.

105. Ibid.; Craig, *From Bismarck to Adenauer,* 110–23.

106. Quoted in Kordt, *Nicht aus den Akten,* 332.

107. Dahlerus, *Last Attempt,* 119.

108. Erich Kordt to Weizsäcker, 21 September 1938, *DGFP, 1918–1945,* ser. D, 2: 864.

109. Helmuth Groscurth, diary entry of 27 September 1938, in Groscurth, *Tagebücher eines Abwehroffiziers,* 125.

110. On Hitler's desire for war, see also Murray, *Change in the European Balance of Power,* 204–5.

111. The British record of this meeting is in *DBFP, 1919–1939,* 3rd ser., 2: 338–51; the German record is in *DGFP, 1918–1945,* ser. D, 2: 786–98.

112. British records of the Godesberg meetings are found in *DBFP, 1919–1939,* 3rd ser., 2: 463–73, 499–508; German records are in *DGFP, 1918–1945,* ser. D, 2: 870–79, 898–908. The German demands were laid out in a memorandum presented to Chamberlain on 23 September. See *DGFP, 1918–1945,* ser. D, 2: 908–10.

113. For a record of Anglo-French discussions of the Godesberg demands, see *DBFP, 1919–1939,* 3rd ser., 2: 520–35, 536–41. On the British side, the decision to reject Hitler's demands was contrary to Chamberlain's wishes and was essentially forced upon him by a rebellious cabinet. See Murray, *Change in the European Balance of Power,* 206–8.

114. *DBFP, 1919–1939,* 3rd ser., 2: 550.

115. On 26 September, Chamberlain sent Wilson the following message: "Since you

left, French have definitely stated their intention of supporting Czechoslovakia by offensive measures if latter is attacked. This would bring us in: and it should be made plain to Chancellor that this is inevitable alternative to a peaceful solution." Halifax to Henderson, *DBFP, 1919–1939,* 3rd ser., 2: 550.

116. The British record is in *DBFP, 1919–1939,* 3rd ser., 2: 564–67; the German record is in *DGFP, 1918–1945,* ser. D, 2: 963–65.

117. For the text of the Munich Agreement, see *DBFP, 1919–1939,* 3rd ser., 2: 627–29; *DGFP, 1918–1945,* ser. D, 2: 1014–17.

118. On the differences between Hitler's Godesberg demands and the Munich Agreement—and the importance attached to these differences by members of the British government—see MacLeod, *Neville Chamberlain,* 253.

119. Although at variance with the conventional wisdom, this interpretation is not entirely novel, having been advanced recently by several historians. For a summary, see Richardson, "New Perspectives on Appeasement," 311–12. Some political scientists have also viewed the Munich Crisis as a deterrence showdown won—at least temporarily—by Britain and France. See Snyder and Diesing, *Conflict Among Nations,* 111–13; and Lebow and Stein, "Deterrence: The Elusive Dependent Variable," 364–65.

120. See Weinberg, *Foreign Policy of Hitler's Germany,* 448–53. Despite this, much of the German leadership quickly convinced itself that Britain and France would *not* have fought over Czechoslovakia, perhaps another example of the attribution of one's own weakness to one's adversary. See Weizsäcker, diary entry of 2 February 1939; *Weizsäcker-Papiere,* 149.

121. François-Poncet, *Souvenirs,* 336.

122. Dietrich, *Hitler,* 40.

123. See Weinberg, *Foreign Policy of Hitler's Germany,* 463.

124. Aigner, *Ringen um England,* 354.

125. *TMWC,* 26: 343.

126. Weinberg, *Foreign Policy of Hitler's Germany,* 654–55. See also Weinberg, "Germany, Munich, and Appeasement," 16–17.

127. *TMWC,* 41: 21.

128. Alexandroff and Rosecrance, "Deterrence in 1939." John Mearsheimer has articulated a general theory of conventional deterrence that is consistent with this interpretation. He argues that conventional deterrence is likely to fail when a potential attacker perceives the possibility of a successful blitzkrieg strategy—where short-term capabilities are crucial—but likely to succeed when it believes it would have to fight a war of attrition—in which long-term capabilities are most relevant. See Mearsheimer, *Conventional Deterrence.*

4. Anglo-American Appeasement of the Soviet Union, 1941–1945

1. Voigt, "Yalta," 104.

2. *San Francisco Examiner,* 5 April 1945, quoted in Levering, *American Opinion and the Russian Alliance,* 196–97.

3. Diary entry of 27 February 1945, Nicolson, *War Years,* 437.

4. The initial reaction in the United States to the Yalta Agreements was generally positive, even among those suspicious of the Soviet Union, but the tide of opinion began to turn within several months.

5. Reaction was particularly vehement among those with a special connection to

Poland and its prewar government. See, for example, Lane, *I Saw Poland Betrayed;* Ciechanowski, *Defeat in Victory;* Umiastowski, *Poland, Russia and Great Britain,* 292–93.

6. Lyons, "Appeasement in Yalta," 465.

7. For an excellent discussion of the historiography of American diplomacy during the Second World War, see Stoler, "Half Century of Conflict," 375–403.

8. Bullitt, "How We Won the War and Lost the Peace" (30 August 1948), 91–92.

9. Dallek, *Franklin D. Roosevelt and American Foreign Policy,* 296.

10. Welles, *Seven Decisions That Shaped History,* 143.

11. Dallek, *Franklin D. Roosevelt and American Foreign Policy,* 338.

12. Welles, *Seven Decisions That Shaped History,* 143.

13. Joint Chiefs of Staff minutes of meeting at the White House, 7 February 1943, U.S. Department of State, *Conferences at Washington and Casablanca,* 506.

14. Kennan, *Russia and the West under Lenin and Stalin,* 362.

15. Welles, *Seven Decisions That Shaped History,* 134.

16. Kimball, *The Juggler,* 40. This information appeared in the Soviet press in the spring of 1989. As Kimball notes, it has not been verified by archival materials.

17. Harriman to Roosevelt, 4 November 1943, U.S. Department of State, *Conferences at Cairo and Tehran,* 154.

18. Memorandum from Burns to Hopkins, 10 August 1943, U.S. Department of State, *Conferences at Washington and Quebec,* 625. The document from which this language was alleged to have been taken has not been found in U.S. archives.

19. Memorandum of 9 September 1944, U.S. Department of State, *Conference at Quebec,* 266.

20. Memorandum of 23 January 1945, *Malta and Yalta,* 396.

21. Report of the Combined Chiefs of Staff to President Roosevelt and Prime Minister Churchill, 9 February 1945, *Malta and Yalta,* 830.

22. Stimson and Bundy, *On Active Service in Peace and War,* 618–19.

23. On the evolution of Roosevelt's thinking regarding the nature of the postwar international organization, see Divine, *Roosevelt and World War II,* chap. 3, "Roosevelt the Realist."

24. Forrest Davis, "Roosevelt's World Blueprint." Davis continued his presentation of FDR's "great design" in a later two-piece article, "What Really Happened at Teheran." As Alex George has pointed out to me, Davis's essays may have been intended as "trial balloons." Had the articles provoked a public outcry, FDR could have shifted direction without major embarrassment since he had never officially declared the "great design" to be his policy.

25. Churchill to Roosevelt, 25 August 1944, Churchill and Roosevelt, *Roosevelt and Churchill, Their Secret Wartime Correspondence,* 567–68.

26. Roosevelt to Churchill, 26 August 1944, Churchill and Roosevelt, *Roosevelt and Churchill, Their Secret Wartime Correspondence,* 568. "U. J." of course was short for "Uncle Joe," the Anglo-American leaders' nickname for Stalin.

27. The best account of the Teheran Conference is Eubank, *Summit at Teheran.* Discussions at the Teheran Conference were not confined to the issue of Poland. Many of the meetings were devoted to debate over the timing of operation OVERLORD, the Allied invasion of Europe on the coast of Normandy, which took place in June 1944.

28. U.S. Department of State, *Conferences at Cairo and Tehran,* 596–604.

29. The best treatment of the Yalta Conference (albeit from an essentially revisionist perspective) remains Clemens, *Yalta.* See also *Malta and Yalta.*

30. For a contrary view, see Stettinius, *Roosevelt and the Russians,* 295.

31. *Malta and Yalta,* 974.

32. Ibid., 973.

33. Roosevelt to Churchill, 7 February 1944, Churchill and Roosevelt, *Roosevelt and Churchill, Their Secret Wartime Correspondence,* 430.

34. Leahy, *I Was There,* 315–16.

35. Hickerson, memo of 8 January 1945, *Malta and Yalta,* 95.

36. Gaddis, *The United States and the Origins of the Cold War,* 133–34.

37. Memorandum of conversation with Joseph Davis, 3 February 1943, *FRUS, 1943,* 3: 503.

38. State Department Advisory Committee on Postwar Foreign Policy, "Soviet Attitudes on Regional Organization," 23 September 1943, quoted in Lynn Davis, *Cold War Begins,* 85.

39. Welles, *Where Are We Heading?* 105.

40. See DeSantis, *Diplomacy of Silence,* for an excellent discussion of the views of American diplomats regarding Soviet motives and objectives.

41. Bullitt to Roosevelt, 29 January 1943, quoted in Kimball, *The Juggler,* 83.

42. Bohlen, *Witness to History,* 160–61.

43. Harriman to Hopkins, 9 September 1944, U.S. Department of State, *Conference at Quebec,* 198–99.

44. Department of State Briefing Paper, September 1944, U.S. Department of State, *Conference at Quebec,* 193.

45. Forrest Davis, "What Really Happened at Teheran," 37.

46. Conversation between Roosevelt and Austrian Archduke Otto, 15 September 1944, U.S. Department of State, *Conference at Quebec,* 368.

47. Miscamble, "Foreign Policy of the Truman Administration," 481.

48. Leahy, *I Was There,* 317–18.

49. Bullitt, "How We Won the War and Lost the Peace" (30 August 1948), 94.

50. Quoted in Eubank, *Summit at Teheran,* 39.

51. Eubank, *Summit at Teheran,* 39.

52. Lynn Davis, *Cold War Begins,* 381.

53. Minutes of Yalta Conference, recorded by Bohlen, 5 February 1945, *Malta and Yalta,* 617.

54. Quoted in Lynn Davis, *Cold War Begins,* 79.

55. Leahy to Hull, 16 May 1944, *Malta and Yalta,* 107–8.

56. Lynn Davis, *Cold War Begins,* 274–75.

57. Quoted in Edmonds, "Yalta and Potsdam," 203.

58. 27 November 1945, *Congressional Record* (Senate), 79th Cong., 1st sess., 91: 11025.

59. W. Averell Harriman, *America and Russia in a Changing World,* 69.

60. Lynn Davis, *Cold War Begins,* 373.

61. Minutes of the Sixteenth Meeting (Executive Session) of the United States Delegation to the United Nations Conference, 25 April 1945, *FRUS, 1945,* 1: 390.

62. Miscamble, "Foreign Policy of the Truman Administration," 481.

63. Roosevelt had, of course, died, while Attlee's Labour Party defeated Churchill's Conservatives in a late-July election. Churchill, in fact, was replaced by Attlee in the middle of the Potsdam negotiations.

64. The literature on containment is vast. The best history of the policy remains Gaddis, *Strategies of Containment.* A good recent work is Larson, *Origins of Containment.*

65. *FRUS, 1977,* 1: 237, 283–84. NSC-68 remained classified until 1975.

66. Stoler, "Half Century of Conflict."

67. Bullock, *Hitler and Stalin,* 871.

68. Taubman, *Stalin's American Policy,* 131.

69. Forrest Davis, "What Really Happened at Teheran," 37.

70. Eubank, *Summit at Teheran,* 485.

71. Djilas, *Conversations with Stalin,* 73.

72. Stalin to Roosevelt, 3 April 1945, *FRUS, 1945,* 3: 743–44.

73. Taubman, *Stalin's American Policy,* 9, 32, 39.

74. Ulam, *Expansion and Coexistence,* 399.

75. Bohlen, *Witness to History,* 124.

76. Lynn Davis, *Cold War Begins,* esp. 170–71, 370–77, 391–95.

77. Quoted in Taubman, *Stalin's American Policy,* 133. The interview was published in the *Washington Post,* 21–25 January 1952.

78. Taubman, *Stalin's American Policy,* 74. See also Mastny, *Russia's Road to the Cold War,* 110.

79. Mastny, *Russia's Road to the Cold War,* 72.

80. Taubman, *Stalin's American Policy,* 74.

81. Stettinius, *Roosevelt and the Russians,* 91.

82. Taubman, *Stalin's American Policy,* 9.

83. Kennan, memo of May or June 1945, "Russia's International Position at the Close of the War with Germany," *FRUS, 1945,* 5: 854.

84. Kennedy, speech at the University of Virginia Law School Forum, 12 December 1950, *Vital Speeches,* 17: 171.

85. *Economist,* 22 May 1982, 60.

86. The best analysis of the Soviet "burden of empire" is Wolf et al., *Costs of the Soviet Empire.* See also Goldman, *U.S.S.R. in Crisis,* chap. 6; and Holzman, *Soviet Economy, Past Present and Future.*

87. Mueller, "Enough Rope." George Liska has argued more generally that appeasement will weaken an adversary if the resultant territorial "advance will cause dispersion of the resources and attrition of the forward thrust of the gradually saturated if not softened expansionist" and if "the advance will activate so far unengaged dormant forces or uninvolved reserve powers." See Liska, *Russia and the Road to Appeasement,* 209.

88. For an opposing view, see Mueller, "Enough Rope." Whether and to what extent the U.S. military buildup under President Ronald Reagan helped bring about an end to the Cold War was an issue of intense debate among policymakers, politicians, and pundits. For one of the better scholarly analyses, see Chernoff, "Ending the Cold War."

89. Taubman, *Stalin's American Policy,* 74.

90. Kennan, "Sources of Soviet Conduct," 574–76.

5. American Appeasement of Iraq, 1989–1990

1. George, *Bridging the Gap,* chap. 4.

2. Brent Scowcroft, quoted in *Washington Post,* 16 July 1991.

3. The best study of U.S. policy toward Iraq in the years leading up to the invasion of Kuwait is Jentleson, *With Friends Like These.* A good, though more journalistic, account of the background of the Gulf War is Sciolino, *Outlaw State.*

4. Seymour M. Hersh, "U.S. Secretly Gave Aid to Iraq Early in Its War Against Iran," *New York Times,* 26 January 1992.

5. A concise overview of U.S. policy toward Iraq in the 1980s is Gigot, "Great American Screw-Up."

6. Waas, "What We Gave Saddam for Christmas," 35.

7. Ibid.

8. A series of articles by Douglas Frantz and Murray Waas provides a detailed examination of the Reagan and Bush administrations' policies toward Iraq and especially Bush's role in policy formulation and implementation as vice president under Reagan. See "Bush Secret Effort Helped Iraq Build Its Secret War Machine," *Los Angeles Times*, 23 February 1992; "Long History of Support for Iraq Aid," *Los Angeles Times*, 24 February 1992; "U.S. Loans Indirectly Financed Iraq Military," *Los Angeles Times*, 25 February 1992.

9. Jentleson, "Enemy of My Enemy," 19.

10. Jentleson, *With Friends Like These*, 61–62.

11. Hersh, "U.S. Secretly Gave Aid to Iraq."

12. Stuart Auerbach, "$1.5 Billion in U.S. Sales to Iraq," *Washington Post*, 11 March 1991; Waas, "What We Gave Saddam for Christmas," 33.

13. Quoted in Waas, "What We Gave Saddam for Christmas," 33.

14. Quoted in Jill Abramson and Edward T. Pound, "If Crisis Eases, Iraq Would Still Pose a Threat for Which the U.S. Must Shoulder Some Blame," *Wall Street Journal*, 7 December 1990.

15. Auerbach, "$1.5 Billion in U.S. Sales to Iraq."

16. Abramson and Pound, "If Crisis Eases, Iraq Would Still Pose a Threat."

17. Seymour M. Hersh, "U.S. Linked to Iraqi Scud Launchers," *New York Times*, 26 January 1992.

18. Waas, "What We Gave Saddam for Christmas," 27–33.

19. Ibid., 30–31.

20. Jentleson, *With Friends Like These*, 87.

21. Ibid., 86–92; Gigot, "Great American Screw-Up," 6.

22. Jentleson, *With Friends Like These*, 95.

23. Critical analyses of Bush administration policy are found in Oberdorfer, "Missed Signals in the Middle East"; and Hedges and Duffy, "Iraqgate."

24. Oberdorfer, "Missed Signals in the Middle East," 21.

25. Quoted in Elaine Sciolino, "Bush Ordered Iraqis Plied With Aid," *New York Times*, 29 May 1992.

26. Sciolino, "Bush Ordered Iraqis Plied With Aid."

27. Statement before the House Committee on Banking, Finance, and Urban Affairs, 21 May 1992, U.S. Department of State, *U.S. Department of State Dispatch*, 3 (25 May 1992): 398.

28. Oberdorfer, "Missed Signals in the Middle East," 21.

29. Frantz and Waas, "Bush Secret Effort." An Agriculture Department Memo of 13 October 1989 stated: "There are currently 10 separate investigations of BNL lending activity to Iraq. Indications are that in addition to violating United States banking laws, BNL activities with Iraq may have led to the diversion of CCC guaranteed funds for commodity programs into military sales either directly, through barter arrangements during transit, and/or through requiring fees to be paid on various transactions in violation of United States regulations. In addition payments required by Iraq of exporters wishing to participate in the Iraq market may have been diverted into acquiring sensitive nuclear technologies." U.S. Congress, House, *Iraq's Participation in Agricultural Guaranteed Loan Programs*, 52.

30. Quoted in Oberdorfer, "Missed Signals in the Middle East," 22.

31. Oberdorfer, "Missed Signals in the Middle East," 36.

32. Speech printed in *FBIS-NES-90–039*, 27 February 1990, 1–5.

33. Karsh and Rautsi, "Why Saddam Hussein Invaded Kuwait," 23.

34. Speech printed in *FBIS-NES-90–064*, 3 April 1990, 32–36.

35. Oberdorfer, "Missed Signals in the Middle East," 23, 36.

36. Ibid., 36.

37. Clyde H. Farnsworth, "Official Reported to Face Ouster After His Dissent on Iraq Exports," *New York Times*, 16 April 1991.

38. Auerbach, "$1.5 Billion in U.S. Sales to Iraq."

39. Waas, "What We Gave Saddam for Christmas," 33.

40. Auerbach, "$1.5 Billion in U.S. Sales to Iraq."

41. Abramson and Pound, "If Crisis Eases, Iraq Would Still Pose a Threat." Commerce Department officials subsequently sought to shield themselves by altering details of a list of licenses granted for exports to Iraq before submitting the list to a House subcommittee. According to one report, the "alterations included several references to the department's knowledge that goods headed for Iraq had potential military use." A particularly egregious example was a change in the designation of trucks "designed for military use" to "commercial utility cargo trucks." R. Jeffrey Smith, "Subpoenaed Committee Material Reported Altered," *Washington Post*, 12 July 1991.

42. Quoted in Gigot, "Great American Screw-Up," 9.

43. Quoted in Salinger and Laurent, *Secret Dossier*, 40.

44. Quoted in Karsh and Rautsi, "Why Saddam Hussein Invaded Kuwait," 25.

45. Gigot, "Great American Screw-Up," 10.

46. Oberdorfer, "Missed Signals in the Middle East," 40.

47. Margaret Tutwiler, quoted in Oberdorfer, "Missed Signals in the Middle East," 39.

48. Quoted in Oberdorfer, "Missed Signals in the Middle East," 39.

49. Testimony of 31 July 1990, U.S. Congress, House, *Developments in the Middle East, July 1990*, 14.

50. See, for example, Karsh and Rautsi, "Why Saddam Hussein Invaded Kuwait," 27. A transcript of Glaspie's meeting with Saddam Hussein was released by the Iraqi government. See *New York Times*, 23 September 1990, for excerpts. The ambassador subsequently denounced the transcript as "a fabrication," claiming that it did not adequately reflect the strength of the warnings she had given the Iraqi government. See *New York Times*, 21 March 1991 and 22 March 1991. Glaspie's cables to the State Department reporting on the meeting were released to the Senate Foreign Relations Committee in July 1991, and excerpts were published by the *New York Times* on 13 July. For the most part, they seem to confirm the Iraqi account. See David Hoffman, "U.S. Envoy Conciliatory to Saddam," *Washington Post*, 12 July 1991.

51. Jentleson, "Enemy of My Enemy," 37. The importance of requiring reciprocity as part of an accommodative strategy is a major theme of Jentleson, *With Friends Like These*.

52. Unnamed senior Iraqi official, quoted in Miller and Mylroie, *Saddam Hussein and the Crisis in the Gulf*, 19.

53. Miller and Mylroie, *Saddam Hussein and the Crisis in the Gulf*, 224; Saddam Hussein's speech of 24 February 1990, *FBIS-NES-90–039*, 27 February 1990, 5.

54. Remarks at a Republican campaign rally in Manchester, New Hampshire, 23 October 1990, Bush, *Public Papers*, 1449.

55. Sciolino, *Outlaw State*, 50–52, 64–69.

56. Dawisha, *Arab Radicals,* 30.

57. Quoted in Sciolino, *Outlaw State,* 132.

58. Miller and Mylroie, *Saddam Hussein and the Crisis in the Gulf,* 106.

59. Sciolino, *Outlaw State,* 111.

60. Quoted in Bulloch and Morris, *Saddam's War,* 122.

61. Stein, "Deterrence and Compellence in the Gulf," 167.

62. Dawisha, *Arab Radicals,* 41, 60–61.

63. Ibid., 62.

64. Oberdorfer, "Missed Signals in the Middle East," 21; Karsh and Rautsi, "Why Saddam Hussein Invaded Kuwait," 19.

65. Stein, "Deterrence and Compellence in the Gulf," 158.

66. Speech at a closed session of the Arab League summit, 30 May 1990, *FBIS-NES-90–139,* 19 July 1990, 21.

67. Note to the Secretary-General of the Arab League, 15 July 1990, Salinger and Laurent, *Secret Dossier,* 227.

68. Karsh and Rautsi, "Why Saddam Hussein Invaded Kuwait," 19–20.

69. Speech to closed session of Arab League Summit, 30 May 1990, *FBIS-NES-90–139,* 19 July 1990, 21.

70. Note to the Secretary-General of the Arab League, 15 July 1990, quoted in Salinger and Laurent, *Secret Dossier,* 228–30.

71. Viorst, "Report from Baghdad" (24 September 1990), 91.

72. *FBIS-NES-90–039,* 27 February 1990, 2, 4.

73. *FBIS-NES-90–103,* 29 May 1990, 5.

74. Jerrold Post, Testimony of 11 December 1990, U.S. Congress, *Persian Gulf Crisis,* 394. Post's testimony was subsequently published as Post, "Saddam Hussein of Iraq." Post is a professor of psychiatry, political psychology, and international affairs at George Washington University.

75. Viorst, "Report from Baghdad" (24 September 1990), 91.

76. Lawrence Freedman and Efraim Karsh argue that Iraq's economic difficulties provided the driving force behind the attack on Kuwait: "We do not . . . believe that Saddam would have resorted to such a desperate measure if Iraq's economic condition had not been so dire." Freedman and Karsh, *Gulf Conflict,* 61.

77. Testimony of 21 March 1991, U.S. Congress, House, *United States-Iraqi Relations* (1991), 14.

78. Viorst, "Report from Baghdad" (24 June 1991), 67.

79. Testimony of 11 December 1990, U.S. Congress, *Persian Gulf Crisis,* 394.

80. Oberdorfer, "Missed Signals in the Middle East," 36.

81. Karsh and Rautsi, "Why Saddam Hussein Invaded Kuwait," 25.

82. Miller and Mylroie, *Saddam Hussein and the Crisis in the Gulf,* 15.

83. Karsh and Rautsi, "Why Saddam Hussein Invaded Kuwait," 26.

84. Stein, "Deterrence and Compellence in the Gulf," 157.

85. Testimony of 21 March 1991, U.S. Congress, House, *United States-Iraqi Relations* (1991), 12–13.

86. 21 March 1991, U.S. Congress, House, *United States-Iraqi Relations* (1991), 13–14.

87. Minutes of this meeting, contained in a secret cable, are printed in *Congressional Record* (House), 102nd Cong., 2nd sess., 138: H864–H866.

88. Oberdorfer, "Missed Signals in the Middle East," 21.

89. Viorst, "Report from Baghdad" (24 June 1991), 64.

90. Oberdorfer, "Missed Signals in the Middle East," 22.

91. April Glaspie, diplomatic cable, quoted in Oberdorfer, "Missed Signals in the Middle East," 22.

92. Glaspie's message to Aziz, quoted in Oberdorder, "Missed Signals in the Middle East," 22.

93. Jentleson, *With Friends Like These,* 147.

94. The report is printed in U.S. Congress, Senate, *United States Policy Toward Iraq,* 12–19.

95. Excerpts from Glaspie's cable to State Department, *New York Times,* 13 July 1991.

96. Testimony of 21 March 1991, U.S. Congress, House, *United States-Iraqi Relations* (1991), 13.

97. Testimony of 15 June 1990, U.S. Congress, Senate, *United States Policy Toward Iraq,* 5–8.

98. Mylroie, "Baghdad Alternative," 350.

99. Hedges and Duffy, "Iraqgate," 48.

100. Jentleson, "Enemy of My Enemy," 25.

101. Gigot, "Great American Screw-Up," 7.

102. Frantz and Waas, "Bush Secret Effort."

103. Gigot, "Great American Screw-Up," 10.

104. Testimony of 26 April 1990, U.S. Congress, House, *United States–Iraqi Relations* (1990), 1.

105. 26 April 1990, U.S. Congress, House, *United States-Iraqi Relations* (1990), 22–23.

106. Testimony of 15 June 1990, U.S. Congress, Senate, *United States Policy Toward Iraq,* 40.

107. Frank Gaffney, quoted in David Hoffman, "U.S. Obsession with Iran Underlies Confrontation," *Washington Post,* 19 August 1990.

108. Jentleson, *With Friends Like These,* 235–36.

109. Kondracke, "Baker's Half Dozen," 11.

110. Jentleson, "Enemy of My Enemy," 45.

111. Statement before the House Committee on Banking, Finance, and Urban Affairs, 21 May 1992, U.S. Department of State, *U.S. Department of State Dispatch* 3 (25 May 1992): 398.

112. Gigot, "Great American Screw-Up."

113. See Jentleson, *With Friends Like These,* 15, 33–42.

114. Hoffman, "U.S. Obsession with Iran."

115. Testimony of 15 June 1990, U.S. Congress, Senate, *United States Policy Toward Iraq,* 30–31.

116. Oberdorfer, "Missed Signals in the Middle East," 41. One of the paradoxes of deterrence for the United States is that it may be—this case and the case of the North Korean invasion of South Korea in 1950 are examples—incapable of threatening in advance what it is capable of doing after an attack has taken place. I am indebted to Alex George for this point.

117. Quoted in Hedges and Duffy, "Iraqgate," 51.

118. Viorst, "Report from Baghdad" (24 June 1991), 64–65, 67.

119. Stein, "Deterrence and Compellence in the Gulf," 161.

120. Freedman and Karsh write that "If the Kuwaitis had taken a conciliatory line in immediate response to Saddam's demarche of 17 July and given in to his demands, then there might have been a peaceful resolution. . . . Kuwait's failure to appease Saddam confirmed its fate." Freedman and Karsh, *Gulf Conflict,* 62.

121. The need for deterrence or "deterrent credibility" to accompany efforts at ac-

commodation is a central theme of Jentleson, *With Friends Like These.*

122. Quoted in Oberdorfer, "Missed Signals in the Middle East," 41.

123. Quoted in Viorst, "Report from Baghdad" (24 June 1991), 67. Whether this after-the-fact statement can be taken at face value is, of course, open to question. At the very least, Iraqi officials were uncertain as to the "scope" of the U.S. retaliation. They may have decided to seize all of Kuwait rather than just a part in order to deprive the United States of the chance to launch a counterattack from bases in the unoccupied portion of the country. See Stein, "Deterrence and Compellence in the Gulf," 167–68.

124. For a similar conclusion, see Stein, "Deterrence and Compellence in the Gulf." Bruce Jentleson, by contrast, argues that Iraq could have been deterred from attacking Kuwait. See Jentleson, *With Friends Like These,* 203–6. However, Jentleson does not address the severe economic pressures facing Iraq. Nor does he make a convincing argument that it would have been feasible for the United States to present Iraq with a credible deterrent threat.

6. American Appeasement of North Korea, 1988–1994

1. "U.S. Stepped Up Warnings," *New York Times,* 21 November 1991.

2. Elaine Sciolino, "Clinton Ups Atom Stakes," *New York Times,* 20 October 1994. A superb study of North Korea's nuclear program and of U.S. efforts to stop it is Mazarr, *North Korea and the Bomb.*

3. U.S. Congress, Senate, *Implications of the U.S.-North Korea Nuclear Agreement,* 44.

4. Gallucci, quoted in Andrew Pollack, "North Korea to Get Plants from Rival," *New York Times,* 14 June 1995.

5. Details of the agreement, which had become known in advance, were widely reported in the American press. A good summary is in "U.S., Pyongyang Reach Accord on North's Nuclear Program," *Arms Control Today,* 25, 32.

6. *Forbes,* 21 November 1994, 35.

7. A concise history of North Korea's nuclear program, and of the U.S.-North Korean dispute over it, is provided in Reiss, *Bridled Ambition,* chap. 6. A time line of important events is found in "Promises, Promises (While Building the Bomb)," *New York Times,* 20 March 1994.

8. Statement of Leonard Spector, U.S. Congress, Senate, *Threat of North Korean Nuclear Proliferation,* 21; David E. Sanger, "Nuclear Activity by North Koreans Worries the U.S.," *New York Times,* 10 November 1991.

9. Reiss, *Bridled Ambition,* 234.

10. Sanger, "Nuclear Activity."

11. David E. Sanger, "Delay on North Korea Leaves Nasty Choices," *New York Times,* 1 December 1991.

12. See statements of Gary Milhollin and Leonard Spector in U.S. Congress, Senate, *Threat of North Korean Nuclear Proliferation,* 15–16, 22; statement of Paul D. Wolfowitz in U.S. Congress, House, *Tensions on the Korean Peninsula,* 2–3; statement of Richard Perle in U.S. Congress, House, *Policy Implications of North Korea's Ongoing Nuclear Program,* 21–22. See also Thomas W. Lippman, "Perry Offers Dire Picture of Failure to Block North Korean Nuclear Weapons," *Washington Post,* 4 May 1994.

13. This fear was not unfounded. See David E. Sanger, "South Korea, Wary of the North, Debates Building a Nuclear Bomb," *New York Times,* 19 March 1993; and Daniel Williams, "Japan Hedges on Nuclear Arms Treaty," *Washington Post,* 9 July 1993.

14. Reiss, *Bridled Ambition,* 235.

15. U.S. Congress, House, *Korea: North-South Nuclear Issues,* 4–5, 9.

16. Ibid., 11.

17. Steven R. Weisman, "Japan and North Korea Set Talks on Ties," *New York Times,* 29 September 1990. The talks began in early November.

18. Reiss, *Bridled Ambition,* 235.

19. T.R. Reid, "N. Korea Seeks Separate U.N. Membership," *Washington Post,* 29 May 1991.

20. Don Oberdorfer and T.R. Reid, "North Korea Issues Demand for Mutual Nuclear Inspections," *Washington Post,* 21 June 1991. Ten days earlier, a U.S. State Department spokesman had said that the United States would not use nuclear weapons against any signatory of the NPT, including North Korea, but Pyongyang said it regarded this assurance as "insufficient."

21. Don Oberdorfer, "U.S. Decides to Withdraw A-Weapons from S. Korea," *Washington Post,* 19 October 1991.

22. Robin Bulman, "No A-Arms in S. Korea, Roh Says," *Washington Post,* 19 December 1991.

23. Statement of Arnold Kanter, U.S. Congress, Senate, *Threat of North Korean Nuclear Proliferation,* 104.

24. David E. Sanger, "Seoul to Permit Nuclear Inspections," *New York Times,* 12 December 1991.

25. Robin Bulman, "Koreas Sign Declaration Banning Nuclear Arms," *Washington Post,* 1 January 1992.

26. *FBIS-EAS-92–004,* 7 January 1992, 9.

27. "U.S., N. Korea Meet at U.N. on Nuclear Issues," *Washington Post,* 23 January 1992.

28. Reiss, *Bridled Ambition,* 239.

29. Michael Z. Wise, "N. Korea Signs Agreement for Inspection of Nuclear Sites," *Washington Post,* 31 January 1992.

30. Don Oberdorfer, "N. Korea Releases Extensive Data on Nuclear Effort," *Washington Post,* 6 May 1992.

31. Reiss, *Bridled Ambition,* 242–43. The words "inspectors" and "inspections" were carefully avoided.

32. R. Jeffrey Smith, "N. Korea and the Bomb: High-Tech Hide-and-Seek," *Washington Post,* 27 April 1993; Albright, "How Much Plutonium Does North Korea Have?" See also the testimony by Blix in U.S. Congress, House, *North Korean Nuclear Program.*

33. Reiss, *Bridled Ambition,* 246.

34. Michael R. Gordon, "North Korea Rebuffs Nuclear Inspectors, Reviving U.S. Nervousness," *New York Times,* 1 February 1993; David E. Sanger, "In Reversal, North Korea Bars Nuclear Inspectors," *New York Times,* 9 February 1993.

35. Reiss, *Bridled Ambition,* 244.

36. Ibid., 248.

37. David E. Sanger, "West Knew of North Korea Nuclear Development," *New York Times,* 13 March 1993; Smith, "N. Korea and the Bomb."

38. R. Jeffrey Smith, "North Korea Gets More Time to Accept Nuclear Inspections," *Washington Post,* 26 February 1993. Since the IAEA lacks any enforcement capability, "further measures" presumably meant referring the case to the U.N. Security Council.

39. "North Koreans Reject Atomic Inspections," *New York Times,* 27 February 1993.

40. Nicholas D. Kristof, "A North Korean Warning," *New York Times,* 13 March 1993.

41. "Sanctions on North Korea May Get Tighter," *New York Times,* 26 March 1993.

42. Douglas Jehl, "U.S. May Bargain with Korea on Atom Issue," *New York Times,* 27 May 1993.

43. Douglas Jehl, "North Korea Says It Won't Pull Out of Arms Pact Now," *New York Times,* 12 June 1993.

44. David E. Sanger, "Clinton, In Seoul, Tells North Korea to Drop Arms Plan," *New York Times,* 11 July 1993.

45. David E. Sanger, "Squeezing North Korea: Getting Blood From a Stone," *New York Times,* 23 March 1994.

46. Testimony of 21 November 1991, U.S. Congress, House, *Policy Implications of North Korea's Ongoing Nuclear Program,* 41. Not everyone agreed with Perle's assessment. See testimony of Gen. John Wickham, which immediately followed that of Perle.

47. U.S. Congress, House, *Security Situation on the Korean Peninsula,* 19.

48. Though not particularly sympathetic to Pyongyang, Beijing was initially opposed even to discussing the issue in the U.N. Security Council. Nicholas D. Kristof, "China Opposes U.N. Over North Korea," *New York Times,* 24 March 1993. The Chinese government later softened its position somewhat. See below.

49. David E. Sanger, "North Koreans in Japan Are Seen as Cash Source For Nuclear Arms," *New York Times,* 1 November 1993, and Sanger, "Tokyo Reluctant to Levy Sanctions on North Koreans, Opposes Clinton's Plan," *New York Times,* 9 June 1994. In testimony before a congressional subcommittee, Robert Gallucci took issue with the latter article, presenting a very different picture of the Japanese position. See U.S. Congress, House, *Developments in North Korea,* 15–16, 19.

50. David E. Sanger, "U.S. Delay Urged on Korea Sanction," *New York Times,* 4 November 1993.

51. Quoted in David E. Sanger, "Seoul's Big Fear: Pushing North Koreans Too Far," *New York Times,* 7 November 1993.

52. Sanger, "Seoul's Big Fear."

53. Quoted in Sanger, "Seoul's Big Fear."

54. Quoted in David E. Sanger, "North Koreans Say Nuclear Fuel Rods Are Being Removed," *New York Times,* 15 May 1994.

55. Thomas W. Lippman, "U.S. Considered Attacks on N. Korea, Perry Tells Panel," *Washington Post,* 25 January 1995.

56. Quoted in Steven Greenhouse, "Administration Defends North Korea Pact," *New York Times,* 25 January 1995.

57. Greenhouse, "Administration Defends North Korea Pact."

58. Statement by William J. Taylor Jr. in U.S. Congress, House, *Tensions on the Korean Peninsula,* 55–56. See also Mack, "A Nuclear North Korea," 33.

59. Sanger, "Clinton, In Seoul."

60. Quoted in Sanger, "Clinton, In Seoul."

61. Statement by Jeremy J. Stone, in U.S. Congress, Senate, *Threat of North Korean Nuclear Proliferation,* 10.

62. Unnamed State Department official, quoted in Reiss, *Bridled Ambition,* 263. See also David E. Sanger, "U.S. Revising North Korea Strategy," *New York Times,* 22 November 1993.

63. Sanger, "U.S. Revising North Korea Strategy."

64. David E. Sanger, "U.S. Gets Warning From North Korea," *New York Times,* 1 December 1993.

65. David E. Sanger, "Hard Line on Arms From North Korea," *New York Times,* 18 December 1993.

66. Michael R. Gordon, "U.S. Sees Progress on Nuclear Talks with North Korea," *New York Times,* 31 December 1993.

67. David E. Sanger, "North Korea Reported to Balk at Inspection Terms," *New York Times,* 21 January 1994.

68. Michael R. Gordon, "U.S. Said to Plan Patriot Missiles for South Korea," *New York Times,* 26 January 1994.

69. Michael R. Gordon, with David E. Sanger, "North Korea's Huge Military Spurs New Strategy in South," *New York Times,* 6 February 1994.

70. "North Korea Warns U.S." *New York Times,* 6 February 1994.

71. David E. Sanger, "North Koreans Agree to Survey of Atomic Sites," *New York Times,* 16 February 1994.

72. David E. Sanger, "North Korea Said to Block Taking of Radioactive Samples From Site," *New York Times,* 16 March 1994.

73. Michael R. Gordon, "U.S. Cancels Talks With North Korea Over Atom Inspections," *New York Times,* 17 March 1994.

74. Michael R. Gordon, "U.S. Will Urge U.N. to Plan Sanctions for North Korea," *New York Times,* 20 March 1994.

75. David E. Sanger, "North Korea Bars A-Plant Survey; Threatens to Quit Nuclear Treaty," *New York Times,* 21 March 1994.

76. Michael R. Gordon, "U.S. Goes to U.N. to Increase the Pressure on North Korea," *New York Times,* 22 March 1994.

77. Paul Lewis, "U.S. and China Reach Accord at U.N. on Korean Nuclear Issue," *New York Times,* 1 April 1994.

78. Sanger, "North Koreans Say Nuclear Fuel Rods Are Being Removed."

79. Michael R. Gordon, "White House Asks Global Sanctions on North Koreans," *New York Times,* 3 June 1994.

80. "Warning from the North," *New York Times,* 7 June 1994.

81. U.S. Congress, House, *Developments in North Korea,* 29.

82. David E. Sanger, "Carter Optimistic After North Korea Talks," *New York Times,* 17 June 1994; Sanger, "Two Koreas Plan Summit Talks on Nuclear Issue," *New York Times,* 19 June 1994; Michael R. Gordon, "Back From Korea, Carter Declares The Crisis Is Over," *New York Times,* 20 June 1994.

83. Michael R. Gordon, "Clinton Offers North Korea a Chance to Resume Talks," *New York Times,* 22 June 1994.

84. Douglas Jehl, "Clinton Says the North Koreans Really May Be Ready for Talks," *New York Times,* 23 June 1994.

85. Alan Riding, "U.S. and N. Korea Say They'll Seek Diplomatic Links," *New York Times,* 13 August 1994.

86. Andrew Pollack, "Seoul Offers Help On Nuclear Power to North Korea," *New York Times,* 15 August 1994.

87. James Sterngold, "North Korea Turns Away From Nuclear Inspection Condition," *New York Times,* 21 August 1994; Andrew Pollack, "North Korea May Rebuff South's Offer," *New York Times,* 29 August 1994.

88. Alan Riding, "U.S. and North Korea Announce Pause in Talks, but No Progress," *New York Times,* 30 September 1994.

89. Steven Greenhouse, "U.S. and North Korea Agree to Build on Nuclear Accord,"

New York Times, 18 October 1994.

90. U.S. Congress, Senate, *Implications of the U.S.-North Korea Nuclear Agreement,* 47.

91. R. Jeffrey Smith, "N. Korea Accord: A Troubling Precedent?" *Washington Post,* 20 October 1994.

92. Thomas W. Lippman, "U.S. Considered Attacks on N. Korea."

93. "Mr. McCain's Risky Korea Strategy," *New York Times,* 27 October 1994. McCain had previously written a letter to the editor of the *New York Times* (28 March 1994) that condemned Clinton's "concession-laden" policy toward North Korea and said, "I take it as an article of faith that appeasement of tyrants makes war more, not less, likely."

94. U.S. Congress, Senate, *Implications of the U.S.-North Korea Nuclear Agreement,* 24.

95. See testimony of Mitchell Reiss, U.S. Congress, Senate, *Implications of the U.S.-North Korea Nuclear Agreement,* 86.

96. See, for example, Mathews, "Good Deal with North Korea."

97. U.S. Congress, Senate, *Implications of the U.S.-North Korea Nuclear Agreement,* 52.

98. Ibid., 25–26, 36.

99. David E. Sanger, "Clinton Approves a Plan to Give Aid to North Koreans," *New York Times,* 19 October 1994.

100. Robert Gallucci, statement of 9 June 1994, U.S. Congress, House, *Developments in North Korea,* 11.

101. Easily the best analysis of North Korean motives is Mazarr, *North Korea and the Bomb.* See esp. 16–34 and 182–83.

102. See, for example, the statement of Paul D. Wolfowitz, professor of national security strategy at the National War College, in U.S. Congress, House, *Tensions on the Korean Peninsula,* 2–3.

103. Statement of 21 November 1991, U.S. Congress, House, *Policy Implications of North Korea's Ongoing Nuclear Program,* 21.

104. Mack, "Nuclear North Korea," 27–29.

105. Ibid.

106. Jeremy Stone in U.S. Congress, Senate, *Threat of North Korean Nuclear Proliferation,* 5.

107. Hayes, "What North Korea Wants," 9. Hayes, the author of *Pacific Powderkeg: American Nuclear Dilemmas in Korea,* had discussed nuclear issues with North Korean leaders on several occasions.

108. Statement of William Taylor in U.S. Congress, Senate, *Threat of North Korean Nuclear Proliferation,* 80; Mack, "Nuclear North Korea," 29; David E. Sanger, "Journey to Isolation," *New York Times,* 15 November 1992.

109. Nicholas D. Kristof, "Hunger and Other Hardships Are Said to Deepen North Korean Discontent," *New York Times,* 18 February 1992.

110. Statement of William Taylor in U.S. Congress, Senate, *Threat of North Korean Nuclear Proliferation,* 80; Mack, "Nuclear North Korea," 29; Sanger, "Journey to Isolation."

111. Harrison, "North Korean Nuclear Crisis," 18.

112. William Taylor and Michael Mazarr, "Defusing North Korea's Nuclear Notions," *New York Times,* 13 April 1992.

113. Kim Dal Hyon, quoted in David E. Sanger, "North Korea Asks Investors to Look Beyond Bleakness of Communist Decay," *New York Times,* 21 May 1992.

114. See Mazarr, *North Korea and the Bomb,* esp. 16–34 and 182–83. Mazarr argues that not only did North Korea's nuclear program serve a variety of motives, but that these motives changed and evolved over time.

115. Harrison, "North Korean Nuclear Crisis," 18–19. An earlier version of this essay

was presented in testimony before a congressional subcommittee. See U.S. Congress, House, *Tensions on the Korean Peninsula*, 29–48.

116. Harrison, "North Korean Nuclear Crisis," 18. According to Reiss, Harrison's views were widely held: "*Most observers* perceived a rough division of North Korean policy elites into two factions: "hard-liners" and "pragmatists." Reiss, *Bridled Ambition*, 247; emphasis added. However, as Mazarr notes, Harrison was the "anchor [of] the liberal wing of North Korea watchers." Mazarr, *North Korea and the Bomb*, 1. Not surprisingly, conservative analysts tended to reject the liberals' assessment, instead regarding the North Korean leadership as dominated by, if not composed entirely of, hard-liners.

117. On the importance of incentives in convincing North Korea to abandon its nuclear program, see Scott Snyder, "North Korea's Nuclear Program."

118. Quoted in William Drozdiak, "N. Korea, U.S. Sign Broad Pact," *Washington Post*, 22 October 1994.

119. R. Jeffrey Smith, "N. Korea, U.S. Reach Nuclear Pact," *Washington Post*, 18 October 1994.

120. U.S. Congress, House, *Security Situation on the Korean Peninsula*, 8.

121. U.S. Congress, House, *Developments in North Korea*, 24, 31.

122. U.S. Congress, Senate, *Threat of North Korean Nuclear Proliferation*, 80.

123. For some of these points, see "North Korea's Nuclear Program: Challenge and Opportunity for American Policy," A Report of the North Korea Working Group of the United States Institute of Peace, in U.S. Congress, House, *Security Situation on the Korean Peninsula*, 58–59. North Korea's rapidly deteriorating economic condition may have given Washington and Seoul some sense of urgency regarding the conclusion of negotiations. South Korean officials particularly feared that the North Korean regime might collapse, leaving South Korea "with a multibillion-dollar bill for feeding and reindustrializing its enemy of five decades." Sanger, "U.S. Revising North Korea Strategy."

124. U.S. Congress, Senate, *Implications of the U.S.-North Korea Nuclear Agreement*, 55.

125. Ibid., 18.

126. "Don't Demonize North Korea," *New York Times*, 17 April 1991.

127. Harrison, "North Korean Nuclear Crisis," 19.

128. Ibid., 19–20.

129. Reiss, *Bridled Ambition*, 244.

130. Sanger, "Clinton, In Seoul."

131. Michael Mazarr arrives at a similar conclusion. He writes that "the evidence . . . seems overwhelming on one point: in the Korean case at least, nonproliferation policy appears to have been successful to the degree that the United States and South Korea adopted a strategy of engagement as opposed to confrontation. On balance, talking and offering incentives seem to have worked far better than threats." Mazarr, *North Korea and the Bomb*, 229–30.

132. Philip Shenon, "Breakthrough Is Announced in U.S.—North Korea Nuclear Talks," *New York Times*, 8 June 1995.

133. Pollack, "North Korea to Get Plants from Rival."

134. Andrew Pollack, "U.S. and North Korea Agree on Deal for Nuclear Reactors," *New York Times*, 13 June 1995.

135. "U.S. Korea Nuclear Accord Remains on Track Despite Incident," *Arms Control Today*, 20, 26.

136. "U.S., Allies Create Consortium for Korean Nuclear Deal," *Arms Control Today*, 28.

137. Statement by Gallucci, U.S. Congress, Senate, *Implications of the U.S.-North Korea Nuclear Agreement,* 16.

138. Don Oberdorfer, "Silence of a Strange Land," *Washington Post,* 5 February 1995.

139. See Sigal, "Averting a Train Wreck with North Korea," 11–15.

140. Oberdorfer, "Silence of a Strange Land."

141. Pollack, "North Korea to Get Plants from Rival."

142. Hayes, "What North Korea Wants," 9.

143. U.S. Congress, House, *Security Situation on the Korean Peninsula,* 24.

144. "North Korea's Nuclear Program," 59; Bracken, "Nuclear Weapons and State Survival in North Korea," 150.

145. R. Jeffrey Smith, "U.S. Accord With North Korea May Open Country to Change," *Washington Post,* 23 October 1994.

7. Toward a Theory of Appeasement

1. I do not mean to suggest here that conciliation of Nazi Germany was possible in any practical sense; in addition to the fact that Hitler sought war, his tangible ambitions were such that it was infeasible and dangerous for Britain to meet even his minimum demands.

2. Indeed, the South Korean leadership tended to act as a counterweight to U.S. policy generally. As Mazarr notes, "it seemed that whenever Washington got tough, Seoul became concerned and urged a softer line; when U.S. officials talked of compromise, South Korean leaders worried about a collapse of will and demanded a firm stance against the North." Mazarr, *North Korea and the Bomb,* 141. See also Reiss, *Bridled Ambition,* 282.

3. It is, of course, possible that a dissatisfied state might perceive concessions to be *more* rather than less important than they really are. Misperceived concessions of this type would actually be beneficial to the cause of appeasement. However, the occurrence of positive misperceptions in adversarial relationships is surely rare.

4. Tuchman, *March of Folly,* chap. 4.

5. Jervis, *Logic of Images in International Relations,* 197–98.

6. Iklé, *Every War Must End,* 115.

7. Ibid., 114–15.

8. See Larson, *Anatomy of Mistrust,* 31–34, on the problems for conciliatory policies created by mistrust. Larson's concluding chapter identifies some of the factors that may help states to overcome mistrust of one another.

9. The idea that socialization requires not simply setting an example, but also addressing a state's perceived interests, is not new. Alexander George, for example, has suggested that "rogue" states and leaders might be resocialized by offering them benefits and concessions in a strategy of "conditional reciprocity." He writes, "Insofar as possible, concessions and benefits should give leaders of the outlaw state and its people *a stake in continuing the process of conditional reciprocity and an awareness of the advantages of accepting and participating in the international system.*" George, *Bridging the Gap,* 56; emphasis added. Most students of socialization (or learning), including regime theorists, recognize that states initially develop and adhere to norms because they serve their interests. They argue, however, that over time, such norms exert influence independent of interests and may even affect how interests are defined.

10. Whether these kinds of relationships between leaders of friendly states may sometimes be beneficial in smoothing over differences is a different question. The close relationship between Ronald Reagan and Margaret Thatcher, for example, may have

contributed to enhanced Anglo-U.S. cooperation during the time they served as their countries' leaders.

11. Lebow and Stein, "Beyond Deterrence," 36.

12. It is instructive in this regard to compare British efforts to appease the United States around the turn of the century with American attempts to conciliate the Soviet Union during the 1940s and U.S. efforts to ease tensions with the Iraqi government of Saddam Hussein in the late 1980s. U.S. insecurity vis-à-vis Britain was based almost entirely on (alleged) British actions, especially in Latin America. When British behavior changed, American fears were eased. By contrast, Soviet insecurity vis-à-vis the United States and Britain, and Iraqi insecurity vis-à-vis the United States, had strong ideological components. Marxist doctrine told Soviet leaders that the capitalist United States was its mortal enemy, while Saddam Hussein, like many Muslims in the Gulf Region, subscribed to the myth of a Zionist-imperialist conspiracy directed against Iraq by Israel and the United States. Because Soviet and Iraqi fears were as much the product of a belief system as American actions, they were much more difficult to efface.

13. Some analysts argue that the U.S. military threat did help to compel North Korea to conclude the Agreed Framework with the United States. It is important to note that, if so, this threat was an implicit, background threat, not an explicit one (e.g., "if you do not abandon your nuclear weapons program, we will strike").

BIBLIOGRAPHY

Achen, Christopher, and Duncan Snidal. "Rational Deterrence Theory and Comparative Case Studies." *World Politics* 40 (January 1989): 143–69.

Adams, Brooks. "The Spanish War and the Equilibrium of the World." *Forum* 25 (August 1898): 641–51.

Aigner, Dietrich. *Das Ringen um England: Das deutsch-britische Verhältnis, Die offentliche Meinung, 1933–1939, Tragödie zweier Völker.* Munich: Bechtle Verlag, 1969.

Albright, David. "How Much Plutonium Does North Korea Have?" *Bulletin of the Atomic Scientists* 50 (September–October 1994): 46–48.

Alexandroff, Alexander, and Richard Rosecrance. "Deterrence in 1939." *World Politics* 29 (April 1977): 404–24.

Allen, H.C. *Great Britain and the United States: A History of Anglo-American Relations (1783–1952).* London: Odhams Press, 1954.

Anderson, Stuart. *Race and Rapprochement: Anglo-Saxonism and Anglo-American Relations, 1895–1904.* East Brunswick, N.J.: Associated University Presses, 1981.

Axelrod, Robert. *The Evolution of Cooperation.* New York: Basic Books, 1984.

Bacon, Nathaniel T. "American International Indebtedness." *Yale Review* 9 (November 1900): 265–85.

Bailey, Thomas A. *A Diplomatic History of the American People,* 7th ed. New York: Appleton-Century-Crofts, 1964.

———. "Theodore Roosevelt and the Alaska Boundary Settlement." *Canadian Historical Review* 18 (June 1937): 123–30.

Baldwin, David A. "The Costs of Power." *Journal of Conflict Resolution* 15 (June 1971): 145–55.

———. "Inter-nation Influence Revisited." *Journal of Conflict Resolution* 15 (December 1971): 471–86.

———. "The Power of Positive Sanctions." *World Politics* 24 (October 1971): 19–38.

———. "Thinking About Threats." *Journal of Conflict Resolution* 15 (March 1971): 71–78.

Beck, Robert J. "Munich's Lessons Reconsidered." *International Security* 14 (fall 1989): 161–91.

Bennett, Andrew, and Alexander George. *Case Studies and Theory Development.* Cambridge: MIT Press, forthcoming.

Bennett, Edward Moore. *Franklin D. Roosevelt and the Search for Victory: American-Soviet Relations, 1939–1945.* Wilmington, Del.: SR Books, 1990.

Bertram, Marshall. *The Birth of Anglo-American Friendship: The Prime Facet of the Venezuelan Boundary Dispute.* Lanham, Md.: University Press of America, 1992.

Black, Naomi. "Decision-making and the Munich Crisis." *British Journal of International Studies* 6 (October 1980): 278–303.

Blechman, Barry M., and Tamara Coffman Wittes. "Defining Moment: The Threat and Use of Force in American Foreign Policy," a work in progress prepared for the Committee on International Conflict Resolution of the National Research Council, National Academy of Sciences.

Bohlen, Charles E. *Witness to History, 1929–1969.* New York: W.W. Norton, 1973.

Bourne, Kenneth. *Britain and the Balance of Power in North America, 1815–1908.* Berkeley: University of California Press, 1967.

Bracken, Paul. "Nuclear Weapons and State Survival in North Korea." *Survival* 35 (autumn 1993): 137–53.

Brebner, John Bartlet. *North Atlantic Triangle: The Interplay of Canada, the United States, and Great Britain.* New Haven: Yale University Press for the Carnegie Endowment for International Peace, Division of Economics and History, 1945.

Bullitt, William C. "How We Won the War and Lost the Peace." *Life,* 30 August 1948, 83–97, and 6 September 1948, 86–103.

Bulloch, John, and Harvey Morris. *Saddam's War: The Origins of the Kuwait Conflict and the International Response.* London: Faber and Faber, 1991.

Bullock, Alan. *Hitler and Stalin: Parallel Lives.* New York: Alfred A. Knopf, 1992.

Bush, George Herbert Walker. *Public Papers of the Presidents of the United States, George Bush, 1990.* Washington: USGPO, 1991.

Campbell, A.E. *Great Britain and the United States, 1895–1903.* London: Longmans, Green & Co., 1960.

Campbell, Charles S. *Anglo-American Understanding, 1898–1903.* Baltimore: Johns Hopkins University Press, 1957.

Carr, E.H. *The Twenty Years' Crisis, 1919–1939: An Introduction to the Study of International Relations.* London: Macmillan & Co., 1942.

Carroll, Berenice A. *Design for Total War: Arms and Economics in the Third Reich.* The Hague: Mouton, 1968.

Chernoff, Fred. "Ending the Cold War: The Soviet Retreat and the US Military Buildup." *International Affairs* 67 (January 1991): 111–26.

Christian Science Monitor.

Churchill, Winston S. *The Gathering Storm.* Boston: Houghton Mifflin Co., 1948.

Churchill, Winston S., and Franklin D. Roosevelt. *Roosevelt and Churchill, Their Secret Wartime Correspondence.* Edited by Francis L. Loewenheim, Harold D. Langley, and Manfred Jonas. New York: Saturday Review Press, 1975.

Ciechanowski, Jan. *Defeat in Victory.* Garden City, N.Y.: Doubleday & Co., 1947.

Clemens, Diane Shaver. *Yalta.* New York: Oxford University Press, 1970.

Clarke, G.S. "England and America." *Nineteenth Century* 44 (August 1898): 186–95.

Cockett, Richard. *Twilight of Truth: Chamberlain, Appeasement and the Manipulation of the Press.* New York: St. Martin's Press, 1989.

Coker, Christopher. *The United States and South Africa, 1968–1985: Constructive Engagement and Its Critics.* Durham, N.C.: Duke University Press, 1986.

Copeland, Dale C. "Economic Interdependence and War: A Theory of Trade Expectations." *International Security* 20 (spring 1996): 5–41.

Cortright, David, ed. *The Price of Peace: Incentives and International Conflict Prevention.* Foreword by David A. Hamburg and Cyrus R. Vance. Lanham, Md.: Rowman and Littlefield, 1997.

Craig, Gordon. *From Bismarck to Adenauer: Aspects of German Statecraft.* The Albert Shaw Lectures on Diplomatic History. Baltimore: Johns Hopkins University Press, 1958.

Craig, Gordon A., and Alexander L. George. *Force and Statecraft: Diplomatic Problems of Our Time,* 2nd ed. New York: Oxford University Press, 1990.

Dahlerus, Johann Birger. *The Last Attempt.* Introduction by the Rt. Hon. Sir Norman Birkett, P.C. Translated by Alexandra Dick. London: Hutchinson & Co., n.d.

Dallek, Robert. *Franklin D. Roosevelt and American Foreign Policy, 1932–1945.* New York: Oxford University Press, 1979.

Davis, Forrest. "Roosevelt's World Blueprint." *Saturday Evening Post,* 10 April 1943, 20–21, 109–110.

———. "What Really Happened at Teheran." *Saturday Evening Post,* 13 May 1944, 12–13, 37, 39, 41; and 20 May 1944, 22–23, 44, 46, 48.

Davis, George Theron. *A Navy Second to None: The Development of Modern American Naval Policy.* New York: Harcourt, Brace, Jovanovich, 1940.

Davis, Lynn Etheridge. *The Cold War Begins: Soviet-American Conflict Over Eastern Europe.* Princeton: Princeton University Press, 1974.

Dawisha, Adeed. *The Arab Radicals.* New York: Council on Foreign Relations, 1986.

DeSantis, Hugh. *The Diplomacy of Silence: The American Foreign Service, the Soviet Union, and the Cold War, 1933–1947.* Chicago: University of Chicago Press, 1979.

Dietrich, Otto. *Hitler.* Translated by Richard and Clara Winston. Chicago: Henry Regenery Co., 1955.

Divine, Robert A. *Roosevelt and World War II.* Baltimore: Johns Hopkins University Press, 1969.

Djilas, Milovan. *Conversations with Stalin.* Translated from the Serbo-Croat by Michael B. Petrovich. New York: Harcourt, Brace & World, 1962.

Douglas, Roy. "Chamberlain and Appeasement." In Wolfgang J. Mommsen and Lothar Kettenacker, eds., *The Fascist Challenge and the Policy of Appeasement,* 79–88. London: George Allen & Unwin, 1983.

————. *In the Year of Munich.* New York: St. Martin's Press, 1977.

Draper, Theodore. "Appeasement and Detente." *Commentary* 61 (February 1976): 27–38.

Dugdale, Blanche E.C., *Arthur James Balfour, First Earl of Balfour, K.G., O.M., F.R.S., Etc.* 2 vols. New York: G.P. Putnam's Sons, 1937.

Dunbabin, John. "The British Military Establishment and the Policy of Appeasement." In Wolfgang J. Mommsen and Lothar Kettenacker, eds., *The Fascist Challenge and the Policy of Appeasement,* 174–96. London: George Allen & Unwin, 1983.

Dunning, William A. *The British Empire and the United States: A Review of Their Relations During the Century of Peace Following the Treaty of Ghent.* New York: Charles Scribner's Sons, 1914.

Eden, Anthony. *Facing the Dictators.* Boston: Houghton Mifflin Co., 1962.

"Editorial Comment: 'Poisonous' Criticism of Russia." *Catholic World* 161 (July 1945): 289–93.

Edmonds, Robin. "Yalta and Potsdam: Forty Years Afterwards." *International Affairs* 62 (spring 1986): 197–216.

Etzioni, Amitai. *The Hard Way to Peace: A New Strategy.* New York: Collier Books, 1962.

Eubank, Keith. *Munich.* Norman: University of Oklahoma Press, 1963.

————. *Summit at Teheran.* New York: William Morrow and Co., 1985.

Fearon, James D. "Signaling versus the Balance of Power and Interests: An Empirical Test of a Crisis Bargaining Model." *Journal of Conflict Resolution* 38 (June 1994): 261–65.

Feiling, Keith. *The Life of Neville Chamberlain.* London: Macmillan & Co., 1946.

François-Poncet, André. *Souvenirs d'une ambassade á Berlin, Septembre 1931– Octobre 1938.* Paris: Flammarion, 1946.

Frank, Hans. *Im Angesicht des Galgens; Deutung Hitlers und seiner Zeit auf eigener Erlebnisse und Erkenntnisse.* Munich: F.A. Beck, 1953.

Freedman, Lawrence, and Efraim Karsh. *The Gulf Conflict, 1990–1991: Diplomacy and War in the New World Order.* Princeton: Princeton University Press, 1993.

Friedberg, Aaron L. *The Weary Titan: Britain and the Experience of Relative Decline, 1895–1905.* Princeton: Princeton University Press, 1988.

Fuchser, Larry William. *Neville Chamberlain and Appeasement: A Study in the Politics of History.* New York: W.W. Norton & Co., 1982.

Gaddis, John Lewis. *Strategies of Containment: A Critical Appraisal of Postwar American National Security Policy.* Oxford: Oxford University Press, 1982.

————. *The United States and the Origins of the Cold War, 1941–1947.* New York: Columbia University Press, 1972.

Gelber, Lionel M. *The Rise of Anglo-American Friendship: A Study in World Politics, 1898–1906.* London: Oxford University Press, 1938.

George, Alexander L. *Bridging the Gap: Theory and Practice in Foreign Policy.* Washington: United States Institute of Peace Press, 1993.

———. "Case Studies and Theory Development: The Method of Structured, Focused Comparison." In Paul Gordon Lauren, ed., *Diplomacy: New Approaches in History, Theory and Policy,* 43–86. New York: Free Press, 1979.

———. "Case Studies and Theory Development." Paper presented at the Second Annual Symposium on Information Processing in Organizations, Carnegie Mellon University, Pittsburgh, 15–16 October 1982.

———. *Forceful Persuasion: Coercive Diplomacy as an Alternative to War.* Washington: United States Institute of Peace Press, 1991.

———. "The Role of Force in Diplomacy: A Continuing Dilemma for U.S. Foreign Policy," paper prepared for the Dedication Conference of the George Bush School of Government and Public Service, Texas A&M University, 9–10 September 1997.

George, Alexander, and Richard Smoke. "Deterrence and Foreign Policy." *World Politics* 41 (January 1989): 183–207.

———. *Deterrence in American Foreign Policy: Theory and Practice.* New York: Columbia University Press, 1974.

George, Alexander, and William E. Simons, eds. *The Limits of Coercive Diplomacy,* 2nd ed. Boulder: Westview Press, 1994.

Germany. Auswärtiges Amt. *Documents on German Foreign Policy, 1918–1945,* from the archives of the German Foreign Ministry, series C (1933–1937), 6 vols.; series D (1937–1945), 13 vols. Washington: USGPO, 1949–1983.

Gibbs, N.H. *Grand Strategy,* vol. 1, *Rearmament Policy.* London: HMSO, 1976.

Gigot, Paul. "A Great American Screw-Up: The U.S. and Iraq, 1980–1990." *National Interest* (winter 1990/91), 3–10.

Gilbert, Martin. *The Roots of Appeasement.* London: Weidenfeld & Nicolson, 1966.

Gilpin, Robert. *War and Change in World Politics.* Cambridge: Cambridge University Press, 1981.

Glaser, Charles. "Political Consequences of Military Strategy: Expanding and Refining the Spiral and Deterrence Models." *World Politics* 44 (July 1992): 497–538.

Gleig, Charles. "British Food Supply in War." *Naval Annual* (1898): 152–66.

Goldman, Aaron L. "Two Views of Germany: Nevile Henderson vs. Vansittart and the Foreign Office, 1937–1939." *British Journal of International Studies* 6 (October 1980): 247–77.

Goldman, Marshall I. *U.S.S.R. in Crisis: The Failure of an Economic System.* New York: W.W. Norton & Co., 1983.

Great Britain. Foreign Office. *British Documents on the Origins of the War, 1898–1914.* Edited by G.P. Gooch and Harold Temperley, with the assistance of Lillian M. Penson. 11 vols. London: HMSO, 1926–38.

Great Britain. Foreign Office. *Documents on British Foreign Policy, 1919–1939;* 1st series, 27 vols.; series 1A, 7 vols.; 2nd series, 21 vols.; 3rd series, 10 vols. London: HMSO, 1946–.

Great Britain. Parliament. *Parliamentary Debates,* 4th series.

Great Britain. Parliament. *Parliamentary Papers,* 1903, vol. 68 (Accounts and Papers, vol. 33), "Food Supplies (Imported)."

Grenville, J.A.S. *Lord Salisbury and Foreign Policy: The Close of the Nineteenth Century.* London: University of London, Athlone Press, 1964.

Grenville, J.A.S., and George Berkeley Young. *Politics, Strategy, and American Diplomacy: Studies in Foreign Policy, 1873–1917.* New Haven: Yale University Press, 1966.

Groscurth, Helmuth. *Tagebücher eines Abwehroffiziers, 1938–1940, mit weiteren Dokumenten zur Militäropposition gegen Hitler.* Edited by Helmut Krausnick and Harold C. Deutsch with the assistance of Hildegard von Kotze. Stuttgart: Deutsche Verlags-Anhalt, 1970.

Gruner, Wolf D. "The British Political, Social and Economic System and the Decision for Peace and War: Reflections on Anglo-German Relations, 1800–1939." *British Journal of International Studies* 6 (October 1980): 189–218.

Gwynn, Stephen, ed. *The Letters and Friendships of Sir Cecil Spring Rice: A Record.* Boston: Houghton Mifflin Co., 1929.

Harriman, W. Averell. *America and Russia in a Changing World: A Half Century of Personal Observation.* Introduction by Arthur M. Schlesinger Jr. Garden City, N.Y.: Doubleday & Co., 1971.

Harrison, Selig S. "The North Korean Nuclear Crisis: From Stalemate to Breakthrough." *Arms Control Today* 24 (November 1994): 18–20.

Harvey, George. "The United States and Great Britain: Their Past, Present, and Future Relations." *Nineteenth Century* 55 (April 1904): 529–37.

Hayes, Peter. "What North Korea Wants." *Bulletin of the Atomic Scientists* 49 (December 1993): 8–10.

Healy, David. *US Expansionism: The Imperialist Urge of the 1890's.* Madison: University of Wisconsin Press, 1970.

Hedges, Stephen J., and Brian Duffy. "Iraqgate." *U.S. News & World Report,* 18 May 1992, 42–51.

Henke, Josef. *England in Hitlers politischen Kalkül, 1935–1939.* Boppard: Boldt, 1973.

Herz, John. "The Relevancy and Irrelevancy of Appeasement." *Social Research* 31 (autumn 1964): 296–320.

Hesse, Fritz. *Hitler and the English.* Edited and translated by F.A. Voigt. London: Allan Wingate, 1954.

Hildebrand, Klaus. *Vom Riech zum Weltreich: Hitler, NSDAP und Koloniale Frage, 1919–1945.* Munich: Wilhelm Fink Verlag, 1969.

Hillgruber, Andreas. "England in Hitlers Aussenpolitischen Konzeption." *Historische Zeitschrift* 218 (1974): 65–84.

———. *Germany and the Two World Wars.* Translated by William C. Kirby. Cambridge: Harvard University Press, 1981.

Hitler, Adolf. *Hitler's Secret Book.* Introduction by Telford Taylor. Translated by Salvator Attanasio. New York: Grove Press, 1962.

———. *Mein Kampf.* Munich: F. Eher, 1933.

Hofer, Walther. *War Premeditated, 1939.* Translated by Stanley Godman. London: Thames and Hudson, 1955.

Holzman, Franklyn D. *The Soviet Economy: Past, Present, and Future.* Foreign Policy Association Headline Series, no. 260 (September/October, 1982).

Huth, Paul. "Extended Deterrence and the Outbreak of War." *American Political Science Review* 82 (June 1988): 423–43.

———. *Extended Deterrence and the Prevention of War.* New Haven: Yale University Press, 1988.

Huth, Paul, and Bruce Russett. "What Makes Deterrence Work? Cases from 1900 to 1980." *World Politics* 36 (July 1984): 496–526.

Iklé, Fred Charles. *Every War Must End.* New York: Columbia University Press, 1971.

International Military Tribunal (Nuremberg). *Trial of the Major War Criminals Before the International Military Tribunal,* 42 vols. Nuremberg, 1947–49.

Jentleson, Bruce W. "The Enemy of My Enemy . . . May Still be My Enemy, Too: U.S.-Iraqi Relations, 1982–1990, and the Failure of Accommodation." Paper prepared for delivery at the meeting of the American Political Science Association, 1992.

———. *With Friends Like These: Reagan, Bush, and Saddam, 1982–1990.* New York: W.W. Norton & Co., 1994.

Jervis, Robert. "Deterrence Theory Revisited." *World Politics* 31 (January 1979): 289–324.

———. *The Logic of Images in International Relations.* New York: Columbia University Press, 1970.

———. *Perception and Misperception in International Politics.* Princeton: Princeton University Press, 1976.

———. "Rational Deterrence: Theory and Evidence." *World Politics* 41 (January 1989): 183–207.

Jervis, Robert, Richard Ned Lebow, and Janice Gross Stein. *Psychology and Deterrence.* Baltimore: Johns Hopkins University Press, 1985.

Jones, R.J. Barry. "The Study of 'Appeasement' and the Study of International Relations." *British Journal of International Studies* 1 (April 1975): 68–76.

Jones, Thomas. *A Diary with Letters, 1931–1950.* London: Oxford University Press, 1954.

Karsh, Efraim, and Inari Rautsi. "Why Saddam Hussein Invaded Kuwait." *Survival* 33 (January/February 1991), 18–30.

Karsten, Peter. "Response to Threat Perception: Accommodation as a Special Case." In Klaus Knorr, ed., *Historical Dimensions of National Security Problems,* 120–63. Lawrence: University Press of Kansas for the National Security Education Program of New York University, 1976.

Kaufmann, William W. *The Requirements of Deterrence.* Policy Memorandum No. 7. Princeton: Princeton Center of International Studies, Princeton University, 1954.

Kecskemeti, Paul. *Strategic Surrender: The Politics of Victory and Defeat.* Stanford: Stanford University Press, 1958.

Keitel, Wilhelm. *The Memoirs of Field-Marshal Keitel.* Edited with introduction by Walter Gorlitz. Translated by David Irving. New York: Stein and Day, 1966.

Kennan, George F. *Russia and the West under Lenin and Stalin.* Boston: Little, Brown & Co., 1961.

———. "The Sources of Soviet Conduct." *Foreign Affairs* 25 (July 1947): 566–82.

Kennedy, Paul M. "Appeasement." In Gordon Martel, ed., *The Origins of the Second World War Reconsidered: The A. J. P. Taylor Debate After Twenty-Five Years,* 140–61. Boston: George Allen & Unwin, 1986.

———. "'Appeasement' and British Defence Policy in the Inter-war Years." *British Journal of International Studies* 4 (July 1978): 161–77.

———. "The Logic of Appeasement." *Times Literary Supplement,* 28 May 1982, 585–86.

———. "Mahan *versus* Mackinder: Two Interpretations of British Sea Power." In Kennedy, *Strategy and Diplomacy, 1870–1945: Eight Studies,* 41–86. London: George Allen & Unwin in Association with Fontana Paperbacks, 1983.

———. "Reading History: Appeasement." *History Today,* October 1982, 51–53.

———. "The (Relative) Decline of America." *Atlantic Monthly* 260 (August 1987): 29–38.

———. *The Rise and Fall of British Naval Mastery.* London: Allen Lane, 1976.

———. *The Rise and Fall of the Great Powers: Economic Change and Military Conflict from 1500 to 2000.* New York: Random House, 1987.

———. "The Study of Appeasement: Methodological Crossroads or Meeting-Place?" *British Journal of International Studies* 6 (October 1980): 181–88.

———. "The Tradition of Appeasement in British Foreign Policy, 1865–1939." In Kennedy, *Strategy and Diplomacy, 1870–1945: Eight Studies,* 15–39. London: George Allen & Unwin in Association with Fontana Paperbacks, 1983.

Kimball, Warren F. *The Juggler: Franklin Roosevelt as Wartime Statesman.* Princeton: Princeton University Press, 1991.

Koch, H. W. "Hitler and the Origins of the Second World War. Second Thoughts on the Status of Some of the Documents." *Historical Journal* 11 (1968): 125–43.

Kondracke, Morton. "Baker's Half Dozen." *New Republic,* 24 February 1992, 11–12.

———. "Saddamnation." *New Republic,* 7 May 1990, 9–12.

Kordt, Erich. *Nicht aus den Akten . . . Die Wilhelmstrasse in Frieden und Krieg: Erlebnisse, Begegnungen und Eindrüke, 1928–1945.* Stuttgart: Union Deutsche Verlagsgesellschaft, 1950.

Krock, Arthur. *Memoirs: Sixty Years on the Firing Line.* New York: Funk & Wagnalls, 1968.

LaFeber, Walter. "American Business Community and Cleveland's Venezuelan Message." *Business History Review* 34 (winter 1960): 393–402.

Lane, Arthur Bliss. *I Saw Poland Betrayed: An American Ambassador Reports to the American People.* Indianapolis: Bobbs-Merrill Co., 1948.

Lanyi, George A. "The Problem of Appeasement." *World Politics* 15 (January 1963): 316–28.

Laqueur, Walter. "The Psychology of Appeasement." *Commentary* 66 (October 1978): 44–50.

Larson, Deborah Welch. *Anatomy of Mistrust: U.S.-Soviet Relations During the Cold War.* Ithaca, N.Y.: Cornell University Press, 1997.

———. *Origins of Containment: A Psychological Explanation.* Princeton: Princeton University Press, 1985.

Leahy, William D. *I Was There: The Personal Story of the Chief of Staff to Presidents Roosevelt and Truman Based on His Notes and Diaries Made at the Time.* With a foreword by President Truman. New York: Whittlesey House, McGraw-Hill Book Co., 1950.

Lebow, Richard Ned. *Between Peace and War: The Nature of International Crisis.* Baltimore: Johns Hopkins University Press, 1981.

———. "Conclusions." In Robert Jervis, Richard Ned Lebow, and Janice Gross Stein, *Psychology and Deterrence,* 203–32. Baltimore: Johns Hopkins University Press, 1985.

———. "Deterrence Failure Revisited." *International Security* 12 (summer 1987): 197–213.

Lebow, Richard Ned, and Janice Gross Stein. "Beyond Deterrence." *Journal of Social Issues* 43 (winter 1987): 5–71.

———. "Deterrence: The Elusive Dependent Variable." *World Politics* 42 (April 1990): 336–69.

———. "Rational Deterrence Theory: I Think, Therefore I Deter." *World Politics* 41 (January 1989): 208–24.

Leng, Russell J., and Hugh G. Wheeler. "Influence Strategies, Success, and War." *Journal of Conflict Resolution* 23 (December 1979): 655–84.

Levering, Ralph B. *American Opinion and the Russian Alliance, 1939–1945.* Chapel Hill: University of North Carolina Press, 1976.

Levy, Jack S. "When Do Deterrent Threats Work?" *British Journal of Political Science* 18 (October 1988): 485–512.

Lijphart, Arend. "Comparative Politics and the Comparative Method." *American Political Science Review* 65 (September 1971): 682–93.

———. "The Comparable-Cases Strategy in Comparative Research." *Comparative Political Studies* 8 (July 1975): 158–77.

Liska, George. *Russia and the Road to Appeasement: Cycles of East-West Conflict in War and Peace.* Baltimore: Johns Hopkins University Press, 1982.

Lodge, Henry Cabot. "England, Venezuela, and the Monroe Doctrine." *North American Review* 160 (June 1895): 651–58.

———, ed. *Selections from the Correspondence of Theodore Roosevelt and Henry Cabot Lodge, 1884–1918.* 2 vols. New York: Charles Scribner's Sons, 1925.

Loewenheim, Francis L., ed. *Peace or Appeasement? Hitler, Chamberlain, and the Munich Crisis.* Boston: Houghton Mifflin Co., 1965.

Los Angeles Times.

Luard, Evan. "Conciliation and Deterrence: A Comparison of Political Strategies in the Interwar and Postwar Periods." *World Politics* 19 (January 1967): 167–89.

Lyons, Eugene. "Appeasement in Yalta." *American Mercury* 60 (April 1945): 461–68.

MacDonald, C.A. "Economic Appeasement and the German 'Moderates,' 1937–39." *Past and Present* 56 (August 1972): 105–35.

Mack, Andrew. "A Nuclear North Korea: The Choices are Narrowing." *World Policy Journal* 11 (summer 1994): 27–35.

MacLeod, Ian. *Neville Chamberlain*. New York: Atheneum, 1962.

Marder, Arthur J. *The Anatomy of British Sea Power: A History of British Naval Policy in the Pre-Dreadnought Era, 1880–1905*. New York: Alfred A. Knopf, 1940.

Mark, Eduard. "American Policy Toward Eastern Europe and the Origins of the Cold War, 1941–1946: An Alternative Interpretation." *Journal of American History* 68 (September 1981): 313–36.

Mastny, Vojtech. *Russia's Road to the Cold War: Diplomacy, Warfare, and the Politics of Communism, 1941–1945*. New York: Columbia University Press, 1979.

Mathews, Jessica. "A Good Deal with North Korea." *Washington Post*, 30 October 1994.

May, Ernest R. *American Imperialism: A Speculative Essay*. New York: Atheneum, 1968.

———. *Imperial Democracy: The Emergence of America as a Great Power*. New York: Harcourt, Brace, and World, 1968.

———. *"Lessons" of the Past: The Use and Misuse of History in American Foreign Policy*. New York: Oxford University Press, 1973.

Mazarr, Michael J. *North Korea and the Bomb: A Case Study in Nonproliferation*. New York: St. Martin's Press, 1995.

McElroy, Robert. *Grover Cleveland: The Man and the Statesman*. 2 vols. New York: Harper & Brothers, 1923.

Mearsheimer, John J. *Conventional Deterrence*. Ithaca, N.Y.: Cornell University Press, 1983.

Melman, Seymour. "The Limits of Military Power: Economic and Other." *International Security* 11 (summer 1986): 72–87.

Mercer, Jonathan. *Reputation and International Politics*. Ithaca, N.Y.: Cornell University Press, 1996.

Meyers, Reinhard. "International Paradigms, Concepts of Peace, and the Policy of Appeasement." *War & Society* 1 (May 1983): 43–65.

Michalka, Wolfgang. "Conflicts within the German Leadership on the Objectives and Tactics of German Foreign Policy, 1933–9." In Wolfgang J. Mommsen and Lother Kettenacker, eds., *The Fascist Challenge and the Policy of Appeasement*, 48–68. London: George Allen & Unwin, 1983.

Middlemas, Keith. *The Strategy of Appeasement: The British Government and Germany, 1937–39*. Chicago: Quadrangle Books, 1972.

Milburn, Thomas W. "What Constitutes Effective Deterrence?" *Journal of Conflict Resolution* 3 (June 1959): 138–45.

Miller, Judith, and Laurie Mylroie. *Saddam Hussein and the Crisis in the Gulf.* New York: Times Books, 1990.

Miscamble, Wilson D. "The Foreign Policy of the Truman Administration: A Post-Cold War Appraisal." *Presidential Studies Quarterly* 24 (summer 1994): 479–94.

Mitchell, Brian R. *European Historical Statistics, 1750–1975,* 2nd rev. ed. New York: Facts on File, 1981.

Mommsen, Wolfgang J., and Lothar Kettenacker, eds. *The Fascist Challenge and the Policy of Appeasement.* London: George Allen & Unwin, 1983.

Monger, George. *The End of Isolation: British Foreign Policy, 1900–1907.* London: Thomas Nelson & Sons, 1963.

Morgan, Patrick. *Deterrence: A Conceptual Analysis.* Berkeley: Sage Publications, 1977.

———. "Saving Face for the Sake of Deterrence." In Robert Jervis, Richard Ned Lebow, and Janice Gross Stein, eds., *Psychology and Deterrence,* 125–52. Baltimore: Johns Hopkins University Press, 1985.

Morgenthau, Hans. *In Defense of the National Interest: A Critical Examination of American Foreign Policy.* New York: Alfred A. Knopf, 1951.

Morrison, Elting E., ed. *The Letters of Theodore Roosevelt.* 8 vols. Cambridge: Harvard University Press, 1951–54.

Mowat, R.B. *The Life of Lord Pauncefote.* Boston: Houghton Mifflin Co., 1929.

Mueller, John. "Enough Rope." *New Republic,* 3 July 1989, 14–16.

———. *Retreat from Doomsday: The Obsolescence of Major War.* New York: Basic Books, 1989.

Müller, Klaus-Jürgen. "The German Military Opposition before the Second World War." In Wolfgang J. Mommsen and Lothar Kettenacker, eds., *The Fascist Challenge and the Policy of Appeasement,* 61–75. London: George Allen & Unwin, 1983.

Murray, Williamson. *The Change in the European Balance of Power, 1938–1939.* Princeton: Princeton University Press, 1984.

———. "Munich at Fifty." *Commentary* 86 (July 1988): 25–30.

Mylroie, Laurie. "The Baghdad Alternative." *Orbis* 32 (summer 1988): 339–54.

Nevins, Allan. *Grover Cleveland: A Study in Courage.* New York: Dodd, Mead & Co., 1932.

———. *Henry White: Thirty Years of American Diplomacy.* New York: Harper & Brothers, 1930.

New York Times

Newton, Scott. *Profits of Peace: The Political Economy of Anglo-German Appeasement.* Oxford: Clarendon Press, 1996.

Nicolson, Harold. *Diaries and Letters.* Vol. 2. *The War Years, 1939–1945.* Edited by Nigel Nicolson. New York: Atheneum, 1968.

Nuernberg Military Tribunals. *Trials of War Criminals Before the Nuernberg Military Tribunals Under Control Council Law No. 10,* 15 vols. Washington D.C.: USGPO, 1949–.

Nye, Joseph S., Jr. *Bound to Lead: The Changing Nature of American Power.* New York: Basic Books, 1990.

———. "The Case for Deep Engagement." *Foreign Affairs* 74 (July/August 1995), 90–102.

———. "The Misleading Metaphor of Decline." *Atlantic Monthly* 265 (March 1990): 86–94.

Oberdorfer, Don. "Missed Signals in the Middle East." *Washington Post Magazine,* 17 March 1991, 19–41.

Olney, Richard. "International Isolation of the United States." *Atlantic Monthly* 81 (May 1898): 577–88.

Orme, John. "The Circuitous Route to Peace: Generosity from Strength and the Waning of International Rivalry." Unpublished essay.

———. "Deterrence Failures: A Second Look." *International Security* 11 (spring 1987): 96–124.

Osgood, Charles E. *An Alternative to War or Surrender.* Urbana: University of Illinois Press, 1962.

———. "Suggestions for Winning the Real War with Communism." *Journal of Conflict Resolution* 3 (December 1959): 295–325.

Ovendale, Ritchie. *"Appeasement" and the English Speaking World: Britain, the United States, the Dominions, and the Policy of "Appeasement," 1937–1939.* Cardiff: University of Wales Press, 1975.

Overy, R.J. *War and Economy in the Third Reich.* Oxford: Clarendon Press, 1994.

Patchen, Martin. *Resolving Disputes Between Nations: Coercion and Concession.* Durham, N.C.: Duke University Press, 1988.

Perkins, Bradford. *The Great Rapprochement: England and the United States, 1895–1914.* New York: Atheneum, 1968.

Perkins, Dexter. *Hands Off: A History of the Monroe Doctrine.* Boston: Little, Brown & Co., 1941.

———. *The Monroe Doctrine, 1867–1907.* Baltimore: Johns Hopkins University Press, 1937.

Perkovich, George. "The Korea Precedent." *Washington Post,* 28 September 1994.

Peterson, Walter J. "Deterrence and Compellence: A Critical Assessment of Conventional Wisdom." *International Studies Quarterly* 30 (September 1986): 269–94.

Plano, Jack C., and Roy Olton. *The International Relations Dictionary,* 4th ed. Santa Barbara, Calif.: ABC-Clio, 1988.

Podhoretz, Norman. "The Future Danger." *Commentary* 71 (April 1981): 29–47.

Post, Jerrold. "Saddam Hussein of Iraq: A Political Psychology Profile." *Political Psychology* 12 (June 1991): 297–308.

Przeworski, Adam, and Henry Teune. *The Logic of Comparative Social Inquiry.* New York: Wiley Interscience, 1970.

Reiss, Mitchell. *Bridled Ambition: Why Countries Constrain Their Nuclear Capabilities.* Washington, D.C.: Woodrow Wilson Center Press, 1995.

Resis, Albert. *Stalin, the Politburo, and the Onset of the Cold War, 1945–1946.* The

Carl Beck Papers in Russian and East European Studies, no. 701. Center for Russian and East European Studies, University of Pittsburgh, April 1988.

Reynolds, David. *The Creation of the Anglo-American Alliance, 1937–1941: A Study in Competitive Co-operation*. Chapel Hill: University of North Carolina Press, 1982.

Rich, Norman. *Hitler's War Aims: Ideology, the Nazi State, and the Course of Expansion*. 2 vols. New York: W. W. Norton & Co., 1973.

Richardson, J.L. "New Perspectives on Appeasement: Some Implications for International Relations." *World Politics* 40 (April 1988): 289–316.

Rock, Stephen R. *Why Peace Breaks Out: Great Power Rapprochement in Historical Perspective*. Chapel Hill: University of North Carolina Press, 1989.

Rock, William R. "British Appeasement (1930's): A Need for Revision." *South Atlantic Quarterly* 78 (summer 1979): 290–301.

———. *British Appeasement in the 1930s*. New York: W. W. Norton & Co., 1977.

———. *Chamberlain and Roosevelt: British Foreign Policy and the United States, 1937–1940*. Columbus: Ohio State University Press, 1988.

———. *Neville Chamberlain*. New York: Twayne Publishers, 1969.

Rosecrance, Richard. "Reward, Punishment, and Interdependence." *Journal of Conflict Resolution* 25 (March 1981): 31–46.

Rowse, A.L. *Appeasement: A Study in Political Decline, 1933–1939*. New York: W. W. Norton & Co., 1961.

Rystad, Göran. *Prisoners of the Past? The Munich Syndrome and Makers of American Foreign Policy in the Cold War Era*. Lund, Sweden: CWK Gleerup, 1982.

Salinger, Pierre, and Eric Laurent. *Secret Dossier: The Hidden Agenda Behind the Gulf War*. New York: Penguin Books, 1991.

Santayana, George. *The Life of Reason, or the Phases of Human Progress*. Vol 1. *Reason in Common Sense*. New York: Charles Scribner's Sons, 1905.

Schelling, Thomas C. *Arms and Influence*. New Haven: Yale University Press, 1966.

———. *The Strategy of Conflict*. Cambridge: Harvard University Press, 1960.

Schroeder, Paul W. "Munich and the British Tradition." *Historical Journal* 19 (1976): 223–43.

Schulz, Donald E. "The United States and Cuba: From a Strategy of Conflict to a Strategy of Constructive Engagement." *Journal of Interamerican Studies and World Affairs* 35 (summer 1993): 81–102.

Sciolino, Elaine. *The Outlaw State: Saddam Hussein's Quest for Power and the Gulf Crisis*. New York: Wiley, 1991.

Scruggs, William I. *The Venezuelan Question: British Aggressions in Venezuela, Or the Monroe Doctrine on Trial; Lord Salisbury's Mistakes; Fallacies of the British "Blue Book" on the Disputed Boundary*. Atlanta: The Franklin Printing and Publishing Co., 1896.

Shambaugh, David. "Containment or Engagement of China? Calculating Beijing's Responses." *International Security* 21 (fall 1996): 180–209.

Shepardson, Donald E. "Munich Reconsidered." *Midwest Quarterly* 23 (autumn 1981): 78–102.

Sigal, Leon V. "Averting a Train Wreck with North Korea." *Arms Control Today* 28 (November/December 1998): 11–15.

Singer, J. David. "The Appeasement Option: Past and Future." In Melvin Small and Otto Feinstein, eds., *Appeasing Fascism: Articles from the Wayne State University Conference on Munich After Fifty Years,* 1–8. Lanham, Md.: University Press of America, 1991.

Skidmore, David, and William Gates. "After Tienanmen: The Struggle over U.S. Policy toward China in the Bush Administration." *Presidential Studies Quarterly* 27 (summer 1997): 514–39.

Skocpol, Theda, and Margaret Somers. "The Uses of Comparative History in Macrosocial Inquiry." *Comparative Studies in Society and History* 22 (April 1980): 174–97.

Small, Melvin, and Otto Feinstein, eds. *Appeasing Fascism: Articles from the Wayne State University Conference on Munich After Fifty Years.* Lanham, Md.: University Press of America, 1991.

Smelser, Ronald M. "Nazi Dynamics, German Foreign Policy and Appeasement." In Wolfgang J. Mommsen and Lothar Kettenacker, eds., *The Fascist Challenge and the Policy of Appeasement,* 31–47. London: George Allen & Unwin, 1983.

Snyder, Glen. *Deterrence and Defense: Toward a Theory of National Security.* Princeton: Princeton University Press, 1961.

Snyder, Glen, and Paul Diesing. *Conflict Among Nations: Bargaining, Decision Making, and System Structure in International Crises.* Princeton: Princeton University Press, 1977.

Snyder, Scott. "North Korea's Nuclear Program: The Role of Incentives in Preventing Deadly Conflict." In David Cortright, ed., *The Price of Peace: Incentives and International Conflict Prevention,* 55–81. Lanham, Md.: Rowman & Littlefield, 1997.

Stein, Janice Gross. "Deterrence and Compellence in the Gulf, 1990–91: A Failed or Impossible Task?" *International Security* 17 (fall 1992): 147–79.

———. "Deterrence and Reassurance." In Philip E. Tetlock et al., *Behavior, Society, and Nuclear War.* Vol. 2, 9–72. London: Oxford University Press, 1990.

Stettinius, Edward R., Jr. *Roosevelt and the Russians: The Yalta Conference.* Edited by Walter Johnson. Garden City, N.Y.: Doubleday & Co., 1949.

Stimson, Henry L., and McGeorge Bundy. *On Active Service in Peace and War.* New York: Harper & Brothers, 1948.

Stoler, Mark A. "A Half Century of Conflict: Interpretations of U.S. World War II Diplomacy." *Diplomatic History* 18 (summer 1994): 375–403.

Strausz-Hupé, Robert, and Stefan T. Possony. *International Relations in the Age of the Conflict Between Democracy and Dictatorship.* New York: McGraw-Hill Book Co., 1950.

Tansill, Charles Callan. *The Foreign Policy of Thomas F. Bayard, 1885–1897.* New York: Fordham University Press, 1940.

Taubman, William. *Stalin's American Policy: From Entente to Detente to Cold War.* New York: W.W. Norton & Co., 1982.

Taylor, Telford. *Munich: The Price of Peace.* Garden City, N.Y.: Doubleday & Co., 1979.

Thayer, William Roscoe. *The Life and Letters of John Hay.* 2 vols. Boston: Houghton Mifflin Co., 1915.

Times (London).

Tuchman, Barbara. *The March of Folly: From Troy to Vietnam.* New York: Alfred A. Knopf, 1984.

Ulam, Adam B. *Expansion and Coexistence: Soviet Foreign Policy, 1917–1973.* New York: Praeger, 1974.

Umiastowski, Roman. *Poland, Russia and Great Britain, 1941–1945: A Study of Evidence.* London: Hollis & Carter, 1946.

Ungar, Sanford J., and Peter Vale. "South Africa: Why Constructive Engagement Failed." *Foreign Affairs* 64 (winter 1985/1986): 234–58.

"U.S., Allies Create Consortium for Korean Nuclear Deal." *Arms Control Today* 25 (March 1995): 28.

U.S. Bureau of the Census. *Historical Statistics of the United States, Colonial Times to 1957.* Washington, D.C.: USGPO, 1960.

———. *Statistical Abstract of the United States, 1906.* Washington, D.C.: USGPO, 1907.

U.S. Congress. *Congressional Record.*

U.S. Congress. *The Persian Gulf Crisis.* Joint Hearings Before the Subcommittees on Arms Control, International Security and Science, Europe and the Middle East, and on International Operations of the Committee on Foreign Affairs and the Joint Economic Committee, 101st Congress, 2nd session, 8 August, 18 September, 25 September, 17 October, 28 November, and 11 December 1990.

U.S. Congress, House. *Developments in the Middle East, July 1990.* Hearing before the Subcommittee on Europe and the Middle East of the Committee on Foreign Affairs, 101st Congress, 2nd session, 31 July 1990.

———. *Developments in North Korea.* Hearing Before the Subcommittee on Asia and the Pacific of the Committee on Foreign Affairs, 103rd Congress, 2nd session, 9 June 1994.

———. *Iraq's Participation in Agricultural Guaranteed Loan Programs.* Hearings Before the Subcommittee on Department Operations, Research, and Foreign Agriculture of the Committee on Agriculture, 102nd Congress, 2nd session, 1 July and 30 September 1992.

———. *Korea: North-South Nuclear Issues.* Hearing Before the Subcommittee on Asian and Pacific Affairs of the Committee on Foreign Affairs, 101st Congress, 2nd session, 25 July 1990.

———. *North Korean Nuclear Program.* A Joint Briefing Before the Subcommittees on Arms Control, International Security and Science; Asian and Pacific Affairs; and International Economic Policy and Trade of the Committee on Foreign Affairs, 102nd Congress, 2nd session, 22 July 1992.

———. *Policy Implications of North Korea's Ongoing Nuclear Program and Markup of*

H. Con. Res. 179, H. Con. Res. 189, and H. Con. Res. 240. Hearing and Markup Before the Subcommittee on Asian and Pacific Affairs of the Committee on Foreign Affairs, 102nd Congress, 1st session, 21 November 1991.

———. *Tensions on the Korean Peninsula.* Hearing Before the Subcommittee on Asia and the Pacific of the Committee on Foreign Affairs, 103rd Congress, 1st session, 3 November 1993.

———. *The Security Situation on the Korean Peninsula.* Joint Hearing Before the Subcommittees on International Security, International Organizations and Human Rights, and Asia and the Pacific of the Committee on Foreign Affairs, 103rd Congress, 2nd session, 24 February 1994.

———. *United States-Iraqi Relations.* Hearing Before the Subcommittee on Europe and the Middle East of the Committee on Foreign Affairs, 101st Congress, 2nd session, 26 April 1990.

———. *United States-Iraqi Relations.* Hearing Before the Subcommittee on Europe and the Middle East of the Committee on Foreign Affairs, 102nd Congress, 1st session, 21 March 1991.

U.S. Congress, Senate. *Implications of the U.S.-North Korea Nuclear Agreement.* Hearing Before the Subcommittee on East Asian and Pacific Affairs of the Committee on Foreign Relations, 103rd Congress, 2nd session, 1 December 1994.

———. *Threat of North Korean Nuclear Proliferation.* Hearings Before the Subcommittee on East Asian and Pacific Affairs of the Committee on Foreign Relations, 102nd Congress, 1st and 2nd sessions, 25 November 1991, 14 January and 6 February 1992.

———. *United States Policy Toward Iraq: Human Rights, Weapons Proliferation, and International Law.* Hearing Before the Committee on Foreign Relations, 101st Congress, 2nd session, 15 June 1990.

U.S. Department of State. *The Conference of Berlin: The Potsdam Conference, 1945.* Washington, D.C.: USGPO, 1960.

———. *Conferences at Cairo and Tehran, 1943.* Washington, D.C.: USGPO, 1961.

———. *The Conferences at Malta and Yalta, 1945.* Washington, D.C.: USGPO, 1955.

———. *The Conference at Quebec, 1944.* Washington, D.C.: USGPO, 1972.

———. *The Conferences at Washington, 1941–1942, and Casablanca, 1943.* Washington, D.C.: USGPO, 1968.

———. *The Conferences at Washington and Quebec, 1943.* Washington, D.C.: USGPO, 1970.

———. *Foreign Relations of the United States: Diplomatic Papers.* Washington, D.C.: USGPO, 1861–.

———. *U.S. Department of State Dispatch.*

U.S. Foreign Broadcast Information Service. *Daily Report: East Asia.*

———. *Daily Report: Near East & South Asia.*

"U.S. Korea Nuclear Accord Remains on Track Despite Incident." *Arms Control Today* 25 (January/February 1995): 20, 26.

"U.S., Pyongyang Reach Accord on North's Nuclear Program." *Arms Control Today* 24 (November 1994): 25, 32.

Vagts, Alfred. *Deutschland und die Vereinigten Staaten in der Weltpolitik.* 2 vols. New York: Macmillan Co., 1935.

Viorst, Milton. "Report from Baghdad." *New Yorker,* 24 June 1991, 55–73.

———. "Report from Baghdad." *New Yorker,* 24 September 1990, 89–97.

Voigt, F.A. "Yalta." *Nineteenth Century and After* 137 (March 1945): 97–107.

Waas, Murray. "What We Gave Saddam for Christmas." *Village Voice,* 18 December 1990, 27–37.

Walker, Stephen G. "Solving the Appeasement Puzzle: Contending Historical Interpretations of British Diplomacy during the 1930s." *British Journal of International Studies* 6 (October 1980): 219–46.

Washburn, Charles G. "Memoir of Henry Cabot Lodge." *Proceedings of the Massachusetts Historical Society* 58 (October 1924–June 1925), 324–76.

Washington Post.

Watt, Donald. "The Historiography of Appeasement." In Alan Sked and Chris Cook, eds., *Crisis and Controversy: Essays in Honour of A.J.P. Taylor,* 110–29. London: Macmillan Press, 1976.

Webster's Third New International Dictionary. Springfield, Mass.: G. & C. Merriam Co., 1976.

Weinberg, Gerhard L. "Germany, Munich, and Appeasement." In Melvin Small and Otto Feinstein, eds., *Appeasing Fascism: Articles from the Wayne State University Conference on Munich After Fifty Years,* 9–18. Lanham, Md.: University Press of America, 1991.

———. *The Foreign Policy of Hitler's Germany: Starting World War II: 1937–1939.* Chicago: University of Chicago Press, 1980.

———. "Munich After 50 Years." *Foreign Affairs* 67 (fall 1988): 165–78.

Weizsäcker, Ernst von. *Die Weizsäcker-Papiere, 1933–1950.* Edited by Leonidas E. Hill. Berlin: Propyläen Verlag, 1974.

———. *Memoirs of Ernst von Weizsäcker.* Translated by John Andrews. Chicago: Henry Regnery Co., 1951.

Welles, Sumner. *Seven Decisions That Shaped History.* New York: Harper & Brothers, 1951.

———. *Where Are We Heading?* New York: Harper & Brothers, 1946.

Wendt, Bernd-Jürgen. "'Economic Appeasement'—a Crisis Strategy." In Wolfgang J. Mommsen and Lothar Kettenacker, eds., *The Fascist Challenge and the Policy of Appeasement,* 157–72. London: George Allen & Unwin, 1983.

———. *Economic Appeasement: Handel und Finanz in der britischen Deutschland-Politik, 1933–1939.* Düsseldorf: Bertelsmann Universitätsverlag, 1971.

Wheeler, Joseph, and Charles H. Grosvenor. "Our Duty in the Venezuelan Crisis." *North American Review* 161 (November 1895): 628–33.

Wheeler-Bennett, John. *Munich: Prologue to Tragedy.* New York: Duell, Sloan & Pierce, 1948.

Whelpley, J.D. "American Control of England's Food Supply." *North American Review* 174 (June 1902): 796–806.

White House. *A National Security Strategy of Engagement and Enlargement.* Washington, D.C.: USGPO, 1996.

Wolf, Charles, Jr., K.C. Yeh, Edmund Brunner Jr., Aaron Gurwitz, and Marilee Lawrence. *The Costs of the Soviet Empire.* R-3073/1–NA. Santa Monica, Calif.: Rand, 1983.

INDEX

Adams, Brooks, 45
adversaries: types of and implications
  for appeasement, 156–59, 163–66,
  175–77
aggressive/hostile behavior: motives
  for, 156–59. *See also* greed;
  insecurity
Agreed Framework, 128; criticisms of,
  139–40; defense of, 140; designed
  to avoid exploitation, 146–47;
  future of, 150–53; negotiations
  leading to, 136–39; North Korean
  acceptance of, 144–45; North
  Korean compliance with, 150–52;
  U.S. compliance with, 152
Alaskan boundary dispute, 28–29, 33
Alexandroff, Alan, 66, 75
Allen, H.C., 38
Alverstone, Lord, 29, 41
American appeasement of Iraq: causes
  of failure, 116–20, 124–26;
  continued despite evidence of
  failure, 120–24; U.S. objectives,
  103, 124; under Bush
  administration, 107–12; under
  Reagan administration, 107. *See
  also* Iraq; United States
American appeasement of North
  Korea: avoiding exploitation in,
  146–47; reasons for success, 144–
  45; role of threats in, 147–50; U.S.
  objectives, 127–28; under Bush
  administration, 130–33; under
  Clinton administration, 136–40.

See also Agreed Framework; North
  Korea; United States
Anderson, DeSaix, 131
Anglo-American appeasement of
  Soviet Union: abandoned in favor
  of containment, 92–93; aimed at
  avoiding war with Soviet Union,
  87–92; aimed at Soviet
  cooperation in war against Japan,
  81–83; aimed at obtaining Soviet
  participation in postwar collective
  security organization, 83–87;
  aimed at preventing a separate
  peace, 79–81; contribution to
  collapse of Soviet Union, 100–101;
  reasons for failure (and success) of,
  94–98. *See also* Great Britain;
  Soviet Union; United States
Anglo-Polish Defense Treaty, 70, 74,
  83
Anglo-Saxonism, 46
appeasement: alleged futility of, 2;
  avoiding exploitation, 166–69;
  costs of, 7; criticisms of, 2–3;
  defining, 10–12; defining success
  or failure of, 155–56; effects on
  deterrence, 4–7, 67–76, 167–69;
  and engagement, 21–23; factors
  determining success or failure of,
  155–66; lessons for policymakers,
  169–73; matching strategy to
  adversary, 163–66; "material
  effect" of, 4, 75–76, 168;
  mechanisms of, 14–15; need to